Zhou Enlai
—A PROFILE

Percy Jucheng Fang
Lucy Guinong J. Fang

FOREIGN LANGUAGES PRESS
BEIJING

First Edition   1986

ISBN 0-8351-1712-X

Copyright 1986 by Percy Jucheng Fang and Lucy Guinong J. Fang

Published by Foreign Languages Press
24 Baiwanzhuang Road, Beijing, China

Printed by Foreign Languages Printing House
19 West Chegongzhuang Road, Beijing, China

Distributed by China International Book Trading Corporation
(Guoji Shudian)
P.O. Box 399, Beijing, China

Printed in the People's Republic of China

To the memory of

Zhou Enlai, the people's Premier

Premier Zhou Enlai at the Great Hall of the People on January 9, 1973.

Photo by Giorgio Lotti (Italy)

Contents

Acknowledgements

The idea of writing a book about Zhou Enlai was conceived soon after his death in January 1976. Work pressure, however, did not allow us to take time off from *Beijing Review* and Radio Beijing International until our sabbatical leave in 1979, when an extended stay in the U.S. made it possible for us to begin. Various calls on our time since returning to Beijing left the first draft only partially completed. On and off we took turns revising the manuscript and rewriting chapters, particularly the ones analysing and comparing Zhou Enlai and Mao Zedong and dealing with the tempestuous Cultural Revolution. We are glad that the final version is ready for the printers in time for the tenth anniversary of Zhou Enlai's death.

We are indebted to members of our family, our brother and sisters resident abroad, who helped make our stay in the U.S. enjoyable, and to the loving care they lavished on us: Lily Fong Woo and her grand daughter Angela Tsang of Hong Kong; Frank and Liane Fong of Anaheim, Ca.; Alice F. Fok of Huntington Beach, Ca.; Nancy F. Wu of Rosemead, Ca.; Margaret F. Lam of Houston, Texas; and Rose F. Chung of Concord, Mass. Our thanks also go to our many nephews and nieces in the U.S. who rendered assistance in various ways with the preparation of the manuscript, some reading chapters of the first draft for comments and suggestions. They include: Jackson and Susan Lam of Concord, Ca.; Linda and Austin Staheli of San Ramon, Ca.; Emmy and Peter Nash of New York City; Elaine and Scott Boone of Washington, D. C.; Denis and Georgean Fong of Long Beach, Ca.; Shirley Lam of New York City; Jeffrey Lam of Houston, Texas; Vivien and Willam Tao of Concord, Mass. We also owe thanks to the immediate family: to our daughter Irene and our son Eugene and daughter-in-law Li Mingyang of Houston, Texas, who have been a constant help in looking up sources and materials, checking information, etc.

We are grateful to two very special friends in Houston, Frank C.F. Hsu, M.D., and his wife Grace, our schoolmate at Southwest Associated University in Kunming, Yunnan, and Professor I-Mien Tsiang (retired) and his wife Margaret for their hospitality and many stimulating conversations which improved sections of the book. Dr. Hsu gave much of his time to get the medical terms right, as did Prof. Huang Cuiting, chief surgeon of Beijing's People's Hospital. Prof. Tsiang kindly put his vintage typewriter at our disposal when we set to work, while Margaret read several chapters and gave valuable advice.

It would be invidious of us not to mention the many friends and schoolmates of our Qinghua University days whom we met after a lapse of many years during our journey across the U.S., and who have been so helpful and encouraging: Prof. Ta Liang of Cornell University and his late wife Daisy; Liu Tung-sheng and Wang Man-ming of Huntington Beach, Ca.; Emily and Way Dong Woo of Lincoln, Mass.; John and Lillian Hwang of Naperville, Ill.; Pei Yuan-ling and Hsu Yen-chiu of Palo Alto, Ca.; C.Y. and Joyce Lee of Woodland Hills, Ca.; Jack Huang of New York City; Professor (retired) and Mrs. Hsu Lo of W. Lafayette, Indiana; Lin Tsung-min and Lin Hsia of Indianapolis, Ind.; Mr. and Mrs. K. K. Fong of El Granada, Ca.; Franklin and Jean Chang of Brooklyn, N. Y.; Zhao Jinglun and Zhang Suchu of Queens, N.Y.; and Xie Guangyu, also of Queens.

We would like to acknowledge our special debt to Zhang Wenjin, lately Chinese Ambassador to the United States, to Israel Epstein, Editor-in-Chief of *China Reconstructs*, and to Ma Haide (George Hatem), M. D., Adviser to the Ministry of Health, for giving generously of their time to read through the rough draft of the book and making valuable suggestions. For whatever faults and inadequacies remain, we alone are responsible.

We also owe a debt of gratitude to Fan Jingyi, the new energetic Director of the Foreign Languages Publications and Distribution Administration, for becoming personally involved in the project by helping to expedite the printing process to ensure the scheduled publication date.

We are grateful to our old colleague and friend, Luo Liang, Editor-in-Chief of the Foreign Languages Press, who has been most helpful and patient with us from the very beginning of the project. The co-operation of his hard-working staff was admirable. Huang Youyi, who prepared the index, helped check facts, coordinated the style, and handled many other tasks, and Wu Shousong, who designed the jacket and prepared the illustrations, deserve a special note of appreciation.

Our special thanks also go to Wang Xi, lately Editor-in-Chief of *Beijing Review,* and Ding Yilan, lately Director of Radio Beijing International, for their constant encouragement and help in bringing the book out on time. We are grateful to Chen Hao and Ma Zhisun of the Archives and Research Department of the CPC Central Committee for their assistance in collating essential facts and figures.

And, finally, our thanks to our editor, Dell Bisdorf, whose wisdom and thoroughness appears on every page. We have learned much from her about how to be "ruthless" with verbiage.

Percy Jucheng Fang
Lucy Guinong J. Fang

Beijing, China
December 3, 1985

Chapter One
The Death of a Statesman

Zhou Enali was not expected to be among the mourners at the memorial service that June day of 1975 for He Long, Marshal of the Chinese People's Liberation Army (PLA), and Vice-Premier and Communist Party Politburo member. Under intensive treatment for carcinoma of the urinary bladder since the summer of 1974, Zhou was a very sick man. But he brushed aside his doctors' advice in order to do homage to a man who had been grievously wronged in the Cultural Revolution. The Premier felt he owed it to history to make clear where a man of honour and integrity must stand and to demonstrate his true feelings when matters of principle were at stake.

One of the first casualties of the Cultural Revolution of 1966-1976, He Long (1896-1969) had been hounded to death by Lin Biao, also a Marshal of the People's Liberation Army, who had risen to the number two slot after Mao Zedong in this unprecedented political movement for supremacy. In 1974, however, by order of the Party Central Committee He Long was posthumously vindicated despite fierce opposition by the Gang of Four, led by Mao's wife Jiang Qing. They were the political and ideological allies of Lin Biao, who had died in a plane crash in 1971. To rehabilitate He Long in the public eye was anathema to Jiang Qing and her gang. They had thwarted the proposal and, when it could not be blocked, made sure the ceremony was low-key.

Zhou Enlai arrived with his wife Deng Yingchao to join a restricted number of mourners. Impeccable as ever in a neatly pressed suit and without a hair astray, he appeared to have aged considerably, looking a mere shadow of his former robust self. His emaciated form moved slowly to the roster lying on a table, and the hand holding the brush shook violently as it scrawled the illustrious name. The Premier intended to sign also on behalf of Deng Xiaoping, who was with a visiting foreign delegation, but the effort seemed too much. He left instructions that the roster be sent to

1

the Vice-Premier's home for him to add his signature.

Zhou knew his right-hand man would have liked to be with them at that moment, for both had long memories of He Long. A Robin Hood-like hero in his youth, he and his martial elder sister He Ying had despoiled the rich to help the poor in his native Sangzhi county, Hunan Province, in the early 1920s.[1] When the young man took up soldiering, he rose from the ranks rapidly and became a divisional commanding officer before he turned thirty. In August 1927 when Zhou Enlai led Communist Party forces in an armed uprising in the south China city of Nanchang, Jiangxi Province, He Long turned the tables on the Kuomintang and brought his forces over to the Communist side, serving the revolutionary cause thereafter with devotion and skill. In the 1930s Chiang Kai-shek had offered 100,000 silver dollars for his capture, dead or alive.

Three years after the founding of the People's Republic, he was made Minister in Charge of the State Physical Culture and Sports Commission, in addition to exercising much influence as a member of the Party Central Committee's Military Commission. A pipe-smoker who later developed a weakness for cigars, the general did well at the Sports Commission, for he was a sportsman himself and a lover of horses. The growing stature of China as a sports nation in the 1960s owed not a little to his vigorous leadership.

One of the great names of the Chinese Revolution, He Long had been close to Zhou Enlai as a comrade and friend since Nanchang, a fact that did not endear him to Lin Biao. Lin wielded immense power in the first years of the Cultural Revolution, and from the outset the scheming "crown prince" worked hand in glove with the Cultural Revolution Directorate controlled by Jiang Qing and her cohorts.[2] The two ruthless cliques were determined to gain power by removing Zhou Enlai's closest associates, the first step in their game plan.

In no time He Long became a marked man, branded as a "big bandit" and a "big warlord" and accused of other fantastic crimes. Zhou took He Long and his wife Xue Ming under his wing in Zhongnanhai, the Party-government complex in the Forbidden City. In the initial topsy-turvy days of the Cultural Revolution even Zhongnanhai was not the safest of places. So a hideout known only to his trusted lieutenants was found for the persecuted couple. Lin Biao's prize eluded him for a while. Eventually he got wind of where they were hiding and had He Long taken to a place where his henchmen could grill the old warrior at their leisure. His wife was banished to a remote corner of southwest China. Already in his seventies and suffering from diabetes, He died at the hands of his tormentors on June 9, 1969.

It was to honour the memory of this old comrade-in-arms, whose admission to the Communist Party he had himself sponsored, that Zhou Enlai wrenched himself from his sick bed. No sooner had he signed the roster than he sought out He's widow. With what strength he could summon he called out for her. She ran towards the Premier, who threw his arms around her. "I failed, Xue Ming, I failed to keep him out of harm's way." Tears welled as he spoke. He Long's daughter squeezed his hand. "Uncle Zhou, you must take good care of yourself."

The Premier looked at her for a moment. Then in a trembling voice, succinct and heart-rending, came the words: "It won't be long for me now."[3]

Seven months later, on January 8, 1976, Zhou Enlai, Premier of the People's Republic without break for over a quarter of a century, left this life.

News of the Premier's death struck the nation dumb. People wondered how the void left by his loss could ever be filled. He had pushed himself hard in carrying the crushing load of government, and taxed himself without limit to hold the administration together in the chaotic years of the Cultural Revolution.

Sorrow gripped everyone. He was no ordinary Premier, no ordinary man. He was a man of the people, for the people, with the people. His passing in ordinary times would doubtless have caused grief beyond measure. But these were no ordinary times. To be sure, Lin Biao was gone. But the Gang of Four — Jiang Qing, the evil schemer bent on moving up to the number one spot, Zhang Chunqiao, the calculating usurper coveting the premiership, Yao Wenyuan, the reptilian hack bossing the mass media about and Wang Hongwen the womanizer, who was the gang's hatchet man — were still around, now more impatient than ever to lay hands on the levers of power.

Deng Xiaoping, groomed to take over the premiership since he was transferred from Sichuan Province to Beijing in the late 1950s and made Acting Premier when Zhou Enlai took trips abroad, came under increasingly unbridled attack in the press as an "incorrigible capitalist roader." The spate of media attacks on the Vice-Premier was vicious and vociferous, and often interlarded with invective aimed at the departed

Premier himself.[4]

Jiang Qing and company, believing both Party and state power to be within reach at last, were jubilant. Time-servers jumped on Jiang Qing's bandwagon. And she was unscrupulous enough to do some recruiting herself. All this made the loss of Zhou Enlai all the harder to bear. The nation revealed its mood on January 11, the day set for his cremation.

It was sombre and cold that day. Long before dusk, when the hearse was to emerge from Beijing Hospital to begin its solemn procession to the Babaoshan Cemetery of Revolutionaries, knots and knots of people, including parents carrying babies in their arms, began to collect on the sidewalks. Several million turned out. Every inch of the pavement westwards to Babaoshan was occupied, sometimes three or four deep, with a huge crowd collected at Tiananmen Square. Black armbands were everywhere. Women of all ages wore in their hair home-made white paper chrysanthemums. The cortege moved slowly, very slowly, to the refrains of a funeral march. As it approached subdued sobbing turned into unrestrained wailing all along the capital's main thoroughfare, usually roaring with traffic and now oppressively muted except for the whisper of the crawling vehicle and the sound of people weeping.

The capital's population did not mind standing hours on end in the bitter cold for the Premier's hearse to pass by. They were hardened by something stronger than grief. Put it down to both love for the Premier, and hatred for the Jiang Qing gang, who had tried their best to revile him.

Long revolted by the extraordinary behaviour of Jiang Qing and her gang and the way things were going in the country, people had kept their opinions and feelings private, for the risks of undisguised opposition were too great. People were bolder in the days following Zhou Enlai's death. Dissatisfaction was not registered openly as yet, but a lot of talk was going the rounds which spread and became increasingly defiant.

Jiang Qing's distasteful actions at one particular public function served to pour oil on the flames. When she did homage to the Premier's body as it lay in state, as required of all Politburo members, she wore, of all things[3] a red sweater which was easily visible at the neck of her tunic. She had also donned a rumpled cap, unusual headgear on such a solemn occasion! By time-honoured Chinese convention, black or white, is a proper colour of mourning, while red is associated with felicity or rejoicing. The news spread quickly and everyone was shocked and scandalized. People were even more stunned by what she did on January 15, the day proclaimed for national mourning, with a ban on entertainment in all forms. Of all days, Jiang Qing chose this one to have two films shown at her home, one before noon and another in the evening!

Her attendants were rebuffed for even gingerly reminding her that January 15 was a national day of mourning. Loyal to the memory of the Premier, they were revolted. Perhaps they talked. Anyway, word got around. Still, criticism remained hushed, and was expressed only among friends or relatives. After all, she was Mao Zedong's wife, and in deference to the Chairman people controlled their indignation. Nevertheless, signs of anguish and restlessness were there. What had the country come to if a single individual, however exalted, could behave as she did with impunity, while the multitude were scorned for merely seeking permission to hold a memorial service for the late Premier?[5]

Events three months later were to change things dramatically. It was April, *Qingming* time, the Chinese "Clear and Bright" Festival. At this time of year people in the old China would do their filial duty to their ancestors by "sweeping the graves," and in the new they would remember their dear ones with flowers. So the people of Beijing decided to remember Zhou Enlai with flowers — not real flowers, for the spring weather was still too raw, but paper ones. They also seized this occasion to give vent to their dammed-up discontent and send Jiang Qing a message.

Tiananmen, witness to many great political events, was the rallying point. Now, in 1976, another important political movement was in the making, although few, perhaps none, foresaw its ultimate significance. For here the people of Beijing made a stand which burst open the floodgates of pent-up anger and frustration. It was the beginning of the end of the Jiang Qing gang.

It should be noted that no wreaths for any individual revolutionary leader had ever been laid at the Monument to the People's Heroes at *Qingming* time in the entire history of the People's Republic. Passers-by were intrigued that year to find several lying at the foot of the obelisk, some with the sender's name on them, some without. They were offered to Premier Zhou Enlai. The news electrified Beijing. More came, then more and more. They descended like an avalanche, each one with the sender's name, mostly that of a unit or organization, boldly displayed. People were no longer afraid to stand up and be counted. The wreaths multiplied, grew in size and scale and, what is significant, took on political colouration with the inscriptions attached to them. The timing, the quantity, the identification, the manner of the marchers — often scores strong, who bore the wreaths on their shoulders into the square — and the pledges they made as the garlands were laid before the monument, carried unmistakable undertones of defiance and contempt for Jiang Qing and her minions.

For the first few days these wreaths, as various as they were exquisitely designed and made, held centre stage. Suddenly, they were supplanted by myriads of poems pasted on the balustrades of the monument, on the lampposts and even on trees in and around the square. They were hymns and elegies to Zhou Enlai, written in classical style or free verse. There were also poems of an entirely different character, allegorical attacks on Jiang Qing and company. More than the wreaths, these hard-hitting poems, saturated with anger and scorn, attracted hundreds of thousands of people to the square each day, some to follow suit with poems of their own, and others to jot down the sharpest ones to pass on to friends.[6]

From morn to dusk, and into the small hours, the stream of humanity converging on the square did not cease. The poems of Tiananmen became an engrossing subject of conversation. Many went every day in order not to miss the ones freshly put up. Young people from schools, factories and government offices outnumbered all arrivals, but old folks were in evidence, too.

One old peasant with a weather-beaten face, apparently from a farm on the capital's outskirts, turned up one afternoon dressed in a pair of cotton-padded trousers soiled from field work and a jacket with a sash around his waist. He sought out a quiet spot and there, head down, observed silence for a few minutes. He produced two oranges out of his unbuttoned garment and, as reverently as he could, placed them near a balustrade. After bowing three times he murmured "Premier Zhou, Premier Zhou . . ." and walked away. Wishing to make some gesture, and probably illiterate, he created poetry in his own way.

The explosive developments at Tiananmen Square caught the Gang of Four off guard. On the 5th of April, they acted. Tiananmen Square was cordoned off in one fell swoop, with all hemmed up in the ring taken away by the police. Many arrests were made; Beijing's Chief of Police was the gang's man.

On the 7th, Vice-Premier Deng Xiaoping, shunted aside since delivering the funeral oration at Zhou Enlai's memorial service in January, was stripped of all his posts.[7] He was accused of "instigating counter-revolutionary riots in Tiananmen Square," a trumped-up charge which was finally repudiated only a year later.

In the weeks that followed Beijing people had to account for what they did and where they were in the first week of April — whether one had been to Tiananmen Square, written any poems, copied poems or passed them on to friends, and so forth. Throughout the summer the repressive measures continued. The hunt shifted to rounding up persons suspected of spreading what were called "rumours about Comrade Jiang Qing."

She and her supporters had been scared by the events in Tiananmen Square, but they were now feeling confident again. They miscalculated. Their plot to seize power following Mao Zedong's death on September 9 came to grief. On October 6 these power manipulators who sat on the backs of the people for ten long years were summarily arrested.

The news, though not reported in the press till many days later, spread quickly. It seemed too good to be true. Friends and relatives tried to scoop one another with tidbits about the sensational event. The cathartic joy of the sudden end of ten years of tyranny transformed Beijing into a boozy city overnight. In a matter of days, all the capital's liquor stores were emptied of their stocks. Even those who never touched a drop all drank to celebrate Jiang Qing's downfall.

Strange to say, the better hospitals in the city also found some of their wards emptying of patients overnight. For a number of high-level cadres had ensconced themselves in hospitals in order to put some distance between themselves and Jiang Qing's spite. Feeling safe now, they went back to take up their duties where they had left off and to put things in order again.

The fact that it was October, the beginning of the crab season, helped to make the arrest of the Gang of Four (three men and a woman) really something to be merry about. As a rule, crabs are sold in China by pairs, a male and female each, and October is the month when customers prefer the female because of the seasonal rich eggs. One bright customer is said have given this order to a fishmonger: "Three males and a female, please."

The fishmonger was surprised. "But I can let you have two each, comrade."

The customer repeated the order with a wink. "I can do without the other female. Just let me have my three-and-one." The stress in his voice was on "one." The fishmonger, at last seeing the point, laughed heartily. Other customers took up the bantering and all started to give the same order — three males and one female. Soon this became the standard order at all seafood stores, and the joke was savoured by everyone. The day of reckoning had arrived.

The year 1976 was an eventful one for China. Zhou Enlai passed away on January 8. His death was followed on July 6 by that of Marshal Zhu De (1886-1976), the grand old man of the Chinese People's Liberation Army who was Chairman of the Standing Committee of the National People's Congress (NPC), and then on September 9 by the death of Mao Zedong (1893-1976). The loss of the three great leaders of the Chinese Revolution in quick succession was a terrible blow to the country, and the year's misfortunes were compounded on July 28 by the catastrophe of the Tangshan earthquake, which in a matter of seconds killed a quarter of a million people. In this sense, 1976 was a year of devastation. In another — that the country was rid of the Gang of Four — it was a year of deliverance. The concluding months of 1976 found people in an uplifted mood, hopeful of a change for the better and ready to rebuild the fabric of a shattered nation.

Ten years of upheaval had left China prostrate in every sphere of life. In political respects, the Cultural Revolution had been extremely painful for many once energetic, hard-working cadres holding down jobs at all levels of leadership. They feared exerting themselves too much or getting caught out on a limb once again by pushing too hard to get things done: Once bitten, twice shy. They fell into a state of inertia, the worst enemy of progress. Economically, the country was near bankruptcy, what with production falling or stagnating, the treasury heavily in the red and a population explosion of "Cultural Revolution babies." For China to feed a billion mouths is a mind-boggling proposition. In the sphere of education standards had fallen, so that the general level at institutions of higher learning was described by some wit as: The status is that of a university, the curriculum that of a high school, and actual performance that of a primary school. This was of course an exaggeration. But the policy of Jiang Qing and her cronies of singling out intellectuals for attack put a premium on ignorance and did much to degrade and demoralize people in academic circles. When their pet phrase was "the more one knows the more reactionary one is," knowledge became not an asset but a liability. For learning to become respectable again, the important thing after Jiang Qing's downfall was to create conditions that would let the benumbed intellectuals hold their heads up once more.

Priority was given to resuscitating the economy, for after all a billion people must be fed and clothed. In the meantime, three matters cried out for urgent solution: first, personnel readjustment; second, clearing up the criterion of truth — whether Mao Zedong was infallible, or was he capable of making mistakes, in which case they needed to be set right; and third, passing a verdict on the Cultural Revolution.

In regard to the first, a prudent policy was adopted to maintain stability and solidarity in the Party hierarchy by retaining the errant members of the Politburo for the time being and infusing it with new as well as "good" old blood. Conspicuously, the popular Deng Xiaoping was reinstated in all his four former positions the following year. Four wayard Politburo members, inculpated in one way or another with the Jiang Qing gang, were not dropped until the spring of 1980. They were Wang Dongxing, a Vice-Chairman of the Party Central Committee, Ji Dengkui, a Vice-Premier, Chen Xilian, a Vice-Premier and one time Commander of the Beijing Command of the People's Liberation Army, and the Mayor of Beijing, Wu De.

The second question concerned principally the evaluation of Mao Zedong as leader, thinker and theoretician. Was Mao always right, as the ambitious and fawning Lin Biao pronounced him to be, or could he make mistakes like other mortals? Wang Dongxing, who commanded Unit 8341 — the PLA division detailed to provide security for the Chairman, the Premier and other leaders in Beijing — held the view that Mao Zedong's words, whatever they were, spoken or written, must be adhered to since Mao, Wang claimed, was always right.[8] One Hong Kong China-watching journal coined a new word for this intransigence — *whateverism*.

Many were agitated by the issue, which remained in abeyance until the spring of 1978, when it was resolved by a long and deep-going debate over the criterion of truth — how can one decide what is right and what is wrong? Deng Xiaoping staunchly upheld the position that regardless of who said what, practice is the criterion of truth, the only criterion. This was set forth in a speech before the military in Beijing that summer, which in effect endorsed the thesis first broached by a Nanjing University lecturer in an article appearing in Beijing's *Guangming Daily,* a newspaper published mainly for academics.[9] The point was forcefully carried and the argument of the "whateverists" was punctured. The obvious conclusion, though not spelled out in so many words at the time, was that Mao Zedong, however great were his contributions to the Chinese Revolution, could make mistakes, as was proved in part by the excesses and damage of the Cultural Revoltuion.

In regard to the third question, once there was a consensus on the criterion of truth, it was not difficult to pass judgment on the Cultural Revolution. While Jiang Qing and her coterie had been in power, the subject was of course taboo, for it was they who played the big role in those tumultuous years and naturally would not hear of having their evils exposed. The fact that even after their downfall it should take the Party three years to address itself to the unpleasant task of writing it off shows how intractable the question was. In 1979 Marshal Ye Jianying, delivering the National Day speech in his capacity as Chairman of the Standing Committee of the National People's Congress — but in fact if not in name for the Party Central Committee as well — came to grips with this burning issue. The verdict he pronounced on the ten-year Cultural Revolution? A decade of disaster.

Two years later, in a lengthy resolution adopted by a Party Central Committee plenary session on June 27, 1981, which deals with certain important events since the founding of the People's Republic of China, the Party went a step further to repudiate, in unqualified terms, the Cultural Revolution initiated and directed by Mao Zedong.[10] The Cultural Revoltuion was wrong in every respect, from the beginning to the end, it said: Wrong in conception, wrong in planning, wrong in policy, wrong in execution. It called on the nation, people inside and outside the Party, to recognize it as such and root out its deleterious consequences. "Ultra-Left" ideas and practices which held sway during this deplorable period must not be allowed to exist anymore, in any form or disguise, it warned, for unless the country was freed of such political movements China could not progress or get on with its much-needed modernization.

In thrashing out the momentous issues confronting the nation, the forceful personalities of two men were never far from the thoughts of their former comrades and colleagues as they deliberated what course of action to take. One was of course Chairman Mao Zedong, and the other Premier Zhou Enlai. It is a pity that the recognition of policy errors which marred the image of the Chairman in his last years should have been so long delayed for, warts and all, he, more than any other single individual — not even excepting Zhou Enlai — was the man who conceived and brought the People's Republic into existence. His place in history is assured. Fear of evaluating him soberly can only blur his achievements and so distract from his greatness.

Zhou Enlai's hold over the nation and inside the Party remained undiminished in death. In fact, his stature has increased. In a speech to Party cadres on the tasks facing the country on January 16, 1980, Deng Xiaoping evoked in particular the name of Zhou Enlai, always a model of hard work and plain living, as an example to emulate when he called on all to be true to the austere spirit of the Yan'an days and to be guided by this tradition to bring about the modernization programme in post-Mao China.[11]

Whether as political commissar, army general, Party leader or head of government, Zhou Enlai never spared himself. He worked long hours every day of the year, a characteristic which distinguished his premiership from 1949 to the day he died. He and his wife lived a simple life, frugal to a fault, and only when his staff published their reminiscences did people come to know something more of his self-effacing ways.

As with his personal life, so with the affairs of state. He kept a firm grip on the national purse. All government departments were exhorted to be careful with every penny because China, he never tired of reminding them, is a poor country which must practise economy.

Selflessness personified, these qualities of the man and the statesman made him a folk hero. In the history of modern China no man in his death was more missed and mourned, more loved and revered, than Zhou Enlai when his heart stopped beating on January 8, 1976.

Death comes to every human being. Some cannot bear the thought, while others regard it as a matter of course. Zhou Enlai and Deng Yingchao had discussed the matter a few years before the Cultural Revolution and decided that when the time came for them to go, they would have their ashes dispersed after cremation. From burial to cremation is a revolutionary step in China, they maintained, and from cremation to doing away with the preservation of ashes is still another. In his last days Zhou Enlai asked that his ashes be scattered over the earth and rivers of the land that gave him birth. Before this happened, he requested that the urn holding them repose in the Taiwan Room of the Great Hall of the People. As in his lifetime, Zhou Enlai, as he lay dying held close to his heart the hope of reunification of the island province of Taiwan with the mainland.

Chapter Two
The Youth from Huaian

China's future Premier was born on March 5, 1898, into an impoverished mandarin family in Huaian County, Jiangsu Province, on the eastern seaboard. He was the same age as Liu Shaoqi, China's head of state until the Cultural Revolution swept him into political limbo and destroyed him in 1969.

Until the mid-19th century the ancestral home of the Zhou family was at Shaoxing, in the neighbouring province of Zhejiang, a county famed for two things — rice wine and yamen clerks, or pejoratively, pettifoggers (the drink is still in great demand but pettifoggery has long since gone out of business). Shaoxing claims another honour as the birthplace of modern China's foremost man of letters Lu Xun,[1] the satirist and short-story writer, whose turn of sarcasm compares with the best of Jonathan Swift. Zhou Panlong, Zhou Enlai's grandfather, took the family from Shaoxing to Huaian when he became a magistrate. Nestling by the 560-kilometre Grand Canal — dug in the Sui Dynasty (A. D. 581-618) and connecting Zhuoxian County in Hebei Province, north China, with the lake city of Hangzhou in the south — Huaian, with a history of 1,600 years, was Zhou Enlai's childhood hometown.

His father Zhou Shaogang was a petty official who earned a modest living far from home. His uncle Zhou Yigan, the youngest of four brothers, died in his twenties without issue, and to provide company and comfort for the twenty-year old widow it was arranged for the nephew, then barely a year old, to be adopted as a foster son. So Zhou Enlai was said to have two mothers. Well-read and versed in the classics and romances as well as in the poems of the prolific Tang (A. D. 618-907) age, the foster mother's chief ambition was to bring the boy up to be a scholar. At the age of four, he was taught to read and memorize scores of poems. Before he was nine he had devoured most of the popular old Chinese novels, of which *Romance of the Three Kingdoms, Journey to the West,* and *Outlaws of the Marsh* were his

12

favourites. A firm grounding in the classics, which he learned by heart in his early impressionable years, coupled with a strict self-discipline in later life, gave him a retentive memory which astonished all who came into contact with him.

His boyhood was a relatively hard one. The patriarch of the Zhous died and his father proved an inadequate breadwinner. The family had come down in the world, depending on money from the pawnshop and loans from relatives — extended grudgingly as often as not — to make ends meet. Worry and harassment by debt-collectors made life miserable for his mother and foster mother, who died within a year of each other. By the age of ten Zhou Enlai had the onerous duties of head of family thrust upon him. He had to look after his two younger brothers and try to keep the wolf from the door. In the days when the Zhou family had the resources to maintain some semblance of prosperity, there had been no lack of visitors at their house in Fuma Lane. But when reduced circumstances did not allow even a facade of genteel penury, only debt-collectors showed up. It was young Zhou Enlai's first exposure to the evils of snobbery.

In 1910, the twelve-year-old Enlai left Huaian, never to return, not even when he had become Premier. Still, Zhou Enlai retained happy memories of Huaian, the final resting place of both his mothers, for whom he cherished a lasting affection. In the following three years he studied at a primary school in Shenyang, northeast China, where his uncle Zhou Yigeng had taken him under his roof. He did well and there completed the first stages of formal education.

The boy did not disappoint his foster mother for all the trouble she had taken teaching him to write well and to study the classics and romances. When his school commemorated its second year, Zhou Enlai's essay "Thoughts on Our Anniversary" won the acclaim of both teachers and fellow students, not just for its fine prose but also for its lofty patriotism. The fact that it was later included in two separate anthologies of China's best student essays, one by a publishing house in Shenyang in 1913 and the other by a Shanghai publisher in 1915, speaks much for the boy's literary talent.

Even at that early age Zhou was concerned with the country's future. In the classroom one day the teacher asked the pupils, "Why do you go to school?" Some said more or less the same thing: "To bring honour to the family." One boy replied that he wanted "to learn the ways of good behaviour in society". The son of a shopkeeper gave an earthy answer:

"Just to please my old man." It brought down the house. After the laughter subsided, Zhou replied: "To rouse China from its slumbers and make it strong."[2]

His years in Shenyang coincided with the spread to north China of the ideas of democracy championed by Dr. Sun Yat-sen (1866-1925) of Guangdong, south China, against the imperial Qing (Manchu) rulers. It was sedition to read, possess or disseminate revolutionary literature. Punishment was death by decapitation. But one history and geography teacher named Gao had cut off his pigtail as an act of defiance and was unafraid to teach radical ideas in his classroom. He befriended the lad from Huaian, lending him political pamphlets and explaining to him why the monarchy must be replaced by a republican form of government.[3] His impact on his pupil was largely responsible for Zhou's conversion to the revolutionary cause, which eventually overthrew the Qing rulers in 1911 to usher in a republic as blue-printed by Dr. Sun Yat-sen. An experience outside of school unexpectedly furthered the youth's political progress.

One summer vacation Zhou was invited to stay with the family of a classmate living in the eastern suburbs of the city. The classmate's grandfather was a patriot, as revolutionary-minded as teacher Gao, and he took an immediate liking to his young guest. One day, the grandfather, grandson and their friend explored what remained of an old battlefield near Shenyang. Here, the old man told the youngsters, was where the Russo-Japanese war of 1904-1905 was fought — a war waged to gain control of China's northeastern provinces. And the fighting was right here on Chinese soil, the old man said, punching the air to emphasize his point. The people in these parts, he said, suffered the consequences, and yet the incompetent government in Beijing did not lift a finger to stop the alien invaders from overrunning our country. Worse, it had the temerity to proclaim "neutrality" and mark out limits which the war must not "overspill." Isn't that humiliation in the extreme? he asked the two youths.

The seeds of desire to fight for a strong China were thus sown in the heart of the Huaian youth, who from that time began to take an active interest in national affairs. He vowed to save China from the mortal danger of remaining weak and corrupt.

In 1913 the fifteen-year-old student left Shenyang for Tianjin to enrol at Nankai Middle School. China was in political ferment. The Revolution of 1911 had spurred the nation to a new awakening, agitating the hearts and minds of the young, and heralding an era of new culture which saw its flowering in the May 4th Movement of 1919. Like other youngsters of his age in cities such as Tianjin and Beijing, where new ideas were readily available, Zhou soon found himself drawn into the vortex of this burgeoning nationalism. As a student at Nankai, he was as diligent as before, but he did not allow classroom studies to prevent him from acquiring new knowledge and exploring new horizons after the day's homework was done. He was inspired by ideas in the journals published under Dr. Sun Yat-sen's auspices,[4] and later became a voracious reader of *New Youth* magazine edited by Chen Duxiu (1880-1942) and Li Dazhao (1889-1927) — who later became founding members of the Chinese Communist Party. Zhou Enlai's reading covered a wide range, from the progressive writers of the Qing Dynasty, such as Gu Yanwu (1613-1682) and Wang Fuzhi (1619-1692), to translated works of foreign origin such as Jean Jacques Rousseau's *Social Contract*, Montesquieu's *Spirit of Law* and Thomas H. Huxley's *Evolution*.

Zhou's second year at Nankai saw him coming to the fore as a student leader. Together with two schoolmates, he founded an association called *Jingye Lequnhui* (Respect Work and Enjoy Community Life Fraternity) and brought out a bulletin *Respect Work*. Although he was the group's leader, he stepped aside for one of his fellow co-founders to assume the post of president, he himself playing second fiddle as vice-president. Thus he showed at an early age the fine traits of modesty and lack of personal ambition which later in life often led him to let others take credit for what should have been his due. The association became a lively centre where fellow students came to borrow progressive books, assembled there by Zhou Enlai, to discuss subjects of topical interest, to sing and do other things which interested them. Zhou edited and wrote for the bulletin, and frequently contributed observations on current events and developments to the school magazine *Our School Way*. His commentaries lashed out at the plots of imperialist powers to dismember China, and ridiculed and excoriated Yuan Shikai (1859-1916) for trying to abolish the republic and restore the monarchy with himself as emperor. In his years as Premier, Zhou Enlai often edited articles for *People's Daily*, the Party organ, and it was at Nankai that he cut his journalistic teeth.

Nankai, one of the best secondary schools in pre-liberation China, run by the famed educator Zhang Boling (1876-1951), was administered like many U.S. missionary-financed educational establishments in the country. It adopted textbooks in English for a good number of courses such as algebra, geometry, trigonometry, chemistry, physics, Western history and world geography, and laid great stress on the study of English, requiring the students to work at it ten hours each week.

Zhou Enlai shone at Nankai. According to Zhang Honggao, a friend and classmate who roomed and shared a desk with him for two years,[5] Zhou did their class proud by winning the first prize in the school's 1916 interclass essay contest. The entrants, five from each class chosen through stiff competition, were to select one of two topics: *Honesty Will Win Out*, or *What Is the Most Urgent Problem Facing China?* The prize was awarded to Zhou Enlai for an excellent essay on honesty. He won his spurs too as the star rebutter on the school's debating team, which beat all others in Tianjin two years in a row.

Nankai followed a strict curriculum, prescribing two and a half hours for self-study from seven to half past nine every evening. But Zhou, Zhang Honggao remembered, devoted at most half of the prescribed period to going over the lessons of the day, his mind being preoccupied with extracurricular activities, preparing articles for the magazine he edited and reading up on matters which took his fancy. And yet he managed to come out first virtually every semester and graduated at the top of his class in the summer of 1917. How did he do it? Zhang thought that he knew how to concentrate single-mindedly on what the teacher said in the classroom. Moreover, he added, he was more gifted than the rest. His classmate cited another facet of his talent. Nankai produced a show every year to mark homecoming day on October 17. But not being coeducational, it was left to his friend with his good looks and acting ability, to play the female parts. His portrayal of the heroine in *A Dollar Coin* was so successful that the play became an instant hit in Tianjin.[6]

Two choices faced Zhou Enlai upon his graduation from Nankai: to look for a job or to go to college. He decided on the latter. But where? In China or abroad? He thought it best to continue his studies in Japan, and with the help of some friends, the nineteen-year-old Nankai graduate scraped up enough money to make the journey eastwards in September 1917. He had entertained hopes of finding answers to the questions uppermost in his mind in Japan, to learn how to save and rebuild China, and to acquire the kind of new knowledge that would be needed on his return home. Apart from the United States, Japan was the most appealing country to China's young elite. He was to be disappointed. World War I was raging and militarist Japan, bent on making the most of it while the great powers were embroiled with one another in Europe, stepped up its encroachment on an impotent China.

On arrival in Japan, Zhou set out to study Japanese and soon was able to get an idea of its grammar and learn to read, after a fashion, Japanese newspapers. At the same time, he studied hard to prepare for the college entrance examination. Within two months, however, his attention was drawn to a stirring event — the October Revolution in Russia. A workers' regime had come into being. He tried to understand what the dictatorship of the proletariat meant. He scanned the press, read all he could find about developments in the first socialist country in the world, and began to make a serious study of the doctrine underlying this world-shaking event. It was his first education in Marxism, which was to dominate his whole life.[7]

In spring 1918 Chinese students in Japan were incensed by news reports that the government of Duan Qirui (1865-1936) was bartering away China's sovereign rights to Japan. They held rallies, staged demonstrations and launched a sustained anti-Japanese movement in Tokyo. In all these patriotic activities Zhou Enlai played his usual energetic role. His attention thus divided, he had little time to prepare for the college entrance examination and failed to matriculate. Meanwhile, events in Beijing gave cause for alarm, since the government of warlords with Duan Qirui at its head showed no sign of heeding the popular demand that it terminate its sell-out to imperialist Japan.[8] Zhou decided that there was much more he could do in China. In April 1919 he was homeward bound after a nineteen-month stay abroad.

On his return the young man found a China seething with discontent and crying out for change. The flashpoint came within weeks. On the 4th of May the patriotic students' movement to overthrow the warlord regime shook Beijing with a vehemence and violence that overwhelmed the whole nation. College and high school students in the capital turned out in force to demonstrate in front of Tiananmen against Japan's encroachment and the traitors in high places who permitted it. The protest marchers ended by setting the home of a government minister ablaze.[9] Students in nearby Tianjin responded with a citywide protest march that led to the formation of a student union to direct all patriotic activities. As the nerve-centre for the movement, the student union decided to bring out a newspaper to spread new ideas and trends and mould public opinion in the struggle against imperialism and feudalism. In vain the leaders searched for an editor who could meet their expectations.

Zhou's return from Japan was a windfall, for in the opinion of the union's leaders he filled the bill perfectly. He needed no persuasion to take the job. Now that he was home, he was anxious to get into the thick of the struggle. On July 21 the first issue of the paper appeared on the newsstands, entitled *The Tientsin Student* with "Democracy: A Government for the People, by the People, and of the People — Our Motto" in English adorning the masthead.

Published twice a week, the journal edited by Zhou became an immediate success and soon progressed to a daily with a circulation of over twenty thousand — not bad at all for those days. It was popular with women readers, too, because it espoused their call for equality between the sexes and an end to the feudalistic conventions that shackled them. Designed mainly as a paper for students as its name suggested, *The Tientsin Student* also attracted readers beyond educational circles and received subscriptions from other parts of north China. It was widely read because, apart from news on the domestic and international scenes, it carried articles explaining in simple terms why China's then rulers were subservient to Japan and to other powers just as ready to pounce on China. It appealed to all patriots to carry the struggle to the end to liquidate the rule of feudal bureaucracy. As editor, Zhou Enlai wrote most of the pungent editorials and contributed articles, using the pen-name Fei Fei as his by-line.

But the student movement in Tianjin lacked central direction and united action. This was remedied by the merger of the student union and the Women's Patriotic Association, a separate organization of girl students. The joining of forces took place in September of that year, with each side choosing ten members to form the leading body, which came to be known as the *Juewushe* (Awakening Society). Zhou Enlai and Ma Jun, a Muslim student leader, were the pre-eminent members from the student union side, while from the women's organization the best-known names were Guo Longzhen,[10] also a Muslim, and Deng Yingchao, at fifteen the youngest of them all and later to become Zhou Enlai's wife.

The society published a magazine called *The Awakening,* requiring all members to write for it under pseudonyms. Fifty numerals in lieu of names, and not twenty, were drawn by lot — with an eye to expansion in the future. Zhou Enlai drew number five, and Deng Yingchao number one. To make them sound more like Chinese names, they were rendered into Chinese characters which were homonyms for the numbers. Thus Zhou Enlai became Wu Hao and Deng Yingchao Yi Hao, *noms de guerre* that the two used for many years. The Awakening Society would have liked to see its magazine prosper, but events intervened to limit its publication to just one issue and the organization itself ceased to function in the autumn of the following year. But before folding up it played a final vigorous role in the struggle against the authorities.

Things came to a head in January 1920, when the Tianjin police started cracking down on the student movement and made twenty-eight arrests, among them Zhou Enlai, Ma Jun and Guo Longzhen, who were put behind bars for six months. Execution would have been their fate had not a nationwide movement for justice demanded their immediate release and had not Zhou Enlai and his comrades put up a strong fight inside the prison and gone on a fast.

All this time Deng Yingchao and the others bombarded the police chief with one demand after another. One day they gathered together twenty-eight members and supporters of the society and demanded that they be allowed to substitute for the twenty-eight fasting inmates. After all, they said, the ones imprisoned by the police were their representatives and it was only fair that they take turns. Stung, the police hastened to put the twenty-eight "prisoners" on trial to show that the process of law had not been forgotten, only to find Zhou Enlai in the dock indicting the corrupt government and turning the tables on the prosecution.[11]

On July 17 all the twenty-eight accused were set free, to the rejoicing of their fellow students and supporters, who pinned on them badges bearing the inscription Self-sacrifice for the Nation. Out of his prison experiences Zhou Enlai wrote *Detention by the Police* and *Prison Diary,* his first books, both now out of print.

On August 16 at Taoranting, a park in south Beijing, with other progressive youth organizations taking part, the Awakening Society held its valedictory session after a meteoric career. Prof. Li Dazhao of Beijing University, the first man to introduce Marxist theory and Bolshevism to China, including such articles as *The Victory of the Common People* and *The Victory of Bolshevism,* was the guiding spirit.[12] Zhou Enlai served as the main speaker, summing up the achievements and lessons of Tianjin's patriotic movement. It was his last public appearance before he set sail for Europe on a Sino-French work-study programme.

Zhou Enlai reached France in December 1920, a politically mature twenty-two year old who had been through the revolutionary baptism of the May 4th Movement. His arrival in Paris aroused keen interest among those who had come from China before him on the same study scheme, because he had earned a name for his study of Marxism and the new Soviet state in Japan and also won distinction as a tested and tempered youth leader back home.

Zhou knew exactly what he wanted out of his stay in Europe, and would not allow anything to deflect him from the goal he had set himself. He came to France with two specific aims in mind: To press on with the study of Marxism first begun in Japan and continued in his Tianjin prison days, and second to find a cure for China's ills. He was attracted by the first and impelled to the second. The two were not contradictory but complementary, like key to lock; he came to realize more and more — Marxism being the key to the solution of China's problems. He became a confirmed and dedicated Communist. He read avidly and underlined passages he thought important. A book he read and used during this period, 1921 to be exact, is a precious item in the exhibition in Beijing to commemorate Zhou Enlai. It opens on a page with his pencil marks underlining one famous passage by Marx:

> And now as to myself, no credit is due to me for discovering the existence of classes in modern society or the struggle between them. Long before me bourgeois historians had described the historical development of this class struggle and bourgeois economists the economic anatomy of the classes. What I did that was new was to prove: 1) that the *existence of classes* is only bound up with *particular historical phases in the development of production,* 2) that the class struggle necessarily leads to the *dictatorship of the proletariat,* 3) that this dictatorship itself only constitutes the transition to the *abolition of all classes* and to a classless society.[13]

An assiduous reader of Marxist literature, Zhou was far from being the ivory-tower type. He did not confine himself to the classroom, studying for study's sake, in isolation from reality. He spent his time looking at life around him to see how the French worked and lived and what problems they faced. He took jobs sporadically at French factories, where at close quarters he could get to understand them better and carry on among workers of Chinese origin and work-study trainees like himself the kind of propaganda that would keep them on a patriotic, if not at the same time socialist, course.

In the first days after his arrival he took up lodgings in the suburbs of Paris, where he lived on the meagre allowance received from the work-study programme. For more than two years he stayed at Hotel Godefroy, close by the Place d'Italie in the southern part of the city, and at times worked at the Renault motor-car factory. He cooked his own meals, and though neat in appearance he had an air of shabby gentility about him, accentuated by a pair of trousers which, perhaps worn too often, seemed to shrink and get shorter and shorter at the turn-up. His friends also noticed that he had brought from China a gadget, a sort of shoe-tree with which to darn his own socks. Frugal, thrifty, careful with every penny, these virtues cultivated early on became life habits which were not abandoned when twenty-eight years later, as Premier of China, he could well afford creature comforts but disdained them.

One significant event took place in China the following summer — the birth of the Communist Party of China (CPC) in Shanghai on July 1, 1921. Mao Zedong was one of the founding delegates. Communication between China and France being what it was in those days, the news did not reach Paris until much later. It is however interesting to note that like-minded people, though separated geographically by thousands of miles, should be contemplating the same move more or less at the same time. Zhou Enlai and other Chinese Marxists in Europe had met somewhat earlier in the year to form an organization of their own called the Communist Group, which included Zhang Shenfu, Liu Qingyang, Zhao Shiyan and Chen Gongpei in addition to Zhou Enlai himself.[14]

Prior to that eventful July 1921, there were eight such groups operating within China and abroad, all dedicated to the cause of founding for China a Communist Party. After it came into being, those who had belonged to the Communist Groups were recognized as regular CPC members. The date of admission of all these "pre-Party" members, according to a Party Central Committee Organization Department ruling of May 23, 1985, has been fixed as 1921. Thus the time of Zhou Enlai's admission into the CPC, previously reckoned as dating from 1922, now stands corrected.

The CPC's Paris arm was designated as its European General Branch, with Zhou Enlai elected Secretary — a full-time job which claimed his entire attention, since its bailiwick covered not only France but Germany and Belgium as well. It was only natural for a man of his journalistic bent who knew the full galvanizing value of a publication that he should start one straight away.

La Jeunesse, renamed *Red Ray* in 1923, appeared as the Party's mouthpiece in Europe. Not printed but mimeographed, the magazine exerted wide influence among young Chinese expatriates in Europe and attracted readers in China, too. As usual, Zhou Enlai wrote for the publication and one article "Communism and China" appeared in its second number, signed Wu Hao, his old pen-name. He and Deng Xiaoping the youngest of the work-study trainees, were very close in their Paris days, Zhou treating the younger man affectionately and like a kid brother. They gave much of their time to making stencils. Deng, the paramount leader in post-Mao China, was then so skilled in his job that he earned the nickname Doctor of Mimeography.

As leader of the European branch, Zhou had to shuttle between Paris and Berlin every now and then and often stayed long periods in Germany. During one extended visit to Berlin he made the acquaintance of Zhu De, twelve years his senior. Zhu had tried but failed to gain admission into the Communist Party while in China, and wondered if he was now qualified.[15] Zhou thought he was, and offered to sponsor his application for Party membership. Zhu De was to become famous as Commander-in-Chief of the Communist forces, which were first known as the Chinese Workers' and Peasants' Red Army, then as the Eighth Route Army and the New Fourth Army during the war against Japan and from the late 1940s on as the People's Liberation Army.

In 1924, in response to Dr. Sun Yat-sen's call to embark on what became known as the Northern Expedition from Guangzhou (Canton) to rid China of the warlord regime in the north, the Kuomintang (nationalist) and Communist parties joined forces for the first time. Together they made war and carried it northwards to the Yangtze region. This was the First Revolutionary Civil War Period. The Communist Party, which was in its infancy, needed cadres to fill the ranks. It recalled many of its people from Europe to serve the cause at home. The European branch secretary, too, was ordered home and left for Guangzhou in August. After four years of work and study in Europe, Zhou Enlai, now twenty-six, had come of age politically and intellectually, ready to take on the tasks which lay before him.

Upon his return to the city which Dr. Sun Yat-sen had made the headquarters to direct the national revolution, Zhou Enlai was appointed to the post of Political Director of the Whampoa Military Academy, pre-liberation China's West Point. Also lined up for him was a Party job to

Zhou in Tianjin, 1919.

Zhou Enlai is on far right in back row of this photograph taken in 1918.

Photographed in a traditional Chinese gown in Tianjin, 1920, before sailing for Europe.

The Awakening Society in Tianjin, 1920. Zhou is on far right, back row, and Deng Yingchao, his wife-to-be, is third from right, front row.

Zhou in Berlin, 1922.

Zhou in Paris, 1923.

一九三四年攝於巴黎

Picture taken just before Zhou's departure for Guangzhou, 1924. He is sixth
from right, first row, and Deng Xiaoping is third from right, fourth row.

As chief political instructor at Whampoa Military Academy, 1924.

An up-and-coming political figure in Guangzhou, 1925.

Reaching northern Shaanxi after the Long March, 1935.

With Liu Shaoqi in Yan'an.

With Mao Zedong in Yan'an.

Zhou back at Yan'an airport after holding tripartite talks in Xi'an
in 1936 with Chiang Kai-shek and his captors Generals Zhang
Xueliang and Yang Hucheng.

A rare leisure moment in 1939.

In CPC's liaison office in Chongqing, 1945.

Zhou and Mao greet Patrick Hurley of USA on his visit to Yan'an, 1945.

From left to right: Zhou Enlai, George Marshall, Zhu De, Zhang Zhizhong and Mao Zedong during the American's visit to Yan'an, 1946.

Zhou Enlai (*back to camera*) is welcomed home from negotiations with the Kuomintang in Chongqing, 1946. *From left to right:* Mao Zedong, Zhu De, Liu Shaoqi and Peng Dehuai.

At his desk in Nanjing, 1946.

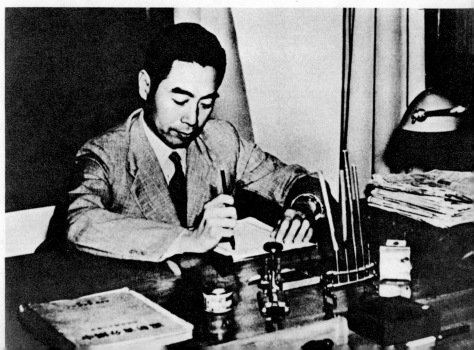

With Mao Zedong and Zhu De at Yan'an airport, 1946.

With Mao at Xibaipo, Hebei Province, in March 1949 before the triumphant march on to Beijing.

guide the work of the Communist Party in Guangdong Province and neighbouring Guangxi. In his position as Political Director, equivalent to political dean of the Academy, and as the Communist Party's representative for south China, Zhou Enlai had many encounters, as in later years, with Chiang Kai-shek. Dr. Sun Yat-sen died early in 1925, and Chiang Kai-shek soon gained control of the Kuomintang. In 1927 he initiated a purge and then a ten-year civil war with the Communists. Japan launched a full-scale invasion of China in 1937, and this brought about between the two political parties a period of precarious peace, which was shattered again when the Kuomintang dictator made a last attempt, starting in 1946, to destroy the Communists and gain absolute control of the country. The outcome is history. So on and off Zhou Enlai found himself in direct confrontation with Chiang Kai-shek for more than twenty years, and in the process became a legendary hero of the Chinese Revolution.

Chapter Three

Character of a Hero

On New Year's Day, 1980, Beijing's *People's Daily* sprang a surprise on its readers, publishing a serialized story about an episode in the Chinese Revolution, a feature without parallel in the history of the usually staid Party organ. The fact-and-fiction serial, actually more fact than fiction, ran for fifteen issues (January 1-21) with a striking title — "Wu Hao's Dagger." Wu Hao was none other than Zhou Enlai himself.

The circumstances of the civil war that broke out in 1927 made it necessary for revolutionaries to adopt pseudonyms. It was often a matter of life or death. Zhou Enlai used various *noms de plume* in his long career as a revolutionary, among them Wu Hao, Fei Fei and Xiang Yu in his student years and Guan Sheng during the 1927-31 period when he directed underground operations against the Kuomintang in Shanghai. During the Third Revolutionary Civil War, that is, the liberation war of 1946-49, top Communist Party leaders were given assumed names in dispatches for the purpose of fooling Chiang Kai-shek's decoders or cryptographers. Mao Zedong was Li Desheng (Li the Victorious) while Zhou Enlai became Hu Bicheng (Hu the Successful). But of all Zhou Enlai's pseudonyms Wu Hao was the best known, and because the name came to have a halo of triumph, his enemies, first the Kuomintang in the early 1930s, and forty years later the Gang of Four, made use of it for their own ends.

On the 16th and 17th of February, 1932, *Shi Bao* (*The Times*) of Shanghai published a notice to the effect that Wu Hao and 242 others had renounced the Communist Party. Who? Wu Hao — Zhou Enlai? The discerning instantly spotted the "notice" as a hoax concocted by Kuomintang propaganda organs to defame Zhou and lead other Party members astray. If there were really well over two hundred people "renouncing" their Party membership along with Wu Hao, the Kuomintang would have maximized such a propaganda windfall and listed in full every single name of the 242. The fact that it didn't, in fact couldn't, made the ploy look all the more spurious and clumsy.

On the 22nd of February, *Shen Bao,*[1] then Shanghai's largest-circulation Chinese newspaper, printed the following in its advertising column:

> Dear Mr. Wu Hao:
> Thank you for sending an advertisement on the 18th to be inserted in the paper. However, since the Fuchang Furniture Co. has refused to stand surety, the formalities are not complete. Hence we regret that we cannot print it as requested.
>
> > Advertising Department
> > *Shen Bao*

If what the advertiser lacked was surety, the paper needed only to ask him to furnish it. Why splash something like this in the paper? It was thought-provoking and meant to be so — to put the reader on guard and hint that the "Wu Hao Notice" in *Shi Bao* was a fake. For *Shen Bao's* unusual feature indicated an important factor — that Wu Hao responded on the 18th instant, the day after *Shi Bao's* publication of the incredible "Wu Hao notice". What the intended ad was to say was not revealed since *Shen Bao* declined to print it — a reply to *Shi Bao* — but there was enough for the reader to put two and two together.[2]

As a matter of fact, Zhou Enlai had left Shanghai months before and by the end of November 1931 was already in Ruijin, Jiangxi Province. He was not even in the city at the time the Kuomintang put this nonsense about. It was his underground lieutenants who countered the Kuomintang hacks with the *Shen Bao* "surety" device. This damp squib would have remained an amusing detail in the history of the Chinese Communist Party but for the machinations of the Lin Biao and Jiang Qing cliques to seize this broken reed to strike at Zhou Enlai.

During the Cultural Revolution they dug up this "affair" again to make grotesque accusations against Zhou of public betrayal of the Party — and set the Red Guards on to embarrass the Premier. But their efforts were in vain. An enraged Zhou Enlai put the case in writing to the Party Central Committee to clear up the matter. The situation came to Mao Zedong's attention and he gave his opinion. It was clear, he said, that the whole thing was a Kuomintang fabrication. Even so Zhou's enemies did not give up, hoping to find some "damaging material" to hurt the Premier. Zhou Enlai, to lay the ghost to rest once and for all, made a special report on this "Wu

Hao Renouncing the Party" canard in June 1972, and requested that the report be filed for the record. He took this unusual step because putting the record straight and in black and white might take the wind out of the sails of would-be mud-slingers in the future.

In September 1975, on the day he was scheduled to undergo a major operation, he asked for a transcript of his recorded report. He read it over carefully once again, signed his name and dated it September 20, 1975. After that he was ready to be wheeled into the operating room. Not sure whether he would survive surgery, he left nothing to chance.

Still, after his death on January 8, 1976, the mud-slingers, Jiang Qing and her cohorts, took up their scurvy tricks again. For weeks the widely circulated *Cankao Ziliao (Reference Material)*, an internal publication of news monitored from foreign sources published daily by Xinhua News Agency, had been carrying tributes to the memory of the late Premier. Then one day it printed a rather unusual article about Wu Hao, reproduced from a Hong Kong journal. It was purposely put in by the gang's hangers-on in Xinhua to malign Zhou Enlai, apparently with the approval of Yao Wenyuan, member of the Gang of Four who controlled the media. Xinhua was bombarded with furious letters and phone calls. People demanded an explanation of this foul insinuation. The heat was such that eventually Xinhua was forced to print an apology, pleading inadvertence, in the next issue. Later in the year, the Gang of Four was swept away forever, and with it the aborted Wu Hao frame-up.

"Wu Hao's Dagger" in *People's Daily* in January 1980 was a timely piece with which to observe the anniversary of Zhou's death. It took the reader back to a time when the Communist Party went into hiding and Zhou Enlai served as an underground revolutionary leader under the Kuomingtang's reign of terror. In April 1927 Chiang Kai-shek, riding on the waves of military successes in the Northern Expedition, took control of the east China provinces of Jiangsu and Zhejiang. He then suddenly renounced the Kuomintang's partnership with the Communists and initiated a bloodbath, first in Shanghai and then in other parts of the country. This put an end to the Kuomintang-Communist collaboration of 1924-27 and marked the beginning of a ten-year internecine strife (1927-36), referred to as the Second Revolutionary Civil War.

This was a bloody period in Chinese history. Many were cut down in the streets. The instruction given to the Kuomintang hounds was to finish off every Communist they could lay their hands on, "rather to kill a thousand by mistake than to let one slip away". Although in hiding, Communist Party members continued to fall into the hands of Kuomintang secret police agents because some of the weak-kneed had turned traitor or informer. In the east China province of Shandong in 1929 the local Kuomintang regime pulled off several raids on Communist cells with the help of traitors, and scores of comrades were seized. This called for swift counter-action.

The *People's Daily* article recounts how Zhou Enlai, as secretary of military affairs in charge of the Party headquarters in Shanghai, decides to strike back at once. A council of war is called and a plan of action mapped out. His bodyguard, a crack shot and an expert in traditional Chinese karate, and another aide are entrusted with the job of eliminating these turncoats. Some time later, a bespectacled Zhou Enlai, dressed in a long Chinese gown, minds a curio store which was used as a front in the city. He waits for the last customers to leave before closing the door behind him to receive news from his aide that the mission has been accomplished. He reminds all present that it is against Party principles to resort to terror, but the circumstances in Shandong make violence necessary to protect the Party and revolutionary cause.

Such in brief is the gist of "Wu Hao's Dagger." It sheds light on Zhou Enlai as Party chief and organizer working against terrible odds underground — bold, composed, resourceful and, if need be, ruthless. It also showed his disdain for physical danger, which expressed itself in ways big and small in his Guangzhou and Shanghai days and later during the years he represented the Communist Party in Chongqing, where he again became a target for Kuomintang assassins. It was demonstrated also on the perilous Long March. While crossing the bitterly cold, swampy grasslands on the march, Zhou gave the last of his ration of barley to his bodyguard Wu Kaisheng, who had been taken seriously ill. By insisting that the young soldier take the food, Zhou Enlai risked his life, for in the next days he would have to eat wild herbs, which the men knew from bitter experience could lead to uncontrollable illness and death. Indeed, men were dying all around them. But Wu Kaisheng, the bodyguard, was in dire need of even a modicum of nourishment. He accepted his Political Commissar's gift under great protest.

Sometimes Zhou Enlai's disregard of personal safety meant courting death even more directly, as when he gave up his own parachute to a fellow passenger in a plummeting plane in 1946. During the negotiations with the Chiang Kai-shek regime at the end of World War II, Zhou frequently had to shuttle between Chongqing and Yan'an. On one Chongqing-bound flight the plane ran into foul weather over the Qinling mountain range and began collecting ice on its propellers and wings, which added considerably to the payload. As the plane was losing altitude fast, the pilot ordered a jettisoning of the baggage and told the dozen or so passengers aboard to get their parachutes ready and wait for his signal to jump. Zhou Enlai got up from his seat and put his on and helped others into theirs. Suddenly a young girl's wail pierced the noise and confusion. It was eleven-year-old Ye Yangmei, daughter of General Ye Ting (1896-1946), one of the best-known military figures of modern China. She was crying because there was no parachute under her seat. The thought of being left behind without a parachute while all the other passengers jumped from the plane terrified her.

As Zhou Enlai rushed over to console her; he unfastened his parachute and fitted it on the child. Lu Dingyi — a Communist delegate to the Chongqing negotiations and later one of Zhou's Vice-Premiers — and the other passengers were distraught. Someone suggested that Zhou Enlai use his own parachute, while Yangmei, small and light, could be tied to one of them to make the jump. Zhou wouldn't hear of it, and the danger passed and the pilot gave the "all clear" signal. This incident has since become an often-told legend about China's beloved Premier.[3]

After his return from Europe in 1924, Zhou Enlai grappled with assignments and situations that were as varied as they were complex, pursuing a career full of challenges, perils and feats of heroism, as well as laurels that he did not seek.

In the spring of 1927, the military campaign against the northern warlords launched from Guangzhou by the democratic and revolutionary forces, and known historically as the Northern Expedition, rolled on irresistibly to engulf the whole of the Yangtze Basin. City after city fell to the revolutionary forces as they advanced northwards. Zhou Enlai was sent secretly by the Communist Party to Shanghai, which was then still held by Sun Chuanfang, the northern warlord. Zhou's mission was to organize an armed uprising of the 800,000 workers there to help take the city from within. It was to be the third uprising since October of the previous year. The first two had failed through lack of strong and properly organized leadership.

Just turned twenty-nine, Zhou then held the posts of Party secretary for military affairs of both Jiangsu and Zhejiang provinces. He set about his new task straight away. Zhao Shiyan of Sichuan Province, who had been on the work-study programme with him in France, and Luo Yinong of Hunan, who had studied Marxism in the Soviet Union years before, were his deputies. It was the third week of March. As the expeditionary troops closed in on the city suburbs, the jittery warlord regime was concentrated on the approaches to Shanghai and was totally unaware that something was happening inside the city. Zhou Enlai had been busy visiting in disguise the more active leaders of the labour unions, frequently conferring with them late into the night. It was decided to stage a general strike at noon on March 21, and to follow this up with an armed attempt to seize control of the government.

Shanghai was divided into seven districts, to be stormed simultaneously according to the strategy mapped out by Zhou and his comrades. He personally led the attack, spearheaded by five thousand hardened industrial workers, most of whom had played a part in the first two insurrections. Within minutes their ranks were swelled by many tens of thousands more insurrectionists. Though up against formidable odds, having less than two hundred rifles among them at the start, they took the enemy completely by surprise. What the rebels lacked in firearms and ammunition was made good, at Zhou's suggestion, by such clever stratagems as setting off fire-crackers in empty gasoline tins to simulate the sound of machine-gun fire. For thirty hours the rebels fought tenaciously, laying siege to police stations and other strongholds throughout the city and overwhelming the enemy by sheer numbers. By six p.m. the following day the authorities were compelled to surrender, and Zhou and his men had Shanghai under control.

The triumph of the third armed uprising in China's largest city, which represents an important milestone in the history of the Chinese Revolution, stamps Zhou Enlai as a brilliant strategist. He was to display these fine qualities a few months later in another insurrection, the famous Nanchang Uprising which, in a different context and on a bigger scale, gave birth to the Chinese Workers' and Peasants' Red Army, the forerunner of the Chinese People's Liberation Army.

In the meantime, the Shanghai workers were betrayed by their own allies. They took over the warlords' administration only to be attacked in turn by Chiang Kai-shek's armies when they moved into the city. In just a few weeks, throwing all scruples to the wind, Chiang broke the long-established Kuomintang agreement with the Communists and turned against the revolution.

Zhou Enlai and his lieutenants went underground and as from April 12 on Shanghai was turned into a slaughter-house. Communists and progressives were massacred in the streets or arrested *en masse* and immediately executed. Luo Yinong was murdered on April 21 and Zhou's other trusted aide Zhao Shiyan was arrested and executed by the Kuomintang on July 19. Zhou Enlai himself eluded the witch-hunt and escaped by the skin of his teeth with the help of underground Party workers.

After giving the Kuomintang the slip, Zhou Enlai arrived by boat at Wuhan where he stayed for some time before proceeding to his next major action at Nanchang, the provincial capital of Jiangxi in south China, near Ruijin where Mao Zedong, Zhou Enlai himself and their comrades were later to establish the first "Soviet Republic" on Chinese soil. Zhou had reached Nanchang at the end of July, having been chosen by the Communist Party to lead a full-scale uprising against the Kuomintang. In part the purpose was to disabuse the rank and file of the then Party General Secretary Chen Duxiu's "Right opportunism" — namely, his illusions of continued collaboration with the Kuomintang despite the April massacre of Communists in Shanghai and elsewhere.[4] Mainly, though, it marked the first independent armed struggle by the Communists to save the revolution that had been betrayed by Chiang Kai-shek and his junta.

After his strong performance in the Shanghai insurrection, which brought him fame at home and internationally as well, Zhou Enlai found his name synonymous with revolutionary insurgence. Since April the Kuomintang had been looking for him without let-up. Zhou vanished from Wuhan and in disguise journeyed by boat down-river to Jiujiang, whence he proceeded to Nanchang, with a trusted escort in the person of Chen Geng (a Whampoa Military Academy cadet who in 1955 was made one of the People's Liberation Army's ten senior generals). They reached their destination safely in the last week of July. Zhu De, a close friend and comrade in Berlin five years before, was, conveniently enough, Chief of the Public Security Bureau of Nanchang. He put up the unannounced visitors at 4 Huayuanjiao, his private residence, which was free from unwelcome prying eyes.

As leader of the uprising carrying the inconspicuous title Secretary of the Frontline Committee, Zhou Enlai lost no time in setting about his work. He called a meeting on July 27 at the Jiangxi Grand Hotel — which was to become the general headquarters of the uprising — of Liu Bocheng, Yun Daiying, Ye Ting, *et al,* devoted Party members who had converged at Nanchang to help. They discussed the situation, which was deemed favourable, decided on a course of action, and picked the dead of night of July 30 as zero hour for launching the uprising.

General He Long, who commanded the Twentieth Army garrisoned in the neighbourhood of Nanchang, had openly shown disgust at Chiang Kai-shek and sympathy for the revolution; he was then ready to embrace the Communist cause. Not yet a member of the Communist Party (after the uprising he was admitted into the Party, with Zhou himself officiating at the ceremony), He Long was not asked to the secret session at the hotel, but Zhou Enlai made a point of calling on him the next day and took him into his confidence. He Long readily agreed to join the uprising, and put his troops at Zhou's disposal. "I'll obey the Communist Party and do what it wants me to," he told Zhou Enlai.

The Twentieth Army under He Long, the crack regiments of the Twenty-fourth Division whose commander was General Ye Ting, (a professional soldier who had joined the Communist Party upon his return from the Soviet Union in 1924), plus the regiment of cadets trained by Zhu De and his public security forces, together added up to a formidable contingent of more than thirty thousand men. In strength, in morale, in fighting trim, this was more than a match for the Kuomintang troops they were to confront, which numbered only a little over ten thousand.

Everything seemed to mesh perfectly. Then on July 29 Zhang Guotao, who stood right of the political spectrum and had qualms about staging the uprising, telegraphed Zhou Enlai twice from Jiujiang in the name of the Party Central Committee that "the uprising must be carried out with particular caution" and that "they must postpone the uprising" until his arrival in Nanchang.[5] Zhou Enlai consulted his associates at the general headquarters. They decided to ignore this intrusion and proceed as planned, and merely to change the time of the uprising to the small hours of August 1. At the eleventh hour Zhang Guotao demanded a revision in the declaration drawn up for the uprising, obviously a ruse to delay action, but Zhou Enlai put his foot down. "If there is any revision to be done, I'll be the one to do it, period."

He Long was made commander-in-chief of the uprising, with Liu Bocheng, an army commander with wide experience in Sichuan, as his chief of staff. The revolutionary forces struck at the appointed time. Zhu De, the Public Security Chief, made an unusual contribution by inviting top Kuomintang officers to a lavish dinner and plying them with drink a few hours before the scheduled uprising. In no time they were immobilized. Fighting ceased after a five-hour exchange of fire, and the enemy laid down their arms. The Nanchang Uprising was one of Zhou Enlai's finest hours.

At nine o'clock on the morning of August 1,1927, the uprising was celebrated by the establishment of a revolutionary committee for Nanchang with twenty-five members, including Zhou Enlai, He Long, Soong Ching Ling (Dr. Sun Yat-sen's widow) and Guo Moruo, the well-known poet and historian. An enraged Chiang Kai-shek regrouped his troops and rushed reinforcements to the Nanchang area, where he expected to annihilate the rebels. The revolutionary forces marched south on August 5 in an attempt to capture Guangzhou and other key parts of Guangdong Province. In this they did not succeed, but the Nanchang Uprising gave birth to the Communist revolutionary armed forces, the famous Workers' and Peasants' Red Army. Soon afterwards the first rural base area was established. The revolutionary army grew rapidly. It would go on to defend the base areas against overwhelming odds, undertake the incredible Long March, win through to northwest China and establish a new headquarters at Yan'an, and begin to play a key role in the resistance against Japanese aggression.

For one stretch of the 1934-35 Long March from the hinterland of Jiangxi Province in the south to the loess plateau in the northwest, Zhou Enlai, ill with typhoid fever, lay on a stretcher. The going was rough for everyone on the trek, from top leaders to common foot soldiers, and often seemed beyond human endurance. Zhou Enlai couldn't bear the thought of being carried by stretcher-bearers, although his position as Political Commissar and Vice-Chairman of the Party's Military Commission fully entitled him to such care. He was in no condition to walk, let alone march, and he was vital to the revolution. His own primary concern was what the physical cost of carrying him on a canvas litter meant to his comrades with their stooped and worn-down shoulders. At times he would insist on walking, but his companions would insist just as stubbornly that he stay put. In later years as chief of the Communist Party delegation in Chongqing, he declined offers to ride in sedan-chairs borne on men's shoulders, then a common means of transport in the hilly wartime city.

On this part of the Long March, one of the stretcher-bearers was Yang Lisan (1900-54), a general in charge of army supplies. When Yang died shortly after liberation, Zhou Enlai attended his funeral and served as pall-bearer, a gesture of personal friendship and perhaps also an expression of kindness reciprocated. But there was more to it. In making a specific request to be one of the pall-bearers Zhou Enlai was motivated by something loftier than mere friendship and gratitude. It was his way of saluting a comrade who in times of great difficulties did more than his share without thought of self.

The next occasion when Zhou Enlai gained world attention was at the time of the 1936 Xi'an Incident, when Chiang Kai-shek was kidnapped by two of his own generals. Generals Zhang Xueliang and Yang Hucheng commanded KMT forces in the northeast and the northwest. In the northeast the Japanese aggressors had already seized large areas of China's territory, and were intent on expanding and consolidating their grip. But Chiang's orders were to keep on fighting the Communists instead of the Japanese, and this struck the patriotic generals as madness. After pleading again and again for a change in policy, Zhang and Yang seized the "Generalissimo," intending to compel him to fight the Japanese invaders.

They invited the Yan'an leaders to send a representative to Xi'an, the provincial capital of Shaanxi, for tripartite talks among the three interested parties — Chiang Kai-shek, the two generals, and his mortal enemy the Communists. Zhou Enlai was chosen and flew on Zhang Xueliang's private plane immediately to Xi'an. The historic negotiations which followed resulted in the second period of Communist-Kuomintang co-operation, a united resistance against the Japanese aggressors. The Communists placed the welfare of the nation above any thought of revenge against their old enemy Chiang. Zhou's great tact and diplomacy helped bring these delicate negotiations to a successful conclusion, and thereafter he would become the Communists' chief representative in the often stormy liaison work with the Kuomintang government.

Unlike earlier days, Zhou Enlai now no longer needed to operate from underground or in the shadows. From the time of the Xi'an Incident in 1936 to the outbreak of the Third Revolutionary Civil War (1946-49), which sent the Kuomintang leader fleeing from the mainland to Taiwan, Zhou Enlai's struggle with his chief protagonist was out in the open as diplomat and negotiator, aboveboard give-and-take pitted against underhand tactics. The multiplicity of Zhou Enlai's talents — whether as revolutionary, in which he was dedicated without being doctrinaire; as negotiator, in which he was tough without being rigid; as diplomat, in which he was fast on his feet without being erratic; or as administrator, in which he tasked himself as severely as his subordinates — made him the natural and manifest choice as Premier of the new China in October 1949. He was then at the ripe age of fifty-one, five years Mao Zedong's junior, and six years Deng Xiaoping's senior.

Running the world's most populous country, Zhou Enlai had a thousand and one duties, especially in the first years of the People's Republic. He had to supply and sustain the Chinese People's Volunteers fighting alongside Kim Il Sung's armies against the American aggressors in Korea, and at the same time take measures to heal an economy shattered by long years of war with the Chiang Kai-shek regime. Yet nothing seemed to escape him.

At one point two rare calligraphy scrolls used as collateral for a bank loan in Hong Kong stood in danger of going by default to some shrewd international art collectors who were eager to pay very high sums for them. The redemption date was before the end of 1951. Zhou Enlai instructed the most concerned government department to recover these two national treasures at any cost. The pair, together with another piece preserved in Beijing, represent the three rarest treasures of Chinese calligraphy, their history going back more than 1,500 years. The trio, specimens of China's all-time great calligraphers, all named Wang, are now on exhibit in Beijing's Palace Museum. Though not widely known at the time, the Premier's expeditious retrieval produced a considerable impact on the country's intellectual elite, because when the Communists first came to power no one knew for sure what their attitude would be towards China's cultural heritage. This was reassuring.

In point of fact, Zhou Enlai had on the eve of nationwide victory, and even before assuming the reins of government, turned his thoughts to the question of preserving important historical sites from gunfire as the People's Liberation Army pursued Chiang Kai-shek's armies across the Yangtze. At a meeting attended by high-ranking officers, as Chief of the General Staff he gave specific orders to the army to see to it that the Tianyige Library in Ningbo (Zhejiang Province) and the Jiayetang Library in Wuxing (Jiangsu Province), which house many of the country's first and rare editions, be protected and preserved intact. At his suggestion a *Catalogue of the Nation's Historical Sites and Ancient Relics* with names and locations was prepared, printed and distributed to all PLA units as an additional reminder to officers and men.

It was, however, not preservation for preservation's sake. When larger interests called for certain sites to be demolished, he acted just as decisively. In 1954 when the *pailou,* or arches, in Beijing's narrow thoroughfares were obstructing traffic and causing accidents, the problem was brought before an enlarged meeting of the State Council (cabinet). Some were for immediate demolition. Others made a strong plea for mercy. The late Professor Liang Sicheng (1901-1972) of Guangdong Province, a Pennsylvania-trained architect, with tears in his eyes pleaded for preservation.[6] It was up to the presiding Premier to say the last word. Like the poet he was in his younger days, he quoted a couple of lines from a Tang poem: "Twilight is a fine time indeed, only it is too close to nightfall." The preservation school, he went on, had been bitten by a "twilight" bug because its case was presented without due regard to the needs of urban development. The demolition school carried the day. Nonetheless, a couple of the arches regarded as worth preserving for their artistic value were moved and re-erected in Taoranting Park. Thus the matter was resolved to the satisfaction of all.

Shortly after the founding of the People's Republic, Zhang Honggao,[7] mentioned earlier in these pages, came to Beijing to see his old classmate who had become the nation's Premier. Twenty years had intervened since their last encounter in 1930, when on his return from the Soviet Union Zhou Enlai had stopped briefly at Harbin, the northeast China city, on his way back to Shanghai.

In the Premier's Zhongnanhai office they talked about old times, something Zhou enjoyed doing with his Nankai schoolmates, for he had a soft spot for his Alma Mater. Naturally the name of Zhang Boling, their old school principal, came up. During the war against Japan, student and principal had both been in Chongqing, the wartime capital, but their paths had not crossed. By then Zhou Enlai had become a nationally known figure as head of the Communist Party delegation, while Zhang Boling, a celebrity in his own way, was nothing more than a functionary in Chiang Kai-shek's government. Through a third party Zhou had asked his former principal for a copy of the Nankai alumni list. The request stumped the old man, for in a moment of zealous anti-communism, perhaps prompted by a desire to please Chiang Kai-shek, he had had the name of China's future Premier struck off the 1917 graduates list. Still, he complied, hastily inserting Zhou's name by hand at the tail-end of the 1917 roll.

After liberation, the Premier confided to his classmate, Zhang Boling had written him a letter. Among other things were these contrite words: "I've not been at home to visitors in order to do some soul-searching." This is a typical Chinese expression *(bi men si guo)* which implies that a person has done something wrong and is trying to make amends. Knowing that the old principal was languishing in Chongqing, Zhou Enlai sent a plane to bring him back to Tianjin, so that he could spend his last days in the comfort of a home he was used to. It was a very special favour, for in those early liberation days there were no commercial flights between the two cities. When Zhang Boling died in 1951, the Premier went to Tianjin to pay a student's last respects. More than that, Zhou made the gesture in an official capacity as a government and Party leader.

It was characteristic of Zhou Enlai not to hold a grudge against anyone, not even someone who had done him an ill turn. It was equally characteristic of him not to forget anyone who had done a good deed for the revolution and the country, in a public or personal way.

On May 2, 1971, Zhou Enlai drove to the Babaoshan Cemetery of Revolutionaries to attend what he had expected to be a memorial service for the Minister of Geology, Li Siguang (Dr. Joseph S.K. Lee), the internationally known Chinese geologist. He came to pay homage to his colleague and personal friend, who more than any one man had made it possible for China to discover and develop the famous Daqing oilfield. But Lin Biao and Jiang Qing, then riding high, had suddenly disparaged all "memorial services" as a feudal practice and decreed that they should be replaced by "farewell rites" — whatever that meant.

If there was not going to be a memorial service, then there wouldn't be any funeral oration. Why? Zhou wanted to know. Why should Li Siguang be made an exception? And why was the Premier not consulted and informed? He was visibly annoyed. He reached into his pocket and took out the letter sent him by the Li family. Unbeknownst to the widow, daughter and other members of the family, he asked Guo Moruo, President of the Chinese Academy of Sciences who was officiating at the service, and others in charge, if they would agree to his reading the letter in lieu of a funeral oration. All nodded. The mourners stood in silence, and as the dirge came to an end, Zhou walked to the microphone. He spoke quietly and solemnly, apologizing on behalf of the State Council for not having prepared a proper funeral oration for a man who had done so much for the country. He wondered if the letter from Comrade Li Lin, the geologist's daughter, would make do. Li Lin, born in 1923 and the only child of the Lis, holds a Ph.D. from Cambridge University and is a scientist in her own right.[8]

Li Siguang(1889-1971), who died at the age of eighty-one, had hoped to live just a few months longer in order to complete some research on seismic forecasting, a project personally assigned him by the Premier. The letter recounted how happy he had been that he could devote the last twenty years of his life to doing something worthwhile for the country. It expressed his feelings of indebtedness to the Party and government for all the assistance and kindnesses coming his way. He would have liked to have a talk, a long talk, with the Premier about the development of science in China, but had thought better of it. Dad, his daughter wrote, could not bring himself to mention it, knowing the Premier was too busy in those Cultural Revolution days. So he committed his thoughts to writing. Among his papers she had found a memo. The Premier, as he read it, raised his voice to put the message across:

> In this great socialist country of ours, we have got courage and the strength in us to overcome whatever stands in our way to scale the heights of science and technology and open up the enormous reservoir of energy in the bowels of the earth for the benefit of our people. If instead of bending our efforts in this direction we should follow the beaten track of capitalism and dissipate the mineral wealth, coal for instance, bequeathed to us by nature and burn it all up in a happy-go-lucky way, then a few score years from now our children's children and their children will not forgive us for our stupidity and recklessness.

He read on and then came to an abrupt stop. It was about the Premier himself, complimentary words of gratitude to himself and Deng Yingchao, his wife. The letter-writer said her father had told the family that the Premier pushed himself too hard, working more than twenty hours a day, seven days a week, and she implored him to guard his health for the sake of the country. Zhou Enlai skipped the entire paragraph.

Zhou Enlai and Li Siguang had come to know each other in the 1940s when they were both in Chongqing. They met only twice during that period, because seeing the head of the Communist Party delegation from Yan'an too often could get Li into trouble. Though their contacts were brief and far between they understood each other well enough to exchange political opinions candidly, and Zhou surmised that Li did not think much of Chiang Kai-shek. The professor had declined Chiang's offer of government appointment at a time when coercion and cajolery were employed to get well-known academics to window-dress his regime and toe the Kuomintang line. As threats were bandied about and persecution might follow, Zhou suggested that Li seek temporary refuge abroad.

Professor and Mrs. Li finally left China at the end of 1947 to stay in Britain, where years before he had been a student. Conveniently, an excuse presented itself to take a trip to Europe, for he had just received from the International Geological Society an invitation to attend its Eighteenth Congress in the British capital the following summer.

In August 1948 the International Geological Society met in Albert Hall in London for its Eighteenth Congress, the first such gathering in eleven years since the Seventeenth Congress was held before the war in Moscow. Professor Li Siguang, on behalf of China, delivered a paper on geomechanics, and shortly after retired to Bournemouth, a seashore resort in south England, where he thought the salubrious sea air might do him and his wife some good. He had coronary troubles and his wife had chronic high blood pressure. During their stay in Bournemouth, events in China were reaching a climax, and the news was encouraging. They began to talk of going home. In the small hours of October 2, 1949, they heard over BBC the news of the birth of the People's Republic. It was the leading item of the broadcast, quoting a dispatch datelined Beijing by the Reuters correspondent. Li was still in his morning gown when the telephone rang. It was a woman's voice which he recognized as that of Ling Shuhua, an old friend, whose husband Chen Yuan had connections with the Kuomintang embassy in London.[9]

"Your name is on the list of members making up the People's Political Consultative Conference. Taiwan has instructed its embassy here to take action. Unless you make a statement to back out, it will try to detain you here abroad." She also intimated that the ambassador himself might be on his way to Bournemouth to apply personal pressure.

There was no time to lose. Li packed a few things, boarded a train to Southampton and there took a freighter to Cherbourg on the other side of the English Channel. Before leaving he discussed with his wife a plan to throw the KMT off the scent. They settled on Basel as their rendezvous in Switzerland.

Two hours after his hurried departure, a secretary, not the ambassador, turned up at his Bournemouth hotel. When told that the professor had left for Turkey to do field work, the secretary grimaced and produced a check for US $ 5,000. "What's that for?" Mrs. Li threw it back in his face. He pocketed the snub but insisted that she read a copy of the telegram from Taiwan without, of course, any words about detention. "You can deliver it in person to the professor when he's back from Turkey," she said and showed him the door.

By May 6, 1950, the Lis were back in China. The following afternoon Premier Zhou Enlai called at their hotel and remained with them for three hours despite his heavy schedule. He had lost track of the professor since he vanished from Bournemouth, and not until recently did he receive word that the couple were expected to arrive in Hong Kong. An aide was sent there to arrange for their trip to the capital. There had been rumours that Li Siguang would not be coming home after all. Some gossips had even darkly hinted that he might have gone to Taiwan. But Zhou Enlai's faith in the professor was not shaken. He insisted that post-liberation China's first geological conference be postponed until Li's return.

In Zhou's conversation with the couple in Beijing, the Premier suggested that they both get a thorough medical check-up. "You have been afflicted with angina pectoris, haven't you? And what about that tuberculosis?" he asked the professor. "No need to worry any more," he said, "since the best medical facilities are now at our disposal." For Zhou Enlai recalled that during the Chongqing years the professor, worried about medical bills, cut down visits to the hospital in order to budget his small income for more urgent outlays. The first business for the geologist before assuming new responsibilities, Zhou maintained, was to be examined by doctors and take a long rest. "Shuping, too," said the Premier, "must have a check-up and her high blood pressure treated." Putting himself in the place of others, coming to the rescue of comrades in trouble, was strikingly characteristic of Zhou Enlai the man and statesman. But in his lifetime he never allowed anything even remotely suggestive of praise to be written about himself, about his role in the revolution or his personal qualities. Only after his death did people come to know the Premier better and the many fine things he did that had gone unrecorded.

During the Cultural Revolution he was often occupied with finding ways to protect and preserve the veterans of the Chinese Revolution from the Guangzhou days through the Long March to Yan'an. Apart from Mao Zedong, he was one of those best placed in those years to cushion, if not to stop, the blows coming from the Lin Biao and Jiang Qing gangs.

Yang Yong (1912-1983), the last commanding general of the Chinese People's Volunteers in the Korean war, was a case in point. Appointed commanding officer of the PLA units in the Xinjiang Uygur Autonomous Region in China's far west on his return from Korea in 1958, Yang was blacklisted at the beginning of the Cultural Revolution by Lin Biao and his crowd. One of the first army veterans so maligned, he was turned over to the Red Guards for "struggle sessions." When Premier Zhou learned what was going on, he ordered a special plane to fly the general to Beijing, ostensibly for medical treatment. Gruesome manhandling had left the general with a broken leg. Later Yang Yong became one of the Deputy Chiefs of the PLA General Staff, and was also a member of the Party Central Committee's Secretariat at the time of his death in 1983.

Not only veterans enjoyed his protection. Wherever glaring injustice caught his eye or ear he would take corrective measures. One such incident in 1973 involved righting a wrong done to a Beijing night-soil collector, Shi Chuanxiang. Shi had been following this calling man and boy until the day when the Jiang Qing gang decided, incredibly, that he was unfit for the job. The fact is that he had done his work well, and because of that had been elected to the National People's Congress. There was a photograph showing him shaking hands with Liu Shaoqi, the head of state. Well, according to the gang's logic, if a man could shake hands with Liu Shaoqi, whom they called the "capitalist roader," then he must be a pretty bad egg. So the night-soil collector was condemned as a "scab" and booted out of the capital.

The accusation was so absurd that the old model worker was driven insane and lost the faculty of speech. On August 20, in the course of presiding over a meeting to review the work of Beijing's Bureau of Public Utilities, Zhou Enlai happened to mention Shi Chuanxiang and was told of the poor man's fate. "What! Is it the purpose of the Cultural Revolution to overthrow a night-soil collector?" he bellowed with rage. It was one of the very few times the Premier is known to have lost his cool. He instructed the municipal government then and there to send someone on behalf of the Party organization to Shi's hometown in Shandong to apologize to him, to invite him back to Beijing and to give him all the medical care he should need. So ended a sordid incident of the Cultural Revolution.[10]

The Cultural Revolution was the most trying period of his long, eventful career. He had to hold the country together. At the same time he was trying to shield colleagues and subordinates from unjust attacks and to fend off barely concealed barbs aimed at himself. He never did things by halves. He would consider all sides of a problem and every eventuality, even the possibility of whether a comrade pressed to the wall might "take a short view" — a Chinese phrase for suicide. Thoroughness was Zhou Enlai's hallmark, a style of work pursued long before the Cultural Revolution.

From 1952 to 1962 Xi Zhongxun served as Secretary General of the State Council. He had been First Secretary of the Northwest Bureau of the Party's Central Committee, the number one man in northwest China, before he was transferred to Beijing to work under Zhou Enlai. At the Tenth Plenum of the Eighth Party Central Committee held in summer 1962, Xi suddenly found all hell breaking loose around him. He was branded a "big anti-Party plotter and schemer" for having fathered an "anti-Party" novel, *Liu Zhidan*.[11] In an article written later to commemorate Zhou Enlai in the *People's Daily*, Xi Zhongxun identified his accuser and nemesis as "that self-appointed theoretical authority."

Who was this enigmatic "theoretical authority"? Until the summer of 1980 when his identity was at last revealed, the Chinese media often referred to this mysterious person by another term, "that adviser of the Cultural Revolution Directorate," sometimes with the epithet "chief" before the word "adviser." When the Cultural Revolution Directorate came into being in 1966 with Chen Boda and Jiang Qing at its head, it had two advisers: Tao Zhu (1908-1969) of Hunan Province and Kang Sheng (1898-1975) of Shandong. Tao Zhu was then the number four man, after Mao Zedong, Lin Biao and Zhou En-lai, in the Party hierarchy. Before that he was First Secretary of the Party Central Committee's Central-South Bureau. Infighting in the directorate dislodged him early on, in 1967. Tao was thrown into prison by Lin Biao and company and held in solitary confinement. In 1969 he died in consequence of persecution. Along with other wrongly condemned veterans, Tao Zhu has since been rehabilitated posthumously.

Kang Sheng, who was held in awe by Jiang Qing's supporters, profited from the turmoils of the Cultural Revolution and prospered. From an alternate Politburo member at the start of the Cultural Revolution, he clawed his way to the top echelon of the Party to sit on the Politburo Standing Committee. Since Jiang Qing's downfall he has never been mentioned except with contempt, because many a foul deed during this traumatic period can be traced to his door.

It was Kang Sheng who slung mud at Xi Zhongxun before the Central Committee meeting. It was a bolt from the blue. Zhou Enlai's close associate was too flabbergasted to defend himself, faced as he was with a farrago of charges hurled at him by people at the meeting who knew nothing about the novel but were egged on by the "theoretical authority." Worse still, Mao Zedong, presiding, read to the gathering a brief note scrawled and handed to him by Kang Sheng: "It is a remarkable invention, using a novel to attack the Party." Whether the Chairman agreed with what was written there or was simply relaying the opinion of a member attending the session, it was hard to tell. In any case those words, given great publicity by Kang Sheng, came to be regarded as "a quotation from Chairman Mao" and used by the unscrupulous as a weapon. Xi Zhongxun was in trouble, as good as drummed out of the Central Committee.

For ten years Xi, who hails from Shaanxi Province in northwest China, had been Zhou Enlai's right-hand man in overseeing the State Council's day-to-day work. To get through their workload they pitched in on Sundays. They often messed together at the State Council's canteen, during which time they would carry on unfinished official business. In 1959 China was in the throes of economic difficulties, and grain and meat were rationed. Each adult was allowed twenty-five to thirty catties of grain per month, with manual workers receiving an extra few catties. Zhou Enlai set himself a low figure. So when he and his wife asked friends to a meal at home, they always reminded them — please come, but bring your own food tickets. The Premier of China just could not be too careful with his meagre allowance.[12]

One day he and Xi Zhongxun were again lunching together at the canteen. As usual, the Premier stood in the queue, and as he waited for his turn he noticed the poor quality of the food served and the pale complexion of the cadres. Back in their office they talked about the matter, about government workers not getting enough calories, about doing something to improve the standard of the staple food and the main dishes. Zhou Enlai suggested setting up "help yourself" production bases to grow crops and vegetables, to raise pigs and poultry, etc.

Acting on the Premier's orders, the Secretary General directed first the State Council offices and then other government departments and Party establishments to get all cadres to take turns to work on their own farm for a certain period each year to produce what they could to supplement their diet. This, Xi Zhongxun recalled, went a long way towards ameliorating life in those lean years 1959-1961.

It was a pleasure and privilege working for a leader who really cared for his subordinates. Xi didn't mind the long hours, for he enjoyed sharing with the Premier the bittersweet political life of the capital. All this would have to end, now that he was on the carpet before the Central Committee.

He needed time to brood over the charges thrust in his face, and he went to the Premier to ask for leave of absence to prepare his defence, or what was called an "examination of mistakes." Then he went home, a very despondent man. He was sinking further into depression when the Premier called and asked him over for a talk. Chen Yi, Vice-Premier and Foreign Minister, was with the Premier, and they said they were speaking not only for themselves but for the Party Central Committee and Chairman Mao as well.

The ebullient Marshal Chen tried to put Xi at ease. "I've made bigger mistakes than you. Nothing to worry about. You need only correct them. Now cheer up." The Premier was solicitude itself. "The Party and Chairman Mao have trust in you. Though there is this *Liu Zhidan* business, you can make amends if you are wrong." Holding Xi's hand, Zhou added: "We remain good friends. Whatever happens, you mustn't do anything foolish." Xi was choked with tears and unable to say a word, but took in the full meaning of the Premier's last words.

Zhou Enlai, however, did not feel reassured. He phoned Xi's wife and told her to take a few days off to stay home with her husband and keep an eye on him. Make sure he doesn't do anything foolish, the Premier warned her.

Xi had a rough time after his dismissal. He eventually got a job in 1965 as a deputy factory manager in Luoyang, Henan Province. He was eventually cleared, and the *Liu Zhidan* affair shown to be nothing but a frame-up by Kang Sheng. He was then eligible for a new appointment more suited to his ability and experience, and the fall of the Jiang Qing gang accelerated his promotion. He was named First Party Secretary of Guangdong Province in south China, and did a fine job in this post. Today Xi Zhongxun is a member of the Politburo, occupying a high place in Beijing's power structure.

From the day he moved into his Zhongnanhai office in 1949 until he left it in 1974 to undergo cancer treatment at the hospital, Zhou Enlai spent most of his waking hours in an austerely furnished office with little decoration except for a bust of Mao Zedong. The walls were lined with bookcases, and his desk, though spacious, looked as though it had seen a good deal of service. Three square tables, joined together to form a rectangular conference table, plus a few chairs, completed the inventory. The single additional piece of furniture acquired during his long tenure was a reclining chair which Mao Zedong sent him as a gift in 1972. Since his already-ill colleague had refused to enter a hospital, Mao thought a chair of this sort would help ease the rigour of long working hours. Otherwise the Premier's office remained much as it was when the occupant first moved into it. Even the telephone number in his outer office, used for receiving calls from ordinary people, remained the same, though an attempt had been made to change it. Some smart bureaucrat in the Telephone Administration, believing too many calls were coming in, suggested that the number be changed or go unlisted. He received in due course a rebuke from the Premier, who said the comrade couldn't think of a better way to divorce the Premier from the masses!

Zhou Enlai's old office, which occupied the Xihuating part of Zhongnanhai, was once part of the official quarters of Prince Zaifeng, the last regent of the Qing (Manchu) Dynasty. It was also used by Yuan Shikai and Duan Qirui of the warlord regimes after 1911, when China became a republic. It was something of a shambles when the revolution finally triumphed in 1949, but the Premier decided that with a little refurbishing he could easily use it as an office. He wanted nothing swanky or impressive around him, and vetoed any spending of the country's money beyond what was absolutely necessary. Thus, when plans were submitted for approval to construct ten "big buildings"[13] to mark the tenth anniversary of the People's Republic, he put his foot down on one project — to build a new office for the State Council. He told Xi Zhongxun and other Vice-Premiers that as long as he remained Premier he would not permit the construction of such a building. He kept such control of the national purse strings that he ticked off a subordinate who took advantage of the Premier's visit abroad to remodel the lavatory in Zhou's living quarters, which in fact needed repair.

In Xihuating the lights were on from sundown to sunrise. The Premier began the day after lunch, worked through the afternoon, stopped for dinner and then at eight in the evening carried on without break until the workload was cleared from his desk. He kept a small box of *qingliangyou* (soothing balm) handy and, if he felt tired, he would rub a bit of this stimulant on his temples to spur himself on. Occasionally the *qingliangyou* failed to do the trick, and he would light a cigarette, though he was generally a non-smoker, to keep him going. He used up many sharpened pencils in each work session, but was more at home wielding a Chinese brush to clear the stack of state papers on his desk. From extreme drowsiness he would occasionally leave a smudge here and there. Because he knew the body did not always obey the spirit, when he had to work over a document long hours after midnight, he would every now and then use a hot towel to keep himself awake.

During the Cultural Revolution, Zhou Enlai rarely got even four hours of sleep, because many unforeseen developments required his attention. He would catnap in his car to and from meetings, and if he ate at all it would be at very irregular hours. He was getting leaner and paler. Worried secretaries, attendants, drivers as well as doctors and nurses in the State Council decided to "rebel" after unsuccessful attempts to persuade him to slow down. On February 3, 1967, they signed and stuck on his office door this poster:

> Comrade Zhou Enlai:
> We are now in a state of rebellion against you. We want you to alter your work pace and daily routine, for only if you do so can you adapt to the changes in your physical conditions and serve the Party longer and better. We are motivated by what we think are the Party's and the revolution's highest interests. Now accede to our demand without fail.

The Premier replied the following day with eight words: "Accept with all sincerity. Please watch my performance." Two days later, five additional suggestions coming from his wife Deng Yingchao and signed with her name were attached to the poster. Colleagues who called, among them Vice-Premiers Li Xiannian, Chen Yi and Nie Rongzhen, saw it and endorsed it with *their* signatures. It became one of the most celebrated posters of the period, revealing a lively give-and-take between the object of criticism and its originators. Although the heat put on the Premier did not lessen, he somehow seemed to get the better of any confrontation. Age, often used as an excuse to do less, in Zhou Enlai's case somehow became an excuse to do more. The older one gets, the fewer the days left to do one's job — that was his invariable excuse.

Deskbound for most of his waking hours, the Premier occasionally took time out in the evening to do some inspection work of his own. Sometimes his aides would send word to warn the place to be inspected that the Premier would be around, and sometimes they didn't, because they themselves knew only at the last minute. One evening he visited Beijing's main department store on Wangfujing near closing time. The minute the manager got word of his coming, he announced over the public address system: "Comrade customers, we've got other business to attend to this evening. Will you please leave earlier than the usual closing time? Thank you." The voice had hardly died down when Zhou Enlai walked in through the side entrance. "Oh, no. You shouldn't do that. You should know better," he ticked the manager off. He smilingly declined the offer of a cup of tea in the lounge before starting his inspection.

The Premier mixed with the shopping crowd and walked straight to the fountain-pen counter. He asked for one, and for permission to dip the pen into the inkstand to try the nib. The shop assistant behind the counter had no idea who was standing in front of him. He was too absorbed with his abacus, totting up the day's sales, or perhaps already thinking about getting home. He just nodded, made no conversation, and didn't even bother to look up. Zhou tried the nib on a writing pad and wrote three legible characters — ZHOU EN LAI. There is no knowing whether the startled salesman muffed his accounts that evening.

The Premier approached the razor counter next, fell to talking with the salesmen, but made no purchase. He asked them, however, to pass on a word to the manufacturers. Just tell them to do something to improve the quality of their blunt razor blades, he said with a smile, for they're no good to me and others. Zhou had sported a bushy beard, a carry-over from his Long March days, during the 1936 Xi'an Incident when he headed the Communist Party delegation in the three-cornered negotiation with Chiang Kai-shek and Chiang's kidnappers Zhang Xueliang and Yang Hucheng. In those days the future Premier was known among his friends as "Zhou the Beard."

He could grow a luxuriant one very quickly. Once, when he took an enforced seaside vacation in Dalian on Mao Zedong's orders, one of his security aides suggested that he grow a beard to avoid being recognized on the beach. Zhou thought the idea was preposterous, and lectured his entourage on "beards and bodyguards." Having too many security men around, he told them, put people off and prevented him from keeping contact with them. Security, to be really effective, must rely on the trust and support of the masses, he stressed. What's the good of just a handful of men like you? Of growing a beard? He laughed and said, "Me? The Premier, the people's servant? How can you suggest that to keep me away from people!"

So he never took more than a couple of security men with him. His nocturnal excursions from his Zhongnanhai office were oftentimes accompanied by a retinue of one.

It was shortly after ten p.m. on September 26, 1958. The last number five bus from the Xijing Road terminal was approaching the stop at Tianqiao, in south Beijing, when the Tianqiao Theatre opened its gates for the home-bound theatre-goers. Two people got on the bus. One paid for two nine-cent fares. As the rookie conductor tore off and handed the tickets to the passenger, he recognized at once who it was. "Premier Zhou!" he cried.

"How are you doing, young man?" the Premier asked him. "Have you got used to the routine yet?" Before he could answer, passengers fell over each other trying to shake Zhou Enlai's hand. The conductor inched his way through the commotion to the driver's cabin to tell him that the Premier was on their bus. As it reached Beihai Park, the stop for Zhongnanhai, the conductor opened the door and leapt to the curb, ready to help the Premier down. Almost as nimble, the Premier got off right behind him, extended a hand and thanked him. The youthful conductor grasped it with both hands. To his horror, he realized too late that he hadn't even thought of saying something proper in return.

This was not the only time the Premier rode a bus to see first hand the growing problems of the capital's mass transit system. He tried the trolley-buses too, standing with other commuters and declining the offer of seats given up for him. He wanted to find out what it was like to be crushed in a bus at rush hour. In 1972, a proposal was up to re-route the number fourteen bus, which passed by the west gate of Zhongnanhai. Easier access and better security for those working and living in Zhongnanhai were reasons put forward for the change by the transport department. "No," Zhou said, "convenience for a few would mean inconvenience to many." The proposal was dropped and to this day the number fourteen bus route remains unchanged.

Zhou Enlai is perhaps unique among prime ministers for taking on the duties of a traffic policeman. He was seen several times directing the heavy flow of traffic arriving for public functions at the Great Hall of the People or the Beijing Hotel. On the occasion of one state banquet there was a bad traffic jam in front of the capital's grand assembly hall. Zhou Enlai took over. As he waved the cars by, he demanded to know why "Hei Da Ge" was not on duty.

Hei Da Ge (Dark, tall and burly) was the nickname of Yu Yufu, hitherto a traffic captain with Beijing's Bureau of Public Security, a policeman who had a knack of directing and controlling traffic with poise. An aide whispered into the Premier's ear that Hei Da Ge had been transferred. Then get him back, the Premier ordered, get him back at once. It is something of a marvel that the name and face of a minor police officer could register so firmly in the Premier's mind.

The fact is, Zhou Enlai seldom forgot a name or face, even years after a first meeting. At a reunion in 1957 with veteran workers of the Shanghai armed uprising thirty years previously, he could call almost every one of them by name.

Throughout Zhou's long career his actions and decisions were guided by a central principle — whether they benefited the people. Matters of policy were of course decided by the Party or government, but since any follow-up measures he took as administrative head of the country would affect the lives and livelihood of several hundred million people, he never failed to consult his colleagues beforehand. He attached importance both to solicited and unsolicited opinions from lower-level cadres. As he saw it, a good leader must not be a one-man band, an oracle, for oracles are dangerous beings. While a good leader must stick to a valid judgment, he must at the same time be ready to abandon a faulty decision with good grace. A good leader must know how to convince and win over skeptics to what he believes to be the right decision, but he must at the same time be big enough and courageous enough to bow to the correct views of others. That, he explaind, is part of democracy.

Because he practised what he preached, people working directly under him felt free to say what they thought, undeterred by the fear of treading on his toes. Zhou wanted no yes-men, or for that matter yes-women, around his office, and he spurned flattery and compliments. Such fulsome babble as "The Premier's opinion is absolutely right and I support it without qualification" put his back up. On one occasion he gave the offender a piece of his mind: "When we talk or hold a meeting, it is to discuss problems, to weigh up pros and cons, to thrash out different opinions and then to arrive at a correct conclusion. I would like to get views different from mine. Don't always say 'I agree' or 'I support that.'"

True indeed, his contribution to the country was an invaluable one. But he always made sure that the credit went to the Party Central Committee and Mao Zedong, that the spotlight fell on others. Unless protocol required, such as when group photographs were taken, he would try to avoid becoming the centre of attraction and would mix freely among the crowd. To borrow his favourite expression, he liked to be "just one of the masses." But when something went wrong, he was the first to come forward to take the blame. He was never one to pass the buck. Open to people inside the Party and out, he never shied away from speaking about his own inadequacies or about his errors in the past, at meetings and in conversations, if some useful purpose could be served. One man's error, he believed, should be another man's warning. He took self-criticism in such earnest that Mao Zedong once remarked, "Comrade Enlai has done far too much self-criticism."

In 1959, to celebrate the tenth anniversary of the People's Republic, the government proclaimed a special pardon for war criminals, mostly of the civil war period. Zhou Enlai allowed himself to get into an expansive mood on the occasion. On the eve of National Day (October lst), with the State Council's Secretary General Xi Zhongxun in attendance, he received in his Xihuating office some of Chiang Kai-shek's once favoured generals before they were to be released to enjoy their first sniff of freedom.

The late Du Yuming (1905-1981), father-in-law of the Chinese-American Nobel prize-winner in physics Yang Chen Ning, was very nervous. In the first place, he did not expect to be set free so soon, much less to be given this honour. He was the commanding general of the Kuomintang forces in central China fighting the People's Liberation Army, whose Chief of General Staff was none other than the man now playing host.

In the last days of 1948 Du had been taken prisoner in the Huaihai campaign in Jiangsu Province, one of the last three battles that sealed the fate of the Chiang Kai-shek regime. Du was visibly ill at ease, not knowing how to conduct himself, or what to say, in this encounter in an entirely different setting. The Premier came to his rescue. Pointing to Secretary General Xi Zhongxun, he told Du that he and Xi hailed from the same province, Shaanxi. Then he asked him his age and whether he was doing all right physically.

The pardoned general straightened up. I am fifty-five, he answered, and in a tone of dubious assurance he added, in the best of health. In that case, the Premier added, you are still young enough to do some useful work for the country. Du regained some poise after unburdening himself of what he called his crimes against the people. Of course you are guilty, the Premier turned didactic, but since you now recognize it and are willing to turn over a new leaf, well and good. Come to that, he said, perhaps I should take part of the blame, too, since you were one of the cadets at the Whampoa Military Academy. Perhaps I didn't do my job as Political Instructor well, didn't educate you and the others in the right direction, so that you went the wrong way.[14]

Chapter Four

Family Circle

Ironically, no record exists of Zhou Enlai's marriage with Deng Yingchao of Guangshan County, Henan Province,[1] though they were acclaimed as a model couple by all who knew them. There had been no formal ceremony, a wedding being out of the question in the circumstances of the time, but August 8, 1925, was always regarded by themselves and their friends as the date when they became man and wife. Of all the top Communist leaders, their union lasted the longest, stretching over half a century.

They first met in the stirring May 4th Movement of 1919 in Tianjin. Deng was then an active student in her mid-teens — vivacious, exceptionally political-minded, and a formidable orator despite her youth. Zhou, six years her senior, a prolific writer and journalist running the influential *Tientsin Student (Tianjin Student)* upon his return from Japan, was equally eloquent and equally energetic in the struggle heralded by the May 4th Movement against imperialism and feudalism. Though they belonged to the same Awakening Society, an organization of patriotic students and other young people, and saw each other often in their political activities, the strait-laced conventions of the time imposed restrictions and kept matters of the heart strictly in the background.

In the winter of 1920, together with close to two hundred other students from China, Zhou sailed for France, as part of a work-study programme sponsored by the French government out of the 1900 Sino-French Indemnity Fund.[2] There he remained for the next four years. Meanwhile, Deng became a primary school teacher, first in Beijing and then back again in Tianjin. The two kept in touch through correspondence, confining themselves at first mainly to discussing the situation at home and in Europe, as was their wont in the Tianjin days. Gradually and inevitably, they allowed themselves to touch on personal subjects. The correspondence became more frequent and more intimate.

Of course, Zhou also wrote to other members of the Awakening

Society, but doubtless "Xiao Chao" (Zhou's nickname for her, "xiao" being an affectionate diminutive meaning "small") received the bulk of his letters and postcards. In 1983, visiting an exhibition in Beijing on Zhou Enlai's early political activities in Tianjin, an old woman friend commented on one of the items on display, a postcard mailed from Paris, and Deng Yingchao, with a twinkle in her eye, told her that she still had in her possession a hundred or so such postcards sent her by Zhou Enlai well over half a century ago.[3]

In response to the Communist Party's summons, Zhou Enlai returned to China in 1924, arriving in Guangzhou in September. A host of jobs awaited him, in Party and other work, the most widely known being the post of Political Director of the new Whampoa Military Academy. He plunged into his manifold duties to the exclusion of all personal matters, and so did not see Deng until nearly a year later. By that time, apart from her job as a school teacher, she was working as head of the women's affairs department of the Tianjin Party organization, which she had joined.

By accident or design, in July 1925 Deng was transferred to Guangzhou, a new assignment which suited her perfectly. She looked forward to her reunion with Zhou Enlai. She travelled south by way of Shanghai, where she stopped over for a few days, and finally reached the south China city on August 8.

If she had counted on Zhou meeting her boat, she was badly disappointed. Guangzhou was then bubbling over with feverish political activities of one kind or another, and Zhou Enlai couldn't get away from headquarters, where his presence was needed from hour to hour to direct the ongoing Great Strike by Guangzhou and Hong Kong workers against the authorities of the British colony.[4] However, he sent his aide Chen Geng (1903-1961) to the wharf, complete with a photograph of Deng to make sure he got the right person, and with instructions to convey his profuse apologies for not being there in person. But for all his ingenuity the alert Chen Geng missed the young woman as the boat discharged its passengers amid the hubbub and commotion on the pier. Deng was obliged to make her own way to the only address she had, Zhou Enlai's living quarters. Late at night he came home and was happy to find his bride-to-be at long last.

Throughout their revolutionary career in Kuomintang China, marked more by separation than togetherness, and often mingled with peril, Zhou Enlai and Deng Yingchao came to accept vicissitudes as routine. Every time they parted, each knew it might be forever. Sudden arrest and execution or outright assassination was the fate of all too many progressives, not to mention Communists, under Kuomintang rule. One particular incident may here be mentioned because of the poignant sorrow that clouded one such separation.

It was 1927, a watershed year in the history of the Communist Party. The Kuomintang's Right-wing, the faction headed by Chiang Kai-shek suddenly broke with its partner and began attacking and massacring Communists, first in Shanghai and then throughout the country. Zhou Enlai was then in Shanghai, while Deng Yingchao was left behind in Guangzhou expecting her first child. It was too dangerous for either to stay where they were. By Party order Deng was to get out of Guangzhou at once. Two comrades, Chen Tiejun[5] and Shen Zhuoqing, were sent to the hospital. Deng under pressure took some traditional Chinese medicine which brought on an abortion. With the help of the attending doctor and a nurse Deng and her mother were smuggled safely out of Guangzhou to Hong Kong. But the getaway cost her the child which would have been born. There was not to be another.

Fond of children, Zhou Enlai and Deng Yingchao always had a soft spot for those born in the same year as their lost child. On one occasion Zhou Enlai said to his wife, "If only I had not left Guangzhou, our only child might have lived."

Filled with remorse, Deng scolded herself. "I should have spoken to you about the abortion first. But I was young then, only twenty-one...."

When they spoke in such a vein, Gong Zhiru, Zhou Enlai's cousin, would chime in, "Yes, it's really a pity that you had no children."

And the Premier would retort: "Who says we have no children? We have ten." He was speaking of the many orphans of revolutionary martyrs, whom he and Deng had taken responsibility for and regarded as part of their family.

Among these may be counted Li Mei, only daughter of Li Shaoshi and Liao Mengxing, whose given name in English is Cynthia. Li Shaoshi, Zhou Enlai's secretary, was killed in Chongqing by Kuomintang bullets in October 1945, a month after Japan surrendered to China and the allies.[6]

Zhandi (Theatre of War), a magazine which was published at irregular intervals by *People's Daily* but has since been incorporated as a supplementary column under a different name, carried prominently on the inside cover of its first issue in 1980 a facsimile of a letter written by Zhou

Enlai to Li Mei in 1949:

> Li Mei:
>   I have received your letter dated today. Whether you should start working or continue your studies, that is a matter for the university authorities and your Youth League to decide. It is not for us to intervene on the side. If however you want my personal opinion, I am not against your taking up some kind of employment, but the place should not be too far away from your mother. Now as to doing work among the masses, you can find that here in the north, too.
>   All the best.
>
> Zhou Enlai
July 23

Several points of interest may be observed, short as the letter is. It is dated July 23, 1949, only a couple of months away from the nationwide triumph of the revolution. Zhou Enlai dispensed with the usual salutation and the addressee became simply Li Mei, a mark of familiarity. He replied the same day, busy as he was with his many duties as a Party leader and Chief of the General Staff in the final months of the Liberation War. He drew a clear distinction between the public and private side of a problem and avoided taking a position which might influence the university authorities. By advising Mei not to take up work far from her mother, he showed consideration for her own desires and also reminded her of her responsibilities.

Mei was thirteen when her father died and she and her mother Cynthia Liao left Chongqing for Shanghai not long afterwards. In 1946 a full-scale civil war was in the offing and the Communist delegation withdrew to Yan'an. Cynthia was detailed to carry on underground Party work, which might well endanger the young girl. So Mei was sent to Hong Kong to stay for the duration with her maternal grandmother He Xiangning, a well-known traditional Chinese painter and champion of progressive causes within the Kuomintang.

Liberation came and the family was reunited in Beijing. Mei enrolled for a political training course at the then North China College and was to be graduated in August, just a few weeks away. But these were exciting times which fired young people with irrepressible eagerness to join the army, then recruiting college and high school students to serve as political workers on their march south. Mei, then seventeen, was no exception. Only she was worried that her mother would not approve, she being an only daughter and the family reunion barely started. She had all the wiles of girls of her age when she wrote to Zhou Enlai, the one person she believed could most sway the family. She did not get Zhou Enlai's backing, and in the end stayed behind to finish her course.

The close relationship between the two families went back to the early 1920s. In 1924, the year Zhou Enlai returned from Paris, preparations were under way in Guangzhou to establish the Whampoa Military Academy under the joint sponsorship of the Kuomintang and Communist parties.[7] Six notables were designated to bring this officer-training institution into existence. One was Zhou Enlai, and another was Liao Zhongkai, Mei's maternal grandfather, representing the Kuomintang. A right-hand man of Dr. Sun Yat-sen and a wizard fund-raiser for the Kuomintang war coffers, Liao Zhongkai had spent some years in Honolulu, U.S.A. He stood on the left of the political spectrum. Liao and his wife He Xiangning both played an active role in the first Kuomintang-Communist collaboration and were close to Zhou Enlai, who was some years their junior but already an up-and-coming political figure.

Cynthia joined the Chinese Communist Party in 1931, but at Zhou's suggestion her membership was kept secret for some twenty years and not disclosed until 1953. Born in 1904, sharing the same birthday with Deng Yingchao, she always called Zhou Enlai "Ah Ge" — the Cantonese version of "elder brother" — with Zhou's and her father's blessing, an indication of the closeness of the two families. Believing secrecy was the best way to work for the Party in conditions then obtaining, Zhou Enlai told Cynthia in 1937: "Far too many Kuomintang people know you. In no circumstances are you to reveal your Party membership. Get in touch with me directly if there is anything you want to discuss." Cynthia adopted her English given name during the years she worked in Hong Kong and in Kuomintang-controlled areas. In the circles where she moved a name with an outlandish sound was a plus.

For many years Cynthia Liao was secretary and burser of the China Defence League, headed by the distinguished Soong Ching Ling, Dr. Sun Yat-sen's widow. The position provided her with a convenient cover for doing confidential Party work. In Chongqing she and her husband kept their status under wraps and lived apart, Cynthia taking a small house in a corner of the wartime city with her daughter, while her husband worked and billeted at Zhou Enlai's headquarters. In those days the China Defence

League served as a conduit for sending funds and medical supplies donated by foreign sources to Yan'an, the nerve centre of the liberated area which, blockaded by Chiang Kai-shek's forces, was short of medical facilities of every description.

One large X-ray machine had arrived at the Chongqing airport from abroad and was waiting to be shipped to Yan'an. Though U.S. aircraft flew between the two cities at the time, not one of them had a big enough door for the machine to be loaded aboard. Madame Sun Yat-sen, after consulting with Zhou Enlai, sent Cynthia to see General Joseph Stilwell's aide-de-camp, Captain Richard M. T. Young, a Hawaiian-born Chinese, who enjoyed the general's implicit trust. Cynthia, fluent in both English and Japanese, spoke English with the captain, who then had little Chinese. Upon hearing a report from his aide, the sympathetic general gave orders to have the door of one plane dismantled and widened and told Captain Young to get it off to Yan'an the moment it was ready. For Stilwell knew full well how interfering Chiang Kai-shek's people could be, and he wanted no delay. Cynthia saw Zhou Enlai the following day and learned that the X-ray machine had been safely unloaded in Yan'an. Stilwell was as good as his word.

Cynthia's husband met his tragic death on October 8, 1945. He was on his way back to the Communist delegation headquarters after having seen a visitor home on Zhou Enlai's behalf when he was struck down. Fatally hit, he was rushed to the hospital. Zhou Enlai, who was attending a banquet given in Mao Zedong's honour by Kuomintang General Zhang Zhizhong (1890-1969) during the Kuomintang-Communist talks, was informed at once of the incident. He dashed to the hospital where his secretary, though still conscious, was unable to utter a word. Within minutes Li Shaoshi was pronounced dead.

While it was Kuomintang bullets that caused Li Shaoshi's death, Zhou Enlai on investigating the incident came to realize that the driver of the car carrying his secretary was partly to blame. Unfamiliar with the motorway in the suburbs, the car driver, newly employed by his office, had been speeding and knocked down a Kuomintang soldier without knowing it. Another soldier fired a shot for the car to stop, but the driver sped on. The angry squad leader sprayed a hail of bullets and Li Shaoshi was killed. Zhou Enlai, informed of all the facts, instructed an assistant to call on the wounded soldier to see if he needed any help. He also directed *Xinhua Ribao* (*New China Daily*), the Party's newspaper in Chongqing, to make an announcement that his office would pay for all medical expenses. Zhou's handling of the incident, marked by propriety and fairness to all, won the admiration of many, including the hill city's foreign community, who had thought the whole thing was probably a political assassination.

In memory of her husband, Cynthia Liao brought out in 1979 a collection of his poems, printed exquisitely in a slender volume entitled *In Memoriam: Shaoshi's Poems*. Cynthia's younger brother Liao Chengzhi (1908-1983) was in his lifetime regarded as China's expert on Japan. An important figure in Chinese officialdom, he was a Communist Party Politburo member, a Vice-Chairman of the Standing Committee of the National People's Congress and the official in charge of overseas Chinese affairs. At the time of his death in the concluding days of the June 1983 National People's Congress he was tipped to be the Party's choice for the high office of Vice-President of the People's Republic.

Liao Chengzhi was a raw lad of sixteen studying at the American-financed Canton Christian College when he first met Zhou Enlai in 1924. One evening he asked his father about the man who had just called at their home, dressed in a Western drill suit. Those sparkling eyes and bushy eyebrows and the conversation carried on in undertones with his father tickled the boy's curiosity. "Who's that?" Liao junior asked.

"Don't you know, son? Zhou Enlai, the Communist Party big shot!" Ten years later, the "big shot" was to save Liao Chengzhi's life on the Long March.

In the meantime, the struggle for power within the Kuomintang assumed ugly proportions in Guangzhou. On August 20, 1925, Chengzhi's father Liao Zhongkai was gunned down by paid assassins of the Kuomintang Right wing. An investigating commission was set up, with both Kuomintang and Communist members, to probe this political murder.

Zhou Enlai played a prominent role and wrote a newspaper article entitled "Forget Not the Party's Enemy" in which he pointed out the "deep plot" behind the killing. By some quirk of fate he was present at the end of two men close to him, Liao Zhongkai in 1925 and his son-in-law Li Shaoshi twenty years later. Liao's death was Chiang Kai-shek's gain. The Right-wingers held responsible for the foul act were purged and the way was thus paved for Chiang Kai-shek to seize the political leverage by which he soon gained ascendancy.

Ten years intervened before young Liao Chengzhi and Zhou Enlai met

again, this time on the Long March. During these years Zhou Enlai had
been organizer and leader of the Shanghai Armed Uprising and the
Nanchang Uprising in Jiangxi Province. Then he returned to Shanghai
once again to direct the Party's underground struggle before he left at the
end of 1931 to make his way to Ruijin, the Central Soviet Base Area in
Jiangxi Province, to join Mao Zedong, Zhu De and other Communist
leaders. In this same period Liao Chengzhi had graduated from the high-
school boy Zhou had met in his Guangzhou days to a full-fledged member
of the Communist Party.

The encounter took place some time after the all-important January
1935 Zunyi Conference in the southwest China province of Guizhou at
which, for the first time, Mao Zedong, with Zhou Enlai's support, was
established as the undisputed leader of the Chinese Communist Party. This
was during the Long March. As the Red Army's Second and Fourth Front
Armies approached the Yellow River after entering Gansu Province and
Ningxia, Zhou Enlai, Political Commissar and Vice-Chairman of the
Party's Military Commission, was looking for Liao Chengzhi and several
other comrades known to be marching with the Fourth Front Army. Little
did he know that Liao was "marching under escort" as a political prisoner
of Zhang Guotao, the principal leading officer of the Fourth Front Army,
who had read the young man out of the Party.

Zhang Guotao, a founding member of the Chinese Communist Party
who had played an inglorious part during the Nanchang Uprising of 1927,
was not the stuff Communists were made of. Sly and shifty, and as cruel as
he was ambitious, he opposed the Central Committee's decision to move
the Red Army soldiers north to Yan'an. He was manoeuvring to withdraw
the forces under his control to Sichuan and Xikang (now part of Sichuan
Province). Quite a few cadres who disagreed with him had been executed,
and the fate of Liao Chengzhi and several others detained at the same time,
including Zhu Guang, mayor of Guangzhou in the early liberation years,
hung in the balance. It was at this juncture that Zhou Enlai by chance ran
into Liao as they were heading for a town called Yuwangbao.

When young Liao caught sight of Zhou Enlai, he was torn by
conflicting inclinations — whether to greet or salute the Political
Commissar as he should, or to look the other way in his present
embarrassing circumstances. He did not want to make trouble for his
father's old friend by seeming to be on familiar terms. While he was musing
on what he should do, Zhou Enlai walked over. There was not a twitch on

his face and he said not a word, but in the presence of the escorts he simply took Liao's hand, gave it a firm shake and was off.

That evening Zhou sent an orderly to summon Liao to headquarters. The room was full of people, and Zhang Guotao was there, too. Zhang, who had begun his career in Guangzhou, was of course aware of Zhou Enlai's friendship with the Liao family. But still he asked, "You knew one another long ago?" Zhou ignored the query. He went for Liao. In a simulated harsh tone he pelted him with question after question: "Now you know you have been wrong? Do you understand how guilty you are? Are you ready to rectify your mistakes?" and so on and so forth. When he was through with Liao he told him to stay for dinner, in the course of which he ignored him, speaking only to Zhang Guotao. He summarily dismissed the young man as soon as dinner was over. Liao had been condemned to face the firing squad that very evening, and only the ingenious show of feigned anger and merciless interrogation put on by his father's friend saved his neck in the nick of time.

Accomplished in the art of intra-Party struggle, Zhou Enlai was to give abundant evidence of this ability in the Cultural Revolution when the fate, indeed the lives, of many veterans depended on his agility and adroitness in fending off the attacks aimed at them by Lin Biao, Jiang Qing and their cohorts. But at times even the master tactician of infighting was thwarted. He was unable to save someone from his own family circle — Sun Weishi, his and Deng Yingchao's daughter by adoption.

Sun Weishi came from a family of revolutionaries. Her father Sun Bingwen and mother Ren Rui, nicknamed "Comrade Mama" in Yan'an circles, were long-standing Communist Party members. Zhou knew Sun well as a close friend of Marshal Zhu De's when all three were students in Berlin in the early 1920s. In fact, it was Zhou who had stood sponsor for their admission to the Party.

Before Sun went to Europe he was a Beijing University student and a newspaperman for some years. A man of culture and a dedicated revolutionary, Sun Bingwen on his return from Germany joined Zhou Enlai at the Whampoa Military Academy and succeeded him as Director of the Political Department and Chief Instructor when the latter left Guangzhou on the 1925 Northern Expedition.

In April 1927 Sun was sent by the Party to Shanghai on another assignment, but before he arrived Chiang Kai-shek had engineered his counter-revolutionary coup of April 12 to liquidate the Communists. On an informer's tip-off, Sun was arrested by the secret police and within a week the Kuomintang dictator had this well-known Communist executed at Longhua, a Shanghai location which in the next few years earned notoriety as the favourite spot for Chiang's executioners.

Back in the mid-1920s in Guangzhou, the Zhous and the Suns often met in secret to discuss Party and other political matters, and Weishi, then hardly five years old, would take up an observation post near a window to keep watch of goings-on outside the house to warn her father and Uncle Zhou should strangers approach. Out on business, the father would take daughter along riding piggyback to see if they were shadowed. She was a bright girl and seemed to understand something of what was happening around her. But her real education in the stark realities of the time came when she was a few years older.

After her father's death, her mother Ren Rui carried on in difficult circumstances as an underground Party worker in Shanghai. Mother and daughter had to keep one jump ahead of the ubiquitous Kuomintang agents, and every time they moved to a new address her mother burned disposable Party documents. Crouching before the fire, she would tell Weishi why the Communist Party was good, and why the Kuomintang was bad. From nine to sixteen, Weishi led an unstable life, switching from one abode to another with her mother, and sometimes without her.

As the Kuomintang reign of terror grew more fierce, Ren Rui arranged in 1935 for her daughter, now fourteen, to lodge and work under an assumed name with two theatrical troupes which maintained clandestine connections with the Party. Jiang Qing, then a struggling actress with one foot in the Communist camp and the other in the Kuomintang camp, made herself available to these troupes and was sometimes given bit parts to play. However, her reputation as a woman of dubious virtue alerted Ren Rui. She warned her daughter to keep her distance from Jiang Qing, who was never to forget this snub.

By 1937 China was at war with Japan. Weishi travelled to Wuhan, the triple central China city on the Yangtze, to seek permission from the office of the Communist Party delegation to go to Yan'an. Nobody there knew her, and anyway she was too young. The sixteen-year-old refused to leave, and stayed sobbing at the entrance. Zhou Enlai, returning to his office at noon, was surprised to find a young girl weeping at the door. It had been many years since he last saw Weishi and he did not recognize her at first.

Then in a flash the familiar features rang a bell. He hugged her, crying out: "Oh, my child . . . ." The Zhous sent Weishi to Yan'an, writing to the girl often and lavishing on her the kind of love and care which could only come from a dear father and mother. They got in touch with "Comrade Mama" and asked to adopt Weishi as their daughter. Ren Rui gladly consented.

Weishi arrived in Yan'an at more or less the same time as Jiang Qing who, tired of Shanghai, was in search of new adventure. Fate threw them together. They were contemporaries at the cadre-training *Kangda* (Anti-Japanese Military and Political University) and once shared the footlights in a play called *Bloodshed in Shanghai.*

The story was about a rich Shanghai capitalist and his mistress who, because of their differences, starts an affair with the chauffeur. The denouement comes when the chauffeur, a patriot, drives a carload of ammunition destined for Japan into the Huangpu River and kills himself. Hence the bloodshed. Jiang Qing took the part of the concubine, while Weishi played the capitalist's daughter.

In the Cultural Revolution thirty years later, Ren Baige, the playwright, paid for what Jiang Qing called her loss of face in playing the capitalist's concubine. The fact is she had sought the role, since she wanted to show off her acting "talent" in her first days in Yan'an and catch the attention of the luminaries there. Before long Jiang Qing married Mao Zedong.

As the Chairman's wife, she took advantage of her position and sought perquisites to which as an ordinary Party member she was not entitled. For in a socialist community the rights and privileges, if any, of a high-ranking cadre do not extend to any member of the family. But she had few scruples and did as she pleased. Horse-riding was one of her hobbies, pursued any time of the day when the fancy took her. One escapade was the direct cause of Zhou Enlai's right elbow being dislocated and crippled for the rest of his life.

One summer evening in 1939 Mao Zedong was scheduled to deliver a lecture at the Party School, and since he was preoccupied with other matters and Zhou happened to be there at his cave-dwelling, he asked that his close associate substitute for him. Zhou got on his horse. As he headed for the Party School he found Jiang Qing riding and spurring her mount on across the shallow Yanhe River. Jiang Qing suddenly drew rein and the horse reared. Zhou pulled up sharply. He was unhorsed and to soften his fall thrust out his elbow, which crumpled beneath him. Jiang Qing would be reprimanded if the Chairman heard of the incident. Zhou saw to it that nothing got to the Chairman's ears and instructed his aides to explain, should anyone ask, that he was simply thrown from his mount.[8] But the fractured elbow needed good surgery, which was beyond Yan'an's medical facilities. Zhou was eventually sent to the Soviet Union, with his wife accompanying him.

Weishi, who had already been approved to continue her studies in Moscow, accompanied her foster parents. They travelled by way of Xinjiang in far-west China, the wartime connection with the Soviet Union. The Zhous remained in Moscow until the following spring, but the treatment was not really successful. Weishi was enrolled first at Moscow's Eastern University and then at the School of Drama, where she graduated at the top of her class. She spent well over six years in the country, mastered the Russian language and was ready to turn her hand to theatre.

In 1946 Weishi returned to China to find the Third Revolutionary Civil War raging. It ended in victory for the Communists three and a half years later. In December 1949 Mao Zedong visited Moscow for negotiations with the Soviet Party and government. Weishi served in the delegation's translation group. Apart from working in her own field, producing and directing a number of plays, including *As the Sun Rises,* her last one, about the life of the Daqing oilfield workers, she had been doing confidential work since the 1950s for both the Chairman and the Premier.

It may be mentioned in passing that it was due largely to Weishi's initiative and love for her foster parents that on August 8, 1950, the celebration of the silver wedding anniversary of Zhou Enlai and Deng Yingchao was organized. In their Zhongnanhai home she pinned on each a big red paper flower to mark the occasion and the smiling Premier explained to the young security guards gathered around the Western custom of "silver" and "golden" anniversaries.[9] It was the only time that the "model couple" ever observed their wedding anniversary.

Jiang Qing never tried to hide her jealousy of Weishi's attachment to the Premier. Believing Weishi to be privy to state secrets and important affairs in both the Chairman's and the Premier's offices, she tried to curry favour with Weishi. She followed an indirect approach: "Weishi, I'm the Chairman's wife and you're the Premier's daughter," Jiang Qing would hint. "We should get together, you know." But Weishi evaded these hints and put off this power-seeking woman. They did not get along, and never had.

With the Cultural Revolution in full swing and Jiang Qing calling the tune in the revolution's directorate, she could hardly wait to get even with Weishi. She made a deal with Ye Qun, Lin Biao's wife, a woman just as thirsty for power and a player of palace politics. Sun Weishi, Jiang Qing told the Defence Minister's wife, was her mortal enemy. Would she get her people to round Sun up for her? One good turn deserved another, she said, promising to return the favour if Ye Qun had enemies she wanted to eliminate.

Thus the two women, one the wife of the Party Chairman, and the other the wife of the Vice-Chairman and Defence Minister, laid their plans. Several ominous developments took place during 1967-68 before Weishi fell into the hands of the goons the two women had in their service.

First Marshal Chen Yi, Vice-Premier and Foreign Minister, was publicly attacked in big-character posters and graffiti put up all over Beijing. Members of a so-called "investigation group" set up by the Jiang Qing gang descended on Sun Weishi's home to demand that she write out "evidence" that Chen Yi had opposed Chairman Mao, the worst crime conceivable. "Never heard of such a thing," Weishi said as she threw the preposterous charge back in their faces.

The inquisitors pressed on. "Chen Yi must be sacked. You just tell us what kind of a man this Chen Yi is." Far from knuckling under to the snoopers, Weishi came to the old man's defence. "Vice-Premier Chen Yi has great respect for the Chairman. He is a fine soldier and seasoned general and his distinguished services have earned him the honours given him by the Party and country."

The next target was Zhu De, Chairman of the Standing Committee of the National People's Congress, who was similarly abused and vilified in posters and graffiti. Jiang Qing's minions pressured Weishi to come up with "evidence" to defame the PLA Marshal, uttering threats if she didn't comply. But she gave them no satisfaction: "Comrade Zhu De is an old comrade-in-arms of Chairman Mao's," she declared in a tone of righteous indignation. "I revere him. Save your breath. You won't get anything out of me." When these types turned up again, she pounded on the table and threw them out.

After Zhu De they shifted their attention, briefly, to a smaller target — Weishi's elder brother, Sun Yang, many years Zhu De's confidential secretary and at that time Deputy Party Secretary and Deputy Chancellor of People's University. He was accused of being a "spy". Enraged by the preposterous charge, Weishi asked for specifics. They prevaricated, simply saying that at any rate Jiang Qing had already made the pronouncement to that effect at a Red Guard meeting. She sent Jiang Qing a letter, denouncing the whole thing as a frame-up and demanding that the Cultural Revolution Directorate make a proper investigation of her brother's case. The letter was never answered. Sun Yang died mysteriously while being detained at People's University.

During this period of violence coupled with lawlessness, the attacks were not confined to a few people close to the Premier. Practically all the Vice-Premiers were tarred with the same brush. Events were falling into a pattern and hinted of things to come. Lin Biao and Jiang Qing seemed no longer reluctant to conceal their ultimate object. They were out to get the Premier himself. At dawn one day Beijing was astounded to find posters splashed on the walls of Tiananmen Square attacking Zhou Enlai by name. Jiang Qing's lackeys turned up at Weishi's home, dropping threats right and left and bellowing at her to confess all that she knew about the Premier. They shouted themselves hoarse but got nowhere.

Then, in December 1967, the police raided her home and arrested her husband Jin Shan, a well-known actor-director, on suspicion of being a spy. Suitcases and trunks were ransacked and all articles of value, particularly photographs with the Chairman and the Premier and letters written her by Zhou Enlai and Deng Yingchao, were confiscated and sent to Jiang Qing, who tore them to pieces.[10] Weishi's arrest and persecution followed. From March 1, 1968, on, even behind prison bars, she was handcuffed and roughed up in a way the petty wardens thought would please their new masters, who now seemed to wield paramount power. The shackles were not removed until October 14, when the bruised flesh could take no more punishment. Sun Weishi had breathed her last.

The question may be asked why Zhou, the country's Premier, could not even save his own totally innocent adopted daughter. What needs to be understood is the situation in China in the first years of the Cultural Revolution. Rebellion, regardless against whom or what, was given the green light by no less a personage than Mao Zedong, the Party Chairman. Though standards of some kind were called for, and indeed enjoined again and again by the Chairman himself, the damage was too devastating and widespread to be contained.

In fact, violence was encouraged by Defence Minister Lin Biao, Jiang Qing and their henchmen, who were then lording it over the country. Red Guards were incited to go for all established authorities, to smash the police departments, the law courts and the procuratorial institutions into the bargain. This was the kind of leadership given to politically naive youngsters. As a result, the routine of government offices was all in disarray, and especially the law enforcement agencies, which were replaced with kangaroo courts, star chambers and the like. Many prisons were simply taken over and run as their fiefdoms.

Imagine the difficulties of a harassed Zhou Enlai, trying to hold the country together in the face of such turmoil, working as best he could to keep up with an interminable schedule of conferences and meetings, often with the Red Guards themselves to decide on affairs of state as head of government, and not least to squeeze into the day's crushing workload an hour or so for foreign visitors.

Then there was this all-important trait of his — never allowing matters of a personal nature to divert his attention from state business. And, finally, try as he would, he was undoubtedly not able to find out where Sun Weishi was being held. That was the way things were in 1968.

On receiving word of Weishi's death, the Premier, suspecting abuse, ordered an inquest to ascertain the cause. But Jiang Qing's retainers had cremated the body right away. When Weishi's younger sister Xinshi went to ask for the ashes, she got a curt reply: "Dealt with as a counter-revolutionary. No ashes preserved."

Weishi had some premonition in her last days of freedom that they were closing in and might arrest her any day. She and Xinshi met several times in Tiananmen Square, instead of at her own home, because she was being watched. At one rendezvous near the Monument to the People's Heroes, she said to Xinshi: "I am of no consequence, a small potato, and it makes little difference whether I live or die. But the Premier... that's different. That involves the welfare of the Party and the country. The Premier must be preserved at all cost."

Then they talked about their brother, who was being subjected to an endless round of grilling by his tormentors. Both knew their brother to be innocent, but were helpless. "But if a person dies, it's hard to clear his or her name," Weishi said. "One must hang on to life. If they ever say I am dead, that I took my own life, don't you believe that. It will be murder." Thus some brave final words from Sun Weishi, Zhou Enlai's adopted daughter, who at the age of forty-seven was done to death by Jiang Qing's executioners.

More fortunate was Li Peng, also a "member" of the Zhou family. In many ways his early career was not unlike that of Sun Weishi's. Both were children of revolutionary martyrs. Both grew up in Yan'an under the guardianship of Zhou Enlai and his wife Deng Yingchao. Both were sent to the Soviet Union, though at different times, to take up further studies, Sun in the humanities and Li in science, chiefly electrical and hydraulic engineering. While Sun died at the hands of Jiang Qing's gang of killers, Li Peng survived the Cultural Revolution.

Fifty-seven years of age, Li Peng is today one of China's four Vice-Premiers, a relatively new face on the political scene, having been appointed to that post as recently as June 1983 by the Sixth National People's Congress. The other Vice-Premiers include Wan Li, Yao Yilin and Tian Jiyun, another fresh face from Sichuan, China's rich and most populous province from which Premier Zhao Ziyang himself soared to national prominence only a few years before. Li Peng's educational background as a technocrat fits him perfectly for the drive to modernize the country by the end of the century. With most of the top Party and government leaders on the wrong side of sixty, his relative youth, not to mention his specialized knowledge, stands in his favour. He has lately been elected to the Politburo and to the Party's important day-to-day working organ — the Secretariat. This was announced after the Central Committee met in September 1985.[11]

Li Peng's father was Li Shuoxun of Sichuan, one of the earliest members of the Communist Party, who took part in the Nanchang Uprising of 1927 as Party representative of the Twenty-fifth Division of the National Revolutionary Army Corps. He was a close comrade-in-arms of Zhou Enlai's and had married the younger sister of Zhao Shiyan, who was executed by the Kuomintang shortly after the Shanghai Armed Uprising. In 1931 Li Shuoxun was made Party Secretary of Military Affairs for Guangdong Province, where he directed guerrilla warfare against the hated enemy regime after the rupture of the Kuomintang-Communist collaboration. He was getting ready to hold a council of war with his comrades on Hainan Island on July 9 when an informer betrayed him to the enemy. Li was arrested, and two months later, on September 16, shot by a firing squad.

Preserved in the Party Archives Office is this letter written by Li Shuoxun before his death:[12]

Tao:

I did not deny my identity here on Hainan Island, and so it looks like a ruling will be handed down in the next few days. This means farewell forever to you all. There are executions every day, some carried out at the front, some in the rear areas, and I will be among them. Don't weep too much over my death. Take good care to bring up our son and send him along to my family. Make an effort to earn a living by yourself, too. Doubtless there will be a burial of a sort. So by all means don't come. This is imperative, absolutely imperative.

Yours,

Xun

September 14

"Tao" is Zhao Juntao, his widow, and "our son" is of course Li Peng. For many years Zhou Enlai lost track of them until 1939, when he learned that Li Peng, now eleven years old, was living with a relative in Chengdu, Sichuan Province. Deng Yingchao had him brought to Chongqing and then sent him on to Yan'an where the boy was given a proper education. They treated him like their own son. To Li Peng, Zhou Enlai was always "Uncle Zhou" and Deng Yingchao "Mama Deng."

Li Peng himself has told how, in November 1945, then not yet out of his teens but already a member of the Communist Party, he went to say goodbye to "Uncle" and "Mama" at their Yan'an cave-dwelling. He had received orders to serve in a unit of the army confronting the Kuomintang forces. Zhou was glad that the young man had won admittance to the Party, but told him in so many words that becoming a Party member organizationally is one thing and being a Party member ideologically, which is more important, is another. In other words, he should emulate the high-mindedness of his father and other revolutionary martyrs. Zhou and his wife gave Li Peng a brand new silk-cotton quilt as a parting gift. It had been sent to them by a friend in Chongqing but never used. The Zhous thought the cotton, not silk, quilts they had, though well-worn with time, were good enough for themselves. One look at the over-laundered quilts on the bed decided Li Peng to decline the gift with all the firmness he could summon. But "Mama" and "Uncle" pressed him to have it, believing that the lightness of a silk cotton quilt, tightly folded and squeezed into a knapsack, would come in handy if and when he had to march.

Li Peng, who later enrolled at the first polytechnic set up in Yan'an and from 1948 on pursued graduate studies in the Soviet Union, did fine work as an electrical engineer and factory director subsequent to his return from abroad in 1955. After holding many posts, mostly in northeast China, he was promoted to Vice-Minister, and then Minister of Power in 1981. Fluent in Russian, his first foreign language, Li Peng began to teach himself English in 1973 in spite of a heavy workload. But in the eyes of Mama Deng he is still the kid who needs a little urging and prodding from his elders from time to time. One sweltering summer day in 1983 the seventy-nine-year-old Deng Yingchao made a personal call at Li Peng's new office in Zhongnanhai to wish him success in becoming a Vice-Premier. But at the same time she warned him "not to think tog well of himself" and "not to keep himself aloof from the masses."[13]

One of Zhou Enlai's nearest blood kin was his niece, Zhou Bingjian, who became a shepherdess in the Inner Mongolia Autonomous Region.[14] In the summer of 1968, at the age of sixteen, she left Beijing to begin a new life on the grasslands with the blessings of her Uncle Zhou and Aunt Deng. Like many youngsters of her age at that time, she was answering the call to go to the countryside, to do a spell of labour away from city life. If they must go, many thought, why not to a place vastly different from China's other rural areas? Bingjian came to say goodbye, and her uncle and aunt gave her a simple send-off supper. The girl never touched beef or mutton, and Zhou advised her to get used to these meats. That would be her first hurdle in a national minority area like Inner Mongolia. She must observe and respect ethnic customs and ways of life, and psychologically must be prepared to overcome more difficulties than she had bargained for. Otherwise, Zhou warned his niece, she would waver and probably not stick it out.

Winter 1970 found Bingjian in army uniform. She had applied to join the People's Liberation Army and been accepted, a long-cherished dream come true. To be able to get into military uniform in those days was something to write home about. She dashed off a letter to tell her uncle and aunt the good news.

On New Year's Day Bingjian, very pleased with herself in a new olive-green tunic, came to Beijing to see them. On crossing the threshold, she was greeted by her uncle, but in a way very different from what she had expected: "Now you take that uniform off. And go back to the grasslands. Didn't you tell me that there is much that can be done in Inner Mongolia? Of course, you've gone through the usual procedure to apply for service in the army and everything seems to be in order. But isn't it a fact that it is because of us that the army has passed over all those applicants in Inner Mongolia to choose you? We should be on guard and not let ourselves be tainted by special privileges. Let the sons and daughters of herdsmen and workers there have the first opportunity. What difference does it make if you stay on in the grasslands?" Nepotism never touched Zhou Enlai. Not even his mortal enemies could accuse him of that.

Although upset and disappointed, and not a little embarrassed, Bingjian was convinced her uncle was right. She should go back to the grasslands. She was unaware of it, but her uncle had inquired into the army's approval of her enlistment soon after receiving her letter. Zhou's main concern was whether the application followed the normal procedure and whether his name had been mentioned to tip the balance in her favour.

Back in the army, Bingjian reported to headquarters her intention to resign and return to the grasslands. The army stalled because they wanted her to stay, believing in a few months' time the busy Premier would forget the whole thing. They reckoned without his thoroughness. He was angry with the army's stalling and reprimanded them. "Now either you send her back or I send you the order to do so." Bingjian duly returned to her job as a shepherdess, to the delight of the herdsmen, who applauded the Premier's decision to keep his niece in their midst.

The next time she went to Beijing she was not permitted to see the cancer-stricken Zhou Enlai, now very ill in the hospital. Nevertheless he called her and in a brief phone conversation encouraged her to study the Mongolian language. Barely able to hold the receiver, he was in fact transmitting his last wish to her.

On January 8, 1976, Bingjian got a telegram from Beijing with the following enigmatic message: "Don't come when you read the newspaper." She was stupefied. Early next morning on the radio she was stunned to hear against a background of funeral music the announcement of her uncle's death. She called Beijing long distance but was persuaded by her aunt to stay at her post. That, Deng Yingchao's message made clear, would be what her uncle would like her to do. For no matter to what lengths Zhou Enlai would go to give some comfort, in similar circumstances, to the bereft families of his comrades, when it came to himself he denied what should easily have been his due as Premier of China. He left word in his last days that he wished his relatives, if they really wanted to do homage to his memory, to stay where they were rather than come to Beijing. But if they should do so, they would have to pay their own expenses. Not a cent was to come from the government. He had the nation's treasury in mind, a stickler for correct behaviour to the last.

For a man closely identified with the Chinese Revolution as leader, organizer and administrator for over half a century, Zhou Enlai had a large "official" family which included secretaries, aides and security guards. These multiplied as the years went by, since he made sure that those who had been with him for some time and proved their worth were transferred and promoted to other posts of responsibility. Many who started working under him in their teens decades past had since raised families. They visited the Zhous whenever they could, bringing their wives and children along. These happy occasions brought back memories of old times together in Chongqing and Nanjing, on the Long March and even back to the early 1930s when they fought the Kuomintang to preserve the independent regime carved out in the hinterland of Jiangxi Province in south China. At such times Zhou would ask, especially his formerly illiterate bodyguards, how they were getting on with their post-liberation education. He would quiz them on the spot to see how well they could read and write. No longer raw lads but officers commanding provincial units of the People's Liberation Army in their fifties or sixties, they were in Zhou Enlai's eyes still the boys who came to work under him after joining the revolution. Zhou and his wife were concerned with their well-being and watched over their progress. They knew when to expect their visits and would have something put aside to give them a treat — nothing special, just snacks, peanuts or seasoned melon seeds or some sweets for the kids.[15]

Zhou Enlai was a taskmaster who expected each and every one of this "official" family to pull his or her weight and to work harder than others. Rather than complain, cadres regarded it is an honour to be assigned to work in his office or in the departments under his immediate control. This was a feather in their cap and put them in a position to benefit from his wisdom and experience. They thought that nothing could be more rewarding than the great man himself taking a personal interest in their joys and troubles.

One of his former aides got a letter from his parents after liberation to tell·him that the money he sent home at regular intervals had been duly received. The puzzled man had done nothing of the kind, nor could he have done so. But then he remembered Zhou asking him once a long time before about his family in the Kuomintang area. He had told his boss about their having a hard time. Without giving him any hint, Zhou had instructed his office to find some money, however small the amount, to be sent to the aged parents to help them survive.[16]

Zhou Enlai liked to share the joys of his subordinates, too. Harvard-educated Pu Shouchang, his secretary-interpreter for many years, was informed by telegram that he was a father for a second time, his wife having given birth to another daughter, and that mother and child were doing well. Pu, later a Vice-Minister of Foreign Affairs, was then away from Beijing with the Premier in the south. As a rule, members of the entourage took turns putting classified material under lock and key at the end of the day's work, which could be any time after midnight. It was Pu's turn that day. As he came in to clear the desk, the Premier mentioned the telegram received earlier in the day. He got a bottle out of the cupboard, poured two glassfuls of *maotai* and then with a smile gave a toast: "Here's to the health of mother and child!"

Chapter Five

The Premier and the People

Forty-three years ago, while heading the Communist Party delegation in Chongqing, the wartime capital, Zhou Enlai, then forty-five, drew up a seven-point resolution concerning his own conduct.[1] In a political career spanning three more decades he had consistently performed according to the high standards he set for himself — except in the area covered by the last point: keeping physically fit and abiding by a rational regimen. This he neglected, especially in the last ten years of his life, which coincided with the Cultural Revolution. As is widely known, Zhou Enlai worked long hours every day of the week, taking little exercise. He occasionally played ping-pong or strolled around Zhongnanhai. A clean-desk man, he pushed himself hard even on Sundays (China works a six-day week) all the year round. He took no vacation unless one was forced on him, and even then would take stacks of papers and documents along.

The other points of the resolution he kept very well, however, especially number six, which stressed keeping in close touch with the masses, learning from them and making himself useful to them.

Keeping in close touch with the masses is one of the three most important principles of the Chinese Communist Party (the other two being criticism and self-criticism and integration of theory with practice). It is required of leaders and rank and file alike. For only in this way, the Party maintains, can a political party in power take the pulse of the nation and gauge what is on the minds of the people, and whether they have complaints that need prompt action. You cannot sit in an office pushing a pen all day; you must go among the people to breathe some fresh air, to look, to listen, and better still, to learn. Keeping in touch with the people is the key, according to the Party.

In this connection it is illuminating to mention a visit by Zhou Enlai to an arts exhibition. Hanging on the wall was a painting supposed to show the easy style of Chairman Mao Zedong and Marshal Zhu De, who were pictured strolling in a park open to the public. Yet not a soul is shown near them or in the background of this so-called work of art. Zhou Enlai looked at it and asked, "Where are the people? Where are the other pleasure-seekers? Have they all been cordoned off?" The exhibition organizer, his face red, was given a lesson on the spot about politics and art.

Zhou Enlai went out of his way to lose himself in crowds and mix with people from all walks of life, regarding himself not as the remote Premier but as just one of the people, affable, agreeable, easy to talk to, and free of official airs. People would unburden their thoughts to him and he would elicit the problems that were bothering them. Often he took up matters that, strictly speaking, should have been the concern and responsibility of subordinates or the departments of the State Council of which he was head. They were not really in his line of duty. But the mere fact that the Premier had made inquiries, which would not have been forthcoming had he not talked to someone, often brought desirable results — for instance, the rectifying of mistakes or reversals of injustices. A case in point is Zhang Quan, one of China's best-known coloratura sopranos.

Talented, American-trained, and at the peak of her career, Zhang Quan was branded a "Rightist" in the 1957 political movement,[2] with all the dire consequences of political disgrace. Demoted, her salary cut, she was dismissed from the Central Experimental Opera House in Beijing to languish in faraway Harbin, a northeastern city close to the Soviet border. Misfortunes seldom come singly, as the Chinese saying goes. Her husband Mo Guixin, an orchestra conductor, was tarred with the same brush and made to suffer worse consequences. For his "sins" as a Rightist Mo was banished to a labour camp, Xingkai Lake Farm, in northeast China, where he was told to "remould himself through labour" — in fact, to rot in detention. He died soon afterwards.

What political offense did this young woman, a musician of considerable achievements, commit that she must be so punished? In 1957, the year the above-mentioned political movement was launched, the *Literary Gazette* published an article written by the magazine's staff but carrying Zhang Quan's by-line. The article took officials to task for not running the Opera House according to the requirements of art, and for good measure said some pretty candid things about the place. It was done with the best will in the world, not for any personal motive but in an attempt to get better operas produced. The criticisms were not taken in the spirit offered, but twisted into "unbridled attacks" on the Party's policies and principles. More ridiculous still was the accusation that Zhang Quan was vilifying an opera house led by the Party when what she did was merely to point up its inadequacies. Thus was a gifted artist who delighted Beijing's music-lovers bundled off the stage until years later, when her case caught Zhou Enlai's attention.

Zhang Quan had worked hard to achieve her eminence. In the summer of 1947, a mother of two daughters, she sailed for San Francisco to take up a musical scholarship at Nazareth College in Rochester, New York. She stayed there for a year and then received a grant to do postgraduate work at the famed Eastman School of Music in the same state, where she took her M.A. degree, studying classical and modern music under Eastman's best teachers. While still a student, Zhang Quan was often invited to sing at concerts.

Eastman's stipend covered her tuition and other school expenses but was not sufficient for her modest upkeep. She took on odd jobs in her spare time — bookkeeping, baby-sitting, giving private lessons and dish-washing in restaurants. She did a stint as a librarian. When summer vacation came round it was always to Eastman Kodak that the young woman returned for a daily grind in the film department. In addition to paying her living expenses, she made a big effort to put money away every week for her passage home. When she had earned her degree and her soloist diploma, teachers and friends pressed her to stay on in the United States. Zhang's heart, however, was in the new-born People's Republic, and in October 1951 she was homeward bound, now a mature thirty-two-year-old coloratura full of hope and expectations and ready to pass on what she had learned in the United States.

Zhang Quan's first concert back in Beijing drew a record crowd. Among the audience was Zhou Enlai, whose unexpected presence seemed to indicate that the government appreciated her return to the homeland. The Premier's appearance was a gesture to all patriots — not least the intellectuals — that they would be welcomed home to help build a new China. When the final curtain call ended with another round of applause, he went to congratulate the singer, praising her patriotism and wishing her greater success.

In her first year back in China, the Eastman graduate taught voice and was much sought after as a soloist. In the prime of her singing career, she worked as never before and went on stage even when she was seven months pregnant with her third child. In 1956 she took the leading role in *La Traviata* in its first performance ever in China, and was feeling on top of the world. A year later that world crashed around her. Even her two school-age daughters were discriminated against because their mother carried the "Rightist" stigma.

Zhang was racked with pangs of guilt mingled with doubt, and a feeling of having been gravely wronged. But even in her darkest hour Zhang Quan did not give up hope, sustained as she was by faith in herself and faith in the higher Party leaders. Sorrow did not interfere with the daily ritual of exercising her vocal chords. She persevered in this over the years.

Zhou Enlai finally learned what had happened to the singer. He reviewed the case and had her "Rightist" label removed. He did more. In 1962, Zhang Quan, then attached to the Harbin Opera House, received a special invitation to come to Beijing to attend a session of the Chinese People's Political Consultative Conference (CPPCC), the Party's united front to maintain contact and unite with non-Party people. Zhou Enlai was then its head.

At that time dance parties were a weekend fixture, and top government officials occasionally dropped by after a long day to take to the floor like other cadres. One was held at the Beijing Hotel during the CPPCC session and Zhang Quan's old friends, glad to see her back among them, pressed her to sing a few tunes. For old time's sake, she stepped on to the hotel's mini-stage and sang folk songs she had made famous. It was her first performance after four years of trouble-ridden absence from the capital. As good as ever, her rich voice filled the room. She had reached her final number when Zhou Enlai quietly entered. Resounding applause exploded at her last note, and the Premier rose from his table and clapped as he walked towards the stage. He greeted her warmly.

"I haven't heard you sing for a long time." The words sent tears coursing down her cheeks. Zhang Quan had never been so sadly happy.

Then the Premier asked for a dance: "May I have the pleasure?" As they waltzed, he kept up a conversation, wishing to know how things were with her and what she had been through in the last few years.

"I didn't know you had been transferred. Are you used to life in the northeast? You're a southerner, and constitutionally you're not strong. Take good care of yourself. If it's not suitable for you in the northeast, you can come back here." The Premier then inquired after her husband. He came to a sudden stop in the middle of the dance when told that Mo had died three months after he was sent to the Xingkai Lake Farm. To distract her from this painful subject, he gave the conversation a new drift and asked about her children. His friendly manner gave her the courage to ask what to her was an important question.

"Premier," there was diffidence in her voice. "Can someone who made a 'Rightist' mistake and has corrected it ever become a 'Leftist'?"

"Of course one can. And why not?"

This from the Premier himself was so reassuring that right after the CPPCC session she sat down to draft a recommendation for pooling the forces of the three northeastern provinces to set up a new opera house with Harbin as its headquarters — and the suggestion was adopted.

Back in the swim, the coloratura was again invited to Beijing in November for concert performances. At one of them, as she was bowing to the audience, Zhou Enlai rose from his seat, and as all eyes turned to him carried a cup of tea to the stage to offer to the singer. It was a wonderful and extraordinary gesture from one who spoke for the Party and government to mollify the wound of an unjustly treated artist.

Then came the Cultural Revolution, and like many others Zhang Quan fell on evil times again. For ten years, particularly in the late 1960s the cream of China's educated, those who had a college or higher education generally came under suspicion. Those who had studied abroad or had overseas connections were most suspect. All intellectuals were called the "stinking ninth category," following other such scum of society as landlords, rich peasants, counter-revolutionaries, bad elements, Rightists, renegades, enemy agents and capitalist-roaders.

In the circumstances, Zhang Quan became a sitting duck, the more so because she was regarded as a protégé of Premier Zhou Enlai by Lin Biao, Jiang Qing and their followers. Her artistic life was cut short again; she was forbidden to appear on stage or sing at concerts. Her background — a returned student from the United States — was enough to condemn her as a "spy" and a "reactionary authority" (on music). She was placed in solitary confinement and insulted. She was so roughed up by Jiang Qing's minions, who tried to make her confess to being a spy, that she suffered a slipped disk.

During all this time Zhang never doubted that it was Zhou Enlai, not Lin Biao and Jiang Qing and their like, who really represented the Party and government. She drew courage from this belief, and in the closing months of 1976 emerged once again from the depths of despair to bask in the sunshine of the new era ushered in by the downfall of China's most hated woman. Zhang was completely rehabilitated, with the 1957 "Rightist" verdict overturned and her salary and status restored. Her husband's name was cleared posthumously.

The number of people, high and low, censured and condemned on flimsy charges during the Cultural Revolution, as Zhang Quan was, is staggering. Practically all have been vindicated and most have returned to their old jobs, many no doubt feeling like Rip van Winkle but only a little more dazed and dumbfounded.

Zhang Quan, back again in Beijing's world of music, included in her repertoire a paean of praise to the late Premier which she sang with great feeling. Her voice pulled at the heart-strings, and audiences were so responsive that perfect empathy seemed to exist between them and the vocalist.

Zhou Enlai personally arranged for Pu Yi, the last emperor of the Qing Dynasty, to watch one of New China's National Day parades on October first. The decision was taken as a gesture of forgiveness to mark the joyous occasion.

Pu Yi had been deposed after the 1911 revolution, when he was still a child, and years later allowed himself to be used as a puppet ruler under the Japanese forces occupying northeast China. After the war he was put in prison, where through patient education he was brought to a new view of the futility of his past life and a hope for a more meaningful future. Freedom for the ex-monarch, along with other war criminals, mostly ex-Kuomintang generals, was announced in a special pardon forty-eight hours before the 1959 National Day.[3] By special arrangements he was installed at a window on the second floor of a Bureau of Public Security building on the edge of Tiananmen Square, safe from curious eyes but still close enough for him to get a ringside view of the march-past and the colourful floats rolling by which, the Premier thought, should be an education for the former emperor about the changes which had come over the country since the Communist take-over.

After Pu Yi's release the Premier granted him an audience. Lean, bespectacled and shabby-genteel in a rather ill-fitting Mao tunic, the former emperor was all courtesy and humility when ushered into the reception room, ill at ease with himself and the surroundings. Perhaps he thought that in the Premier's presence he should first of all make a clean breast of his infamous past. He began rattling off his crimes and misdeeds, such as having been the chief of the country's landlord class, betraying his country to the Japanese occupiers by becoming their puppet, and so on and so forth. The litany was stopped by the Premier, who said he had done his share of self-examination and need do no more. "If you have time," he told the former emperor, "you can write your memoirs, and that would be a service to the country." The words took a load off Pu Yi's mind. He ventured to describe to the Premier how, on his return home, former members of the court went down on their knees in the traditional greeting to royalty. He gave them a dressing-down, he said, pointing out to them how backward their behaviour was. He himself, he told them, was a shade more advanced in his thinking.

By all accounts, China's last emperor took his "ideological remoulding" seriously during and after his prison term, a fact which surprised Japanese visitors who interviewed him. "It's a marvel how the Chinese Communists have managed to do that," remarked one. "They have even transformed an emperor!" Pu Yi was given a job with a modest salary as a special research worker of the CPPCC's Historical Research Committee and acquitted himself well. Before his death in 1967 he had completed, at Zhou Enlai's suggestion, *From Emperor to Citizen,* an autobiography telling the story of how as a boy of three he was carried crying to the throne, the idleness and debauchery of his middle years, his bitter memories of being a pampered puppet, and how his thinking had finally changed.

The Premier did not find it beneath his dignity to deal with Pu Yi, who had been indicted as an "enemy of the people." He thought it worth the trouble because the Party's policy was to help war criminals reform and turn over a new leaf and because Pu Yi belonged to the Manchu ethnic group, one of China's sixty or so national minorities. The Party's policy is to unite all the national minorities to the greatest extent and rally them round the government. In this sphere of endeavour the Premier was as dextrous as he was indefatigable. Not long after the former emperor was given his freedom, Zhou Enlai invited him and his family to dinner along with Lao She, the play-wright and novelist, and his wife, both of Manchu extraction.

It was a time for politicking and the Premier made a brilliant opening gambit. Here we have dinner together, you Pu Yi, a Manchu, and you, Lao She, another Manchu,[4] Zhou said, of old one an emperor and the other a commoner. Now all three of us are sitting at the same table. In the old days, in the presence of the sovereign we would have to go down on our knees to kowtow, but now we are having a meal together as equals. Is that not a remarkable change? And change behooves us to learn things anew. Live and learn and learn to better ourselves as long as we live — this was the theme the Premier stressed. The thrust went home.[5]

One of the best-known literary names in China, Lao She — whose real name was Shu Sheyu — made Zhou Enlai's acquaintance in the early 1940s. He was a prolific writer who felt drawn to the progressive ideas of Zhou Enlai and other Party figures in Chongqing during the war years. Later he had been a teacher of Chinese in the School of Oriental and African Studies in London, and was in the United States in 1949 when Zhou Enlai in his capacity as Premier invited him to return to the liberated China. The author of *Rickshaw Boy,* a novel depicting with rich local idiom the miserable life of a Beijing rickshaw puller, came home at the end of 1949. The following year he was elected President of the Beijing Literary and Cultural Association. Knowing like the back of his hand all facets of Beijing, its sights, sounds and smells, and especially the seamy side of life in the old city, Lao She had hardly settled down after a long absence abroad when he plunged into creative writing. His play *Dragon Beard Ditch,* about the transformation of a slum area in south Beijing, is an indictment of the old and a glorification of the new. Its success and popularity encouraged the Premier to urge the producer to put it on in the Huairentang Auditorium in Zhongnanhai for Mao Zedong and other Party leaders.

   In something like ten years Lao She turned out eleven plays, and on the side other literary pieces.[6] From time to time he benefited from the Premier's personal guidance, especially in regard to political subjects with which he found himself totally at sea. Lao She felt quite comfortable with themes like that of *Dragon Beard Ditch,* but had to navigate between shoals when he turned his hand, for instance, to a play with the ongoing *wu-fan* (five-anti) movement[7] as its background. Entitled *Spring Sowing and Autumn Harvest,* this new creative effort gave Lao She trouble, first because he knew little about industrial workers and capitalists and the way money-bags operated, second because the movement was then in its initial stage, and third because writing a play with a political message as he wanted to do was, he found, full of pitfalls. The playwright might either stress Party policy at the expense of plot, the outcome of which could only be a skit rather than full-blooded theatre, or he might pay undue attention to the plot and distort the policy as a whole. Zhou Enlai was asked to be present at the dress rehearsal and he was, to say the least, not impressed. But at their request he gave the playwright, director and cast members his criticisms.

Spring Sowing and Autumn Harvest deals with an important question — the dual nature of China's capitalists, the national bourgeoisie, under socialism. The Party's thinking was that struggle against and restriction of the capitalists should not be emphasized to the point where a central fact was ignored — that under socialism capitalists are susceptible to transformation. Zhou explained to Lao She and the director the finer shades of the Party's policy towards the national bourgeoisie. He also strongly urged Lao She to guard against turning the play into mere political preaching. He advised his friend to let himself go, where the style of writing was concerned, in order to give rein to his special brand of humour, Lao She's outstanding forte. What the public wanted was a meaty play, a real work of art, he said.

It was not just the substance of the play that interested Zhou Enlai. He inspected the costumes, the lighting, the props and the back-drop with a knowing eye, for in his student days in Tianjin he had been an actor, director and all-round man of the theatre. At one of the rehearsals he attended, he spoke to the girl who was playing the part of the capitalist's daughter. He asked her opinion of one particular scene — whether she felt comfortable in it. "No, it's quite irritating," she told him frankly. He mused on the problem for some time and several days later called Lao She to suggest, tactfully, that perhaps there was something wrong with the scene. It was always a suggestion, for Zhou Enlai hated to impose on others what represented only the opinion of a single individual.

Of Lao She's later works, Zhou Enlai rated most highly *Teahouse*, singling out the first act for special praise — he found it soul-stirring, artistically executed and beautifully acted. *Teahouse*, he said, should be seen by the younger generation to let them understand how terrible things were in the past. He thought it important that all young people should have a visual image of the old China — for preaching and persuasion alone, however effectively done, was not enough.

Years later, Zhou saw *Teahouse* a second time, and after the final curtain he got Lao She and the cast together, returning to the theme of the younger generation. The play, he said, must get a message across to the young people — give them something to ponder over as to what constitutes the motive force of history and the kind of people who play a leading role in the march of time. While there was an improvement on the first production by strengthening it with scenes of a student movement, he thought there was room for further improvement, though he was not sure what episode in modern China should be chosen and typified on the stage. He wanted time to think it over and wanted Lao She especially to chew over it, but neither came round to doing it.

Lao She and his wife Hu Jieqing lived in a narrow lane in east Beijing, occupying an unpretentious small house which Zhou Enlai visited occasionally. He turned up at their courtyard one afternoon in 1959 to inquire after Lao She's health, for the writer had been feeling out of sorts lately. His wife opened the door, and Zhou teasingly reproved her for not letting him know of her husband's illness.

Both Zhou Enlai and Lao She were great conversationalists — Lao She was a witty raconteur as well — and that evening the conversation seemed to go on and on. It was time for dinner, and still they talked. The hostess asked if the Premier cared to stay for a meal, though she knew to her embarrassment there was little in the kitchen. Zhou Enlai sensed her qualms. "I'll be happy to take pot luck," he said, and smiled to put her at ease. It wasn't much even in the way of pot luck, just some scrambled eggs plus a dish of pickled fish. The guest enjoyed the meal, but teased his hostess: "Ah, ha! An intellectual after all, no expert in the kitchen!" — referring to her career as a traditional Chinese painter.

In his young days Lao She, though he had a good number of novels and short stories published before trying his hand at playwriting, was not a success financially and to make ends meet became a schoolmaster. He never dreamed that in the autumn of his life he would be held in such high esteem in the new China. Nor could anyone imagine that a writer of such distinction would die a violent death in the political paranoia of the Cultural Revolution.

In its first months the old and frail writer was hauled to one "struggle" meeting after another by Jiang Qing's Red Guards, on the preposterous charge that he was a "reactionary" who advocated the restoration of capitalism. *Dragon Beard Ditch,* they alleged, was "iron-clad evidence" of the man's crimes.

One evening Lao She's body was found lying by Taiping Lake covered with a straw mattress. When and how he died — the exact circumstances are rather murky even to this day, nearly twenty years after his tragic death. The Red Guards' version was that Lao She committed suicide because he was afraid to face up to his crimes. But several facts are now certain. Lao She was hauled to a meeting one day. He disappeared the next day. Then on the third day he was found dead. His wife was called in the dead of night to identify the corpse. She would remember for the rest of her life the ghastly experience of kneeling beside her husband to wipe clean the blood stains on his head and body.

Shocked and outraged by Lao She's sudden death, the Premier ordered an investigation into the circumstances. But much as he mourned the loss of his friend, there was little he could do since Lin Biao and Jiang Qing wielded such power at the time.

Not until June 3, 1978, was a memorial service held in Beijing to do belated homage to this talented playwright, whom Ba Jin, the octogenarian novelist, lauded as an exemplar of China's intellectuals. The author of *The Family* and a host of other novels, a longtime friend of the playwright's, the prolific Ba Jin said, "It's a shame on the living, a shame on all who survived him, to have allowed Lao She to die the way he did."[8]

Among China's top leaders of his day, Zhou Enlai was undoubtedly the most knowledgeable about the outside world. His grasp of international issues and of the problems of other countries surprised heads of government who came into contact with him. As Premier he was obliged to meet with visitors from different parts of the world, people with very different backgrounds and all shades of political opinion. As a rule, he had interpreters with him, but he would cut them short if the meaning didn't quite come across or the idea to be communicated was not adequately conveyed. He knew English rather well and had some French, German and Japanese, but was not proficient enough to carry on long conversations. While demanding high standards of those who did his interpreting, the Premier was also considerate. At banquets he would pile helpings on the plate of the interpreter sitting next to him — for interpreting at a dinner table is no fun.

As China began to play an increasingly important role in world affairs, the need for more well-qualified interpreters and translators, not to mention academics who must be familiar with one or two foreign languages, was acutely felt. Zhou Enlai took the matter in hand in 1970, meeting at irregular intervals between July and November with the foreign languages faculty and student representatives of Beijing Institute of Foreign Languages and Beijing University in five seminars each lasting over five hours.[9]

They began at midnight and lasted until about five in the morning because the Premier's tight schedule admitted only of these unearthly hours. Though already seventy-two and with an ailing heart (he had a heart attack in 1966), he conducted the seminar as if it were the first business of the day. The initial two sessions were given over to questions from the Premier and answers by the teachers and students. Pen in hand, he would jot down the gist of answers to his searching questions and in the process tried to draw out everyone present. The third session proceeded like a college class, with Zhou sitting there as an auditor but taking the measure of both teachers and students.

The last session was a *tour de force,* a summing up of the seminar by the Premier, who put special stress on grasping "three essentials": political orientation, command of language, and range of knowledge. Combining the three, he said, is required of all those who wish to serve the country in a sphere where mastery of a foreign language is a must, whether as translator, interpreter or diplomat.

He quizzed the university teachers and students. But to put them at ease, he prefaced his remarks with a disarming "nothing but common knowledge" statement. At one session he asked, "Now you have all read today's newspaper, haven't you? Fourteen Latin American countries are on record as demanding to exercise their rights to territorial waters. Those who know the names of these countries raise their hands, please."

They looked at each other but none felt confident enough. Zhou Enlai teased them for modesty and said that since nobody was going to volunteer he would have to pick someone at random. The choice fell on the one sitting closest to him, who gave a far from satisfactory answer. Zhou ticked off the names of the Latin American countries in order from the west coast around to the east. He drove the lesson home by emphasizing that the use of a foreign language was but a medium, and that a correct political attitude alone was not enough. He made it clear that one must have a rich store of knowledge at one's finger-tips. He named five specific keys to success: read, speak, listen, write and translate. Without vigorous training in all these five aspects, one cannot achieve proficiency, he said. He thought it important for students to speak the language both in and outside the classroom, and encouraged teachers to send students out to practise at places like airports or docks, where there was a good chance of making themselves useful as interpreters.

The seminar was frequently interrupted, what with the doctor coming in to remind the Premier to take his medicine, secretaries alerting him to important telephone calls or asking him to initial documents, and the like. Yet throughout he was able to keep his eye on the ball. If he saw a new face at the seminar he would ask the person's name, age, family background and so on in order to register these things in his mind, and nine times out of ten he could address the person by name when he or she turned up at the next session. He asked one of the new arrivals to pronounce "Zhou Enlai" and caught him flatfooted. Southerners sometimes have difficulty in distinguishing "l" from "n", and the newcomer immediately betrayed his origins. "Not very good at distinguishing "l" from "n", are you?" Zhou Enlai, a southerner himself, had him there.

Conducted at Zhongnanhai under his direct guidance, these seminars had a great impact on Beijing University and Beijing Institute of Foreign Languages and even beyond their campuses. It stressed the importance the government placed on study of foreign languages, which in the first place should have been the concern of their foreign languages department or the Ministry of Education. More's the pity, little came of these seminars since both teachers and students, while enthusiastically subscribing to the Premier's ideas, dared not veer from a couple of wishy-washy English textbooks compiled during the Cultural Revolution which were stuffed with political jargon in English of a sort. The Premier's first requirement which meant extensive reading of books in the original languages, was taken to mean perusing those textbooks over and over again, for the spate of directives issued by the Jiang Qing gang to its retainers at Beijing University and other institutions of higher learning in those years amounted to an educational strait-jacket. Professors who were bold enough to recommend a literary work by an established Western author, though harmless by any standard, could be called to account for "corrupting" the minds of young students. In days when Beethoven and Shakespeare were picked to pieces and condemned as "bourgeois" academics were not eager to get out on a limb.

Not until Jiang Qing's fall from power did the significance of the Premier's guidance on the study of foreign languages come to be fully appreciated. Students, no less than teachers, scrambled to find books in the original and foreign language study, of English in particular, became a craze on campuses. *English 900,* a U.S.-published text presenting conversational English, was much sought after by students who put it at a premium so far above its actual worth that it seemed possession of a copy held all the keys to the language.

In his lifetime Mao Zedong himself was an assiduous student of English. Talking to a group of PLA air force officers in 1972, Zhou Enlai told the gathering to follow the Chairman's example: "The Chairman is nearly eighty. Every day he browses over two thick volumes of *Reference Material*[10] (the morning and afternoon editions of this internal publication run to something like three hundred pages) and uses a refresher course to keep up with his English studies. The youngest among you are about thirty and the oldest a little over fifty. Anyway, young by comparison with the Chairman. Don't you think you should do the same and catch up with your study?"

Chapter Six
Maotai for a Ping-Pong Player

Like Deng Xiaoping, Chen Yi, He Long — his Vice-Premiers — and many other close associates, Zhou Enlai was a sports aficionado, as keen on watching a game of table tennis as attending a soccer match. Unique among world government leaders, he pursued this interest further afield. Possibly no other Premier of any country kept a coaching manual in his office for reference. Zhou did. He had on his desk at one time a volleyball coach handbook, *Follow Me,* by the late Hirobumi Daimatsu,[1] the famous Japanese volleyball coach who led his country's women's team to win the world championship. The Premier would leaf through it in between polishing off documents in his in-tray. Japan's success story and Daimatsu's reputation as an exacting taskmaster intrigued him. He mused over the question of what lessons China's sportsmen and sportswomen could draw from Japan's experience.

When Daimatsu's squad visited China to play against the host country's women spikers, Zhou Enlai took time out to watch the Japanese girls and their coach, not at a match but during their workouts, to see how they went through their training and to figure out what made them tick. He sat through one entire workout and, when Daimatsu and his players were through with a gruelling session, he talked to the coach and had nothing but praise for the way he put the team through its paces. Zhou Enlai took a liking to Daimatsu and his coaching method — training in the hardest, strictest way and with the next match in mind — and advised the Sports Commission to see that Chinese players took a leaf out of the Japanese book. He extended, then and there, an invitation to Daimatsu to come to China the following year to coach the Chinese women's volleyball team.[2] Daimatsu, a private in the Japanese army that overran north China during World War II, was overwhelmed by the honour given him by the magnanimous Premier and gratefully accepted.

Zhou Enlai attached importance to sportsmanship, as typified by his famous slogan in the '70s — Friendship First, Competition Second. He would come down hard on top officials of the Sports Commission should any incident or unfriendly behaviour occur when a home team played against one from abroad. There were a couple of minor incidents at one soccer match between China and a visiting Southeast Asian team. The crowds in the stadium hissed and booed the visitors for playing a shade rough. The word got to the Premier's office.

It was three o'clock in the morning when Zhou Enlai, still at work in his office, roused out of bed the Vice-Minister in charge of the Sports Commission and summoned him to Zhongnanhai. The sleepy Minister was put squarely on the carpet. This team, the Premier said, was invited to our country. They are our guests and we ought to respect them. Now even if their sportsmanship leaves something to be desired, we can talk about it and have an exchange of views after the match. How can you allow such rowdyism from the spectators? He held him and his colleagues, not the spectators, accountable — because it showed that the Sports Commission had been doing a sloppy job. It should have taken steps beforehand to remind spectators how to conduct themselves at an international match. Can't you print on the back of the tickets such slogans as Be Courteous to Visitors, Be Fair to Each Side, Respect the Referee's Decisions? asked Zhou Enlai.

Some time after this reprimand, the errant official again saw the Premier, who asked if he had read an article in the magazine *Xintiyu* (New Sports) about a primary school teacher taking responsibility for fumbling his job as referee of the school's soccer match. The teacher-umpire had been punched by a player, but thought he himself was to blame, first because as a teacher he had not taught his pupils to abide by proper conduct and second because there really had been some bad calls.

"A remarkable teacher indeed. Very high-minded. Should be commended," said the Premier as he drove the lesson home. "You are a leading cadre. There is something you can learn from this schoolmaster. In fact, your Sports Commission cadres should follow his example."

On the question of sportsmanship, Kimiyo Matsuzaki, Japan's number one woman table tennis player and the 1959 world women's singles champion, produced a great impression on Zhou Enlai. She took part in the Twenty-Sixth World Table Tennis Championships held in Beijing in 1961, and won the hearts of ping-pong fans right away, for she was a great and graceful player who kept her temperament well under control and never seemed to be flustered. At twenty-three and in top form, Kimiyo Matsuzaki was expected to retain her crown, but was eliminated in the quarter-finals by a Hungarian player. She went down with a smile, a game loser to the end.

The Premier, noticing how Matsuzaki managed a fleeting smile every time she conceded a point, was impressed by this show of sportsmanship. At a send-off dinner given for the Japanese team he came to spend an evening with the guests. He singled out Kimiyo Matsuzaki for congratulations, praised her for being a good sport, and called on Chinese athletes at the dinner to emulate her example. It was the Japanese champion player's first meeting with the Chinese Premier, and from 1961 on she became a friend of Zhou Enlai and his wife's. On later visits to China she was again invited to dinner at the Zhous' home in Zhongnanhai. Matsuzaki regained her world singles title in 1963, and in a cable of congratulations to the Japanese team, the Premier made special reference to her triumph. Kimiyo Matsuzaki enjoyed rare honour in China and was referred to as "Premier Zhou's guest" everywhere she went, even after his death.

Kimiyo Matsuzaki retired from competitive play after winning the world women's singles title for a second time and in October 1964 visited China again as coach of the Japanese women's team. Invited to dinner at the Zhous' home with other well-known ping-pong players, Chinese and Japanese, she confided the secret that she was to be married soon, and her host and hostess promptly presented her with a beautiful length of Chinese brocade — white flowers against a pink background — as a wedding present.[3] The gift made news in Japan, and it was the envy of all in the Matsuzaki family. After her parents and sisters and relatives had inspected it the young woman put the brocade in her bottom drawer. To this day it remains intact and uncut — too precious as a symbol to be put to practical use.

This was not the first present Kimiyo Matsuzaki received from the Zhous. During her first visit in 1961 the Premier had given her a bottle of vintage *maotai* for her parents, who have run a little wine shop in a town in Kagawa Prefecture for some forty years.

The news travelled fast. Kimiyo Matsuzaki's neighbours and friends from afar visited her family to see this bottle of *maotai* from China. The aged couple, who were ordinary folk, were overwhelmed with gratitude at receiving a present from the Chinese Premier.

A year later, Kimiyo Matsuzaki was again on a visit to China. As she stood in the line with other Japanese table tennis players waiting to be received by Zhou Enlai, the thought of the busy Premier remembering that bottle of *maotai* did not cross her mind. She reckoned without his phenomenal memory.

"How about that *maotai*? Did they enjoy it?" The Premier's first words took Matsuzaki by surprise.

"Excellent, really excellent." The Japanese girl was at a loss for a more expansive reply.

"Well, in that case I'll give you another bottle."

As *sake* is to the Japanese, champagne to the French, or Scotch whisky to the British, so *maotai* is to the Chinese, practically the national drink, served on special occasions. A 120-proof liquor distilled from sorghum, *maotai* is produced in a remote village in Guizhou Province, southwest China, its market formerly confined to a few cities in Guizhou and Yunnan because of poor transportation.

Zhou Enlai and other comrades from the Long March ran into it with the greatest of pleasure in 1935. But, pursued by Chiang Kai-shek's forces, they could only make a brief acquaintance with this wonderful intoxicant. *Maotai* was lifted out of its relative obscurity after liberation in 1949. Recognition by the Western world came in 1972 when scores of U.S. reporters descended on Beijing to cover Richard Nixon's historic visit to China and scenes of Premier Zhou Enlai toasting the American President in this fiery drink were televised and shown around the world, alerting oenophiles to this hitherto little-publicized winner.

When the second bottle of *maotai* crossed the ocean to Japan, Kimiyo Matsuzaki's parents took it as a gesture of honour and friendship, not just for themselves but for the Japanese people. They made a fuss, dressed up the two bottles and kept both on the mantelpiece with a large glass cover. Only on very special occasions, and only for close friends and relatives, would the old couple remove the case and uncork the bottle to entertain, limiting the treat to a tiny wine cup for each.

The second bottle lasted fourteen years and at the time of Zhou Enlai's death half of it was still left. The Matsuzaki family decided to preserve it in exactly that state as a permanent testimony of reverence.

When no longer able to withstand entreaties to go to hospital, Zhou Enlai was admitted in 1974, but his ailment was not then divulged. Kimiyo

Matsuzaki wrote the Premier to wish him a speedy recovery, not knowing that he was cancer-stricken. On a visit to China shortly after that she and her husband asked for permission to visit the patient. The request was declined by the panel of doctors at the hospital, but the Premier was informed of their call. He instructed one of his Vice-Premiers to convey his brief reply by word of mouth: "Message received. Thank you very much." Those were Zhou Enlai's last words to Kimiyo Matsuzaki, the Japanese table tennis champion who was privileged to be counted among the Premier's friends.

Zhou Enlai's death sent a crush of reporters to her home in Tokyo, but she was too overwhelmed with grief to collect her thoughts properly to tell the press how she felt.

On a subsequent visit to China in 1978 Matsuzaki wrote an inscription to the late Premier: "Premier Zhou Enlai: You live in my heart. Kimiyo Matsuzaki. October 5, 1978." It was prominently printed in Beijing's *People's Daily.*

"You live in my heart." Zhou Enlai lives not only in the heart of a leading world table tennis player, not only in the hearts of his countrymen, but in the hearts of all who had the pleasure of knowing him at close quarters.

A man of charm and poise, of great warmth and kindness, thoughtful, gregarious but self-denying, Zhou Enlai did not allow the exalted duties of his premiership to confine him merely to affairs of state. He would go out of his way to cultivate the friendships of those outside official circles — people in the arts and sports, for instance — and not only Chinese but people from other countries as well. His thoughtfulness and consideration were legendary.

His friendship for Anna Louise Strong (1885-1970) is a case in point. This American was the author of *China's Millions, The Chinese Conquer China,* and a host of other books, including several on the Soviet Union. She was considered a dangerous revolutionary in some Western quarters for her undying interest in both these countries. When she visited China for the sixth time in 1958, at the age of seventy-two, she decided to make it her home.[4] Zhou Enlai, who had known her since before the war and particularly well in the Yan'an days, put at her disposal a comfortable apartment within a stone's throw from the busy Wangfujing Street, in central Beijing. She was also provided with a woman secretary combining the duties of interpreter and companion, Zhao Fengfeng, and some creature comforts Zhou Enlai thought she should have in the autumn of her life. But in fact she continued to work as vigorously as if she were in her prime, writing a fortnightly broadsheet, *Letters from China,* which later appeared in three-volume book form. When her birthday came round, Zhou and his wife Deng Yingchao would call to wish her many happy returns.

Anna Louise's eightieth birth anniversary in November 1965 was a very special one, celebrated with the blessings of China's Party leaders. She had been invited to Shanghai by Mao Zedong, then wintering in the warmer east coast city, who gave a luncheon party in her honour. This was followed by a big party in a hotel organized by Premier Zhou to mark the occasion. Since most of Anna Louise's friends were in Beijing, and she wouldn't want to have a party celebration without them (they had always been present at each of her birthday parties in Beijing), the Chinese government made a special effort to have them whisked by plane to the east China metropolis to help this senior citizen celebrate her auspicious day. They included among others Dr. Ma Haide (George Hatem) and his actress-director wife Su Fei, the Epsteins (Israel and Elsie), the Coes (Frank and Ruth), the Adlers (Sol and Pat), the Schumans (Julian and Donna), the Miltons (David and Nancy). Sidney Rittenberg, Anna Louise's close and old associate, was there too. So was Rewi Alley, the poet, of New Zealand.

Zhou Enlai's opening remarks took the breath away of all present, and particularly the guest of honour. We are gathered here today, said the urbane and silver-tongued Premier, to wish our dear friend, Anna Louise Strong the writer from America, many happy returns on her fortieth "kilo-year" birthday. Anticipating perplexity among the guests with the use of a strange phrase, the Premier hastened to explain. In China, he said, kilo is double the unit that follows. So forty kilogrammes means, in Chinese, eighty *jin* (catty), and likewise forty kilo-year, unfamiliar as the expression must sound, means eighty years.[5] The several hundred well-wishers present — Chinese, Americans, and others — roared with laughter at this unusual, well-turned phrase. Fortieth kilo-year birthday instead of her eightieth birthday! It made Anna Louise feel very young again indeed.

Zhou laboured the point a bit. Forty kilo-years, he waxed philosophical, is middle, not old, age. Anna Louise Strong, he added, has done a lot for the people of China and people the world over. She deserves to be congratulated on her many achievements in the field of political literature. May she win more and greater success! May she live to a green old age!

Anna Louise thanked the host for a glorious birthday party. She said she was especially pleased that the Premier had cut her age by half.

Israel Epstein, UP correspondent for China back in the 1930s and 1940s, was along with his wife the late Elsie Fairfax-Cholmeley, who used to help Anna Louise Strong in preparing her copy for *Letters from China*. According to Epstein, author of *The Unfinished Revolution in China* and recently *Tibet Transformed*, back in 1965 Premier Zhou sang with gusto at Anna Louise's party, and helped the merry-making along by encouraging others to hum familiar tunes, and in particular the songs of the Long March. At sixty-seven, Zhou still looked the gusty student back in Nankai conducting the school's choir with verve and vivacity. The festivities pleased Anna Louise immensely.

Letters from China, which provided readers every two weeks with a regular glimpse into Chinese developments in the years prior to the Cultural Revolution, was Anna Louise's last major journalistic effort, but certainly not her least. It was Strong who first broke the news about Chiang Kai-shek's treacherous attack against the allied Communist forces during the war against Japanese aggression in January 1941.[6] She was in Chongqing shortly before the attack, and Zhou Enlai had talked to her about the general situation at some length over several evenings. Zhou made an incisive analysis of the war and how it affected the tenuous Kuomintang-Communist relationship. He predicted the likelihood that the KMT would once again turn suddenly against the Communist forces instead of fighting the common enemy, the Japanese invaders. The signs were, Zhou added, that the blow would come soon: "But keep this information confidential for the time being. I'll let you know when it's most propitious for its release."

A month later, Strong was back in New York. Not long afterwards Chiang Kai-shek's army launched a surprise attack on the Communist units in southern Anhui Province. A large portion of the Communist-led New Fourth Army was put out of action. It recalled Chiang Kai-shek's earlier treachery in the sudden massacre of Communists in Shanghai in 1927. He did what the Japanese army had tried but failed to achieve — putting so many units out of action at one swoop. The Kuomintang propaganda organs, which exercised tight control over the press, put out an incredible tale. The incident, they said, occurred because the New Fourth

Army had disobeyed orders and mutinied. Strong received Zhou Enlai's cable asking her to "tell the world" what she knew. So she released her story, to the consternation of the allied countries.[7]

The end of World War II found Anna Louise Strong once again in China, where she spent much of her time in Yan'an. There she often discussed China and the international situation with the Zhous. It was during an interview with Strong at this time that Mao Zedong called the atomic bomb a "paper tiger" and elaborated on the theory that the well-armed imperialist forces were not so invincible as they might seem. Hence the entry of the expression "paper tiger" into the English language.

By then Chiang Kai-shek was prepared to loose several million of his troops in a final assault on the Communist forces. He believed it would take no more than six months to finish them off. With vast amounts of materiel taken from the Japanese after their surrender and the money and munitions given him by Washington, he looked forward to a quick victory.[8] Zhou Enlai advised Strong to leave the country but to return when the whole of China was liberated. She didn't have long to wait.

Another anecdote shows Zhou Enlai's thoughtfulness and sensitivity. The late Choi Yong Kun, a top leader of the Democratic People's Republic of Korea, travelled with the Chinese Premier to Shenyang in northeast China in June 1963. Choi was a very old friend, having spent many years as a military cadet in China and fought alongside Chinese comrades against the Japanese invaders in the northeast China mountains in the 1930s. June 21 was his birthday, and the Premier decided to surprise him with a birthday party in traditional Korean style. Zhou ordered longevity cakes, longevity noodles and the like, plus a special item — sorghum rice cooked until it was very soft. The guesthouse cooks didn't understand. They would never have dreamed of entertaining a distinguished guest with so crude a dish. Choi has been through thick and thin with us, the Premier explained, it is to remind us of all we shared in those difficult days. But the sorghum rice should be soft-cooked, because the two of them were no longer young and could do with something that would not strain their digestive systems. Choi was deeply touched by the party and the simple dish which called up so many memories.[9]

Yet Zhou Enlai allowed no birthday celebrations for himself. His own birthday, March 5, was practically a state secret — not disclosed until his death and only observed in a big way in 1978, his eightieth had he lived.

Zhou Enlai was in Chongqing in March 1943. One very old comrade leaked the secret that he was turning forty-five. Associates and subordinates in the Communist delegation headquarters conspired to mark the occasion. As the day approached, Zhou learned of what was afoot and decided to put a stop to it. They pleaded with him, saying it was not really going to be a birthday party. They just wanted to get the kitchen to cook some noodles for a change. Noodles, with which the Chinese celebrate birthdays, was in fact a favourite dish of Zhou's. Fine, he said, they could certainly have noodles — any day except March 5. And that was that.

Zhou Enlai and his colleagues who were sports fans regarded sports as something more than entertainment. Attending games brought them in touch with foreign dignitaries and world-class players and gave them opportunities to win friends for China and expand contacts with the outside world.

The 1952 Olympics in Helsinki, Finland, took place less than three years after the birth of the People's Republic. The International Olympics Committee, after a convoluted struggle within the organization, asked China to take part in the games. The invitation arrived very late, with the grand opening and some events already finished, and Chinese sports circles were more or less unanimous in opting out. There was no time to organize a team, the chance of putting on a creditable performance was slim, and even if they put a team together it would probably be too late for them to take part in many of the events. Their considered opinion was submitted to the State Council. But at the Premier's urging the decision was made to participate after all. Just running up the new red five-star national flag at this international gathering would be a triumph in itself, he told the athletic officials. What is more, you go there to let people know what the new China is like and make friends. It is an opening not to be missed.

The diplomat in Zhou Enlai also urged seizing the opportunity that presented itself at the World Table Tennis Championships hosted by Japan in Nagoya in the spring of 1971. This brought ping-pong diplomacy into being and set China and the United States, glowering at each other in hostility for over twenty years, on a course of reconciliation. Relaxation of tension was a two-way street. U.S. President Richard Nixon had been sending veiled, indirect signals from Washington that the United States was ready to resume some sort of contact with what he now called the People's Republic of China, instead of the customary "Communist" or "Red"

China. But it was up to the astute Zhou Enlai to decide upon the moment for the sequence of moves he had in mind.

Glenn Cowan, a member of the U.S. team, was waiting for transportation to take him to the stadium. The Chinese coach passed by and stopped to give him a lift. Cowan fell into conversation with one of the Chinese players. They began to exchange gifts, something which worried the leader of the Chinese team, for good reason. China and the United States had been calling each other names, and if he allowed the contact to develop he might be creating an unfortunate political incident. He thought it prudent to wire home for instructions. Premier Zhou not only approved the fraternization but told the head of the Chinese squad to invite the U.S. table tennis team to visit China.

The thirteen-member U.S. team headed by Graham Steenhoven seemed excited but nonplussed. They accepted after some hesitation. Four other countries competing in Nagoya — Canada, Colombia, Great Britain and Nigeria — were invited along to make the move look evenhanded. But naturally it was the Americans who received the greatest attention in Beijing and from the world press. Ping-pong diplomacy was born.

The highlight came when Premier Zhou Enlai met with all the visitors. He moved around the room to shake hands and chat with the leader of each team. Then, seated before a microphone, he addressed the gathering, fielded questions and tossed off a few quips. He made the occasion historic with a statement aimed at the Americans in particular. "We have opened," he said, "a new page in the relations of the Chinese and American people." He added that he was sure this renewal of friendship would meet with the approval and support of the great majority of the Chinese and American people.

The Americans reciprocated by inviting a Chinese ping-pong team to visit the United States later in the year. Two decades of frigid antagonism between the two countries began to thaw with these contacts between the two peoples, set in motion by a tiny ball which started a bigger ball rolling. Dr. Henry Kissinger, President Nixon's National Security Adviser, was invited by Premier Zhou Enlai to make a discreet trip to Beijing in July.[10] He slipped in through Pakistan and made arrangements for the trip of the first American President to visit China. Zhou Enlai took this opportunity in both hands and turned over a new page in the history of China's relations with the United States.

Chapter Seven

Consummate Diplomat in Action

Zhou Enlai's career as a diplomat is often dated from the beginning of the Sino-Japanese War, July 7, 1937, when he publicly assumed charge of foreign affairs for the Chinese Communist Party. Actually his work in this sphere went back to the Xi'an Incident of 1936 which has already been recounted. The need to provide information on this momentous event led Zhou to recruit the services of two sympathetic foreign journalists who happened to be in Xi'an at the time.[1] One was Agnes Smedley (1892-1950) of the United States, the daughter of a Colorado miner who identified herself with the cause of the Chinese Revolution and wrote *The Great Road,* Zhu De's biography. The other was James Bertram, author of *North China Front,* a New Zealander.[2] They prepared manuscripts for Radio Xi'an and Zhou Enlai edited and cleared the more important material, English as well as Chinese, that went on the air.

Institutionally, the Party's first regular office dealing with external affairs was set up in the first year of the war in Wuhan (central China) as part of the Communist-led Eighth Route Army's Wuhan Office. It was called the International Information Section. Housed in a nondescript hotel room which was used both as an office and bedroom, the I.I.S., in its embryo stage, had only a staff of three or four people and a couple of dilapidated typewriters. Here Zhou Enlai received visitors and journalists from abroad and directed the I.I.S. in its routine work of translating Mao Zedong's writings. Among those who called to see Zhou for news and views—some frequently and some only occasionally—were a trio of American writers:—Agnes Smedley, Anna Louise Strong, ad Edgar Snow. These Americans are held in fond memory today by the Chinese people as the "three S's."[3] Rewi Alley the poet, another New Zealander, was also a frequent caller at Zhou's office, sometimes to discuss matters concerning his industrial co-operatives project. Host and guests talked mostly about the war and China's future.

It was also here in Wuhan that arrangements were made for foreign visitors who sought safe-conducts to Yan'an. From Wuhan Norman Bethune (1890-1939),[4] the Canadian surgeon who had served in the Spanish Civil War, and the young Indian doctor, Dwarkanath Santram Kotnis (1910-1942),[5] set out for the Liberated Areas where they were to lay down their lives in the war waged by the Chinese people against militarist Japan. Kotnis and B.K. Basu were with the Indian Medical Mission to China headed by Dr. L. Atal. Dr. Basu recalled Zhou Enlai in those days as a man bursting with energy, knowledgeable and well-informed, who analysed the war and political situation with rare acumen. The correspondents at Zhou's press conferences were many, posted by the United States, Britain, France, etc. Basu remembered one of them predicting that perhaps twenty years from now they would be proud to have known Zhou Enlai. "Why twenty years from now?" Basu interjected. "That's too far into the future, I'm proud right at this moment!"

The young staff Zhou collected for the I.I.S. were green but hard-working and eager to learn. He put great stress on using one's brains and laid down *wu qin* for the foreign service personnel. *Wu* means five, and *qin* means to get busy with — busy with five things: 1) Busy with one's eyes — busy reading and above all studying Marxist literature and Mao Zedong's writings, and the Party's policies and directives; 2) Busy with one's ears — busy seeking out people as sounding boards to find out their views of the war, the Kuomintang, the future of the country, etc., and relaying their opinions back for reference; 3) Busy with one's tongue — busy disseminating the Party's policies and principles and repudiating wrong ideas and views; 4) Busy with one's hands — busy with personal attendance to everything that must be done. The point is to rely on oneself, not on others; and 5) Busy with one's legs — busy with legwork, going out to make friends and not staying indoors waiting for somebody to knock on the door.[6]

Equally valid for other spheres of endeavour, these rules were faithfully adhered to by his staff in Wuhan. Though shorthanded, they managed to achieve much in the space of a year.

Wuhan fell to the Japanese in October 1938. The office of the Eighth Route Army moved to Chongqing, the upriver wartime capital, and in April the following year a Foreign Affairs Section replaced the International Information Section. It was put under the South China Bureau of the Communist Party's Central Committee with Zhou Enlai in charge. While in Wuhan, Zhou had to content himself with a skeleton staff, now, in Chongqing, he had more men and women to do the job, but the problems became more complex as the months went by. The Foreign Affairs Section which met regularly under his guiding hand adhered to the guidelines embodied in his review of the first stage of the war.

According to Zhou Enlai, the Japanese invasion posed threats to the Western powers, and in particular jeopardized British and American interests in China. Since London and Washington were bent on keeping their foothold in the country, the last thing they wanted was the outbreak of civil strife, which would only benefit the invaders. Such being the case, the Party must work on the Americans, the British and the French, and especially the Americans, to win them over to Yan'an's point of view. That would compel the Kuomintang to think twice before attacking the Communists in force and making peace with Japan. While it was important to rely on their own strength, Zhou Enlai pointed out, they must do everything possible to gain international support, moral and material, to carry on the war of resistance, for if they allowed themselves to be isolated that would make things easy for the Japanese.

To win sympathy and support for the resistance war — that was the line of action Zhou Enlai charted for the Communist delegation staff as they moved among Chongqing's foreign community. They sought out the embassy people and aid-China groups and made friends with them, called press conferences for foreign correspondents and encouraged sympathetic visitors to call at the delegation headquarters. Zhou Enlai himself played a big part in all these activities, and by sustained efforts he and his aides succeeded in breaking the ban which forbade all political parties other than the Kuomintang to have contact with the diplomatic corps in the wartime capital. Though Chiang's regime kicked up a furore, much of what it wanted to conceal — its corruption, its incompetence, its manoeuvres to sue for peace with Japan in order to turn their guns instead against the Communists — stood nakedly revealed before the world. Public opinion in the West, the United States specifically, began to be scandalized by what was shaping up in China.

Since much has been written about Zhou Enlai the diplomat in the war years and the late 1940s, there is little point in going over old ground again except to point out that while he spent a good deal of his time with the upper echelons of American military and diplomatic circles, he also made a point of cultivating the friendship of ordinary American G.I.s. His trips back and forth from Yan'an were made on aircraft put at his disposal by the U.S. Army, and to show his appreciation he personally invited the crew to dinners in Yan'an, a job he could well have delegated to his aides. He played host himself because it gave him a chance to mix and talk with young Americans. He also asked enlisted men and N.C.O.s of the U.S. Engineers Corps to dine with him after the work of setting up a radio station for his delegation had been completed. His easy approach and informal ways produced a favourable impression on the Americans, and they said so without reserve, which did not put Chiang Kai-shek in very good humour.

For a time after the outbreak of full-scale war between the Kuomintang and the Communists, Zhou Enlai's responsibility for directing the Foreign Affairs Section was taken over by General Ye Jianying. As Chief of the General Staff of the People's Liberation Army, Zhou Enlai was engrossed in military matters and not until nationwide victory was in sight and he and Mao Zedong had moved in May 1948 to Xibaipo in Hebei Province, the last stop before their leapfrogging march onto Beijing, did he resume his duties as the Party's chief spokesman on foreign affairs.

With final triumph in the air, the cadres of the Foreign Affairs Section were anxious to get their teeth into jobs which now seemed to beckon to them. Zhou Enlai, aware of their impatience, had work cut out for them in the interregnum: 1) To carry on with the translation of Mao Zedong's writings; 2) To train a sufficient number of people well-versed in foreign service work; and 3) To do research on the foreign policies to be pursued after the impending nationwide liberation. As Mao Zedong put it, China must start afresh in the realm of foreign affairs and formulate its policies on a new basis. The job for foreign service officials, he said, was "to sweep the house clean and prepare invitations to be sent to the guests."

On the eve of the inauguration of the People's Republic, which Chairman Mao Zedong was to proclaim at ten a.m. October 1, 1949, on Tiananmen tower, Zhou Enlai turned up at the Foreign Affairs Section for the last time. We have accomplished what has been entrusted to us, he told the beaming young men and women gathered around him. Tomorrow we shall embark formally upon our regular diplomatic work. He gave them detailed instructions on how Chairman Mao's speech next morning, together with his covering letter, was to be delivered to the foreign embassies or consulates in Beijing or Nanjing. Then he left the official seal bearing his name with the staff for stamping the communication to be transmitted to the caretaker diplomatic corps. It was the first document that went out in Zhou Enlai's name as Foreign Minister. In his first decade as Premier he concurrently held the portfolio of foreign affairs, turning the job over to Marshal Chen Yi after the two major international conferences in Geneva and Bandung.[7] Nevertheless he remained the dominant personality in China's foreign relations through the Cultural Revolution years to the day he breathed his last. No other Chinese leader bequeathed as deep an imprint on his country's diplomatic front.

Zhou Enlai is remembered not only as a skilful performer[8] but also as a top-flight preceptor of statecraft. Directives to his staff contained not only precise nuts and bolts but explanations of the whys and wherefores. One speech delivered at the Ministry of Foreign Affairs in the first years of the People's Republic afforded a glimpse into his thinking.

In the life of a nation, he told a crop of fledgling foreign service officials, it must be ready at all times to wage two kinds of war — a war of words and a war of swords. The war of words includes both spoken and written words. Diplomacy falls within the province of the war of words. There may not be a war of swords every year, but as sure as day turns into night, there will be a constant war of words, every day of the year. Those who work in the sphere of diplomacy are expected to fight their battles with words all the time, and to make a success of it. He warned them of the difficulties and obstacles in their way, for the new China, as distinct from the old, had no precedent to go by and must strike new ground.[9] While it is out of the question to follow the practice of the capitalist countries, Zhou maintained, the approach of Soviet diplomacy does not suit China in all respects either. Quite early on, the Premier had put some distance between China and the Soviet Union, for Zhou Enlai was no dogmatist who sanctified every bit of Soviet experience, as was the case of quite a few top officials in those days. He knew the Soviet Union, having made a study of that country as a young man, but he responded to the pulse of his own country and stood firm when it came to what was good for China.

His analysis of the international situation then with reference to the capitalist world boiled down to one central fact — that it is divided and not a solid, impenetrable bloc. As he put it, the old world of capitalist countries is divided into three parts: first, the bellicose forces which do not hesitate to go to war; second, the forces which stand for maintaining the status quo; and third, the forces which stand for preserving peace. In pursuance of this analysis, he laid down China's foreign policy as follows: To win over the peace forces, to influence the status-quo forces and to isolate the forces bent on war — in other words, to build a united front for peace in the international arena. Chance and challenge were there for China to bring its influence to bear on these forces, he said. He cited a minor instance which, in a way, illustrated his point.

Columbia University celebrated its bicentennial in 1954 and invited China to the ceremony in New York. Barely a year had elapsed since the conclusion of the Korean armistice and nothing but antagonism existed between China and the United States. Perhaps it wasn't a propitious moment, even on a cultural level, for contact to be made between the two countries. While declining the invitation, Guo Moruo, President of the Chinese Academy of Sciences, nevertheless cabled China's congratulations to the university. In reporting the message of greetings, Xinhua News Agency mentioned only Guo Moruo, with the name of the President of Columbia University, Dr. Grayson Kirk, omitted. In academic etiquette, this constituted a slight. But there was more to it, as Zhou Enlai indicated when he dressed down the editors responsible for the slip-up. It was not only bewildering to people who read the news, he said, they must wonder why there was the name of the recipient of the invitation but not that of the sender. More important, a chance to influence people went by default.

Seldom did the Premier allow such opportunities to slip through his fingers. The late Dag Hammarskjold, the United Nations Secretary General, was in Beijing in 1955 to use his good offices to obtain the release of captured American airmen who had violated China's airspace. It was winter. Seeing the U.N. Secretary General out to his car, Zhou Enlai found a European-looking stranger sitting beside the driver's seat in freezing weather. On inquiry he was told that the man was an American, Mr. Hammarskjold's security aide. The information got his back up. How could you let such a thing happen here, the Premier berated his aides, letting a guest shiver in the cold? Why was he not asked into the heated lobby? Someone offered an explanation. Well, he was an American. Who would want to have anything to do with an American? It is easy to understand why Hammarskjold's bodyguard was treated as a pariah. The Korean war had just ended and the United States was still the number one enemy. But the Premier thought on a different plane. What we are against, he explained to them, is U.S. imperialism, not an ordinary American functionary. How can you treat a guest like that? Make sure, he added, that he is invited to our next reception. On the eve of Hammarskjold's departure from China, the Premier gave a dinner in honour of the U.N. official. Not only was his American security aide invited, Zhou Enlai saw fit to raise his glass to toast him.

The method he had of making amends for the shortcomings and oversights of his subordinates is typical of Zhou Enlai. In the war years in Chongqing he frequently took advantage of Guo Moruo's standing offer to use his home at Tianguanfu, a rendezvous easy of access and not too conspicuous, to meet with friends politically inclined to the policies espoused by the Communist Party. For it was then not convenient, much less safe, for non-Party people to be seen at the headquarters of the Communist Party delegation. It was closely watched by Kuomintang sleuths, disguised as street cobblers, tea-stand owners, and other more shady types milling around the place. Visitors coming out of the delegation headquarters would be tailed to their homes, their names and addresses taken and often hounded and harassed until they thought it better to keep away.

One day Zhou Enlai made up a list and asked his aides to send out invitations for a get-together at Guo Moruo's residence. The appointed hour arrived, but one invitee did not turn up. Zhou wondered why. The aides discovered to their horror that they had forgotten to send the missing guest his invitation. Zhou quoted an old Chinese saying to reprimand the culprits: "No one will be happy at the table if one guest is left out in the cold." Maybe you regard it as a small matter, an unintended slight, he said. But the person in question will probably take it as a deliberate snub. In that case, it is no longer a small but a big matter, especially in these times when the political struggle with the Kuomintang is so complex and delicate. Isn't there a Chinese phrase "put yourself in the other's place"? Zhou told his aides to chew over his words. Having dressed them down, he sent his car to fetch the forgotten guest, who upon arrival was greeted with profuse apologies. As with Hammarskjold's American bodyguard, Zhou Enlai wanted no guest to be "left out in the cold."

The Geneva Conference on Korea and Indochina in 1954,[10] the first major international conference since World War II, was Zhou Enlai's first exposure to the complexities of diplomacy in a big way. It was also the first international conference after the Korean war which brought China and the United States, the two chief protagonists, to the negotiating table. World attention was focused on the Palais des Nations (the old League of

Nations building) where the two mortal enemies were poised to take up Asia's problems and to cross swords with one another. All eyes were on Zhou Enlai, who brought along a two hundred-member delegation. How the fabled virtuoso, called "the Talleyrand of China," was going to perform on the world stage was a matter of intense interest to the press corps assembled in Geneva. All were impatient to file a juicy story home.

Secretary of State John Foster Dulles, leader of the U.S. delegation, was a hardliner who pursued a policy of hostility to and non-recognition of the Chinese People's Republic. Although members of the two delegations crossed each other's path practically every day in the conference hall, Dulles permitted no contact between his delegation and the Chinese. He encouraged a glacial glare if members of the U.S. delegation were to come face to face with the Chinese in the hall or the lobbies, and he himself vowed to have nothing to do with the Chinese delegation unless his car happened to bump into Zhou Enlai's. It was not surprising that in this frigid aura there was a persistent story about Dulles refusing to shake hands with the Chinese Premier in an unexpected encounter in the lounge of the Palais des Nations.

Richard Nixon referred to it in his *Memoirs* as an "insult" and Henry Kissinger described it as a "slight" in his *White House Years*.[11] fIt would not be in Zhou Enlai's nature in such circumstances to take affront as something personal. No public act of his, at home or abroad, was motivated on a personal basis. What he did was done in the name of his country or government. In Geneva he represented China, and if the U.S. Secretary of State should choose to be insolent, it would not be towards Zhou Enlai as an individual but towards China as a country that the insolence was intended.[12]

What if John Foster Dulles had behaved less belligerently in Geneva, or the Eisenhower Administration had held a less rigid position *vis-à-vis* China in the years immediately following Korea? Would the course of history as it affects the United States have been somewhat different? That is a big if.

Dulles left Geneva shortly after the conference went into its first session, and leadership of the U.S. delegation fell upon the shoulders of General Walter Bedell Smith, Eisenhower's wartime Chief of Staff. The general was asked by a newsman at one stage of the conference, which lasted from April to July, whether and what kind of contact he had with Zhou Enlai. His only contact with Mr. Zhou Enlai was, he joked, sharing the same long rolling towel in the men's room. Bedell Smith, loosening up a bit in the conference's concluding weeks, sought out the Premier's interpreter in the lobby and made conversation. Though they were just shooting the breeze, there was something significant about the gesture. Zhou had a hunch that not everybody in the U.S. delegation saw eye to eye with Dulles regarding China, and he decided on a direct approach to the acting U.S. delegation chief.

His opportunity came soon. As he walked into the lobby one day, Zhou Enlai saw Bedell Smith pouring coffee into his cup. He went straight to the American's table and extended his hand. A startled Bedell Smith was apparently off guard but made a swift response. He had a cigar in his left hand and hastily took the coffee cup with his right, as if to indicate he had his hands full. At any rate the Chinese Premier had broken the ice. They carried on a brief cordial conversation, which ended with the American delegation leader praising China as a country with an old and great civilization and complimenting Zhou on the magnificent contribution China had made to the world.

Some time later, Bedell Smith found a chance to resume the rapport just established. It was the closing session and Zhou Enlai was engaged in a conversation in the lobby. The American went over to say hello to the Chinese Premier. Commenting on the conference, Bedell Smith said he thought it had been fruitful and availed himself of the opportunity to express his warm feelings for the Chinese people. He told the Premier how much he was impressed by his diplomatic savoir-faire and how pleased he was to have made his acquaintance. To which Zhou Enlai responded: "Didn't I extend a hand to you first the last time we met?" The American was rather put out by this reminder of his "hands full" antic, and as he tried to laugh away his embarrassment he gave the Chinese Premier a nudge in the arm before taking his leave.

Why did the acting head of the U.S. delegation never gather enough courage to shake hands with the Chinese Premier? It was baffling to the Chinese delegation and remained so for some time. Only much later was the puzzle unravelled. John Foster Dulles, while still in Geneva, had forbidden it — no handshakes with the Chinese. That explains Bedell Smith's inexplicable juggling with a cigar in one hand and a cup of coffee in the other when Zhou Enlai approached him in the first encounter and the nudge in the arm instead of a handshake in the second. For all his shrewdness as a successful Wall Street lawyer, Dulles had overlooked adding a rider to his ban on handshakes — no arm-nudging allowed.

While he wasted no opportunity to work on members of the American delegation, neither did Zhou Enlai let any challenge go unrebuked. The Indochina question came up for discussion, and speaking for China, he put forward a proposal. Finding it useful for resolving the question, Bedell Smith said so in so many words. Squabbling ensued in the U.S. delegation, some taking exception to the acting leader's favourable response to the Chinese proposal. Walter Robertson, a senior member of the U.S. delegation who had served with the U.S. team to the tripartite (Kuomintang, Communist and United States) Military Mediation Group in China following the war against Japan, disagreed with his boss. Bedell Smith, unable to sink the delegation's differences, made an excuse to absent himself in Berne. Robertson, substituting for Smith, as the chief American spokesman, attacked the Chinese proposal at the next session. Zhou Enlai responded, asking if the U.S. delegation meant what it said. "The acting head of the U.S. delegation who spoke at the last session said that the Chinese proposal was useful in this discussion," Zhou Enlai retorted. "And now you, Robertson, have gone back on his word. Whom are we to believe, you or your delegation leader? Let me remind you, Robertson, that we have crossed swords with you before. If you are spoiling for a fight, we are ready to take you on again." The conference records carry no mention of Robertson's reply, if any, to this rebuttal.

In the end Dulles' restriction went by the board. Through the good offices of the British Foreign Secretary Sir Anthony Eden, the U.S. delegation met with the Chinese to discuss procedures for negotiations on the repatriation of personnel held by each side. This finally led to Sino-American talks at the ambassadorial level, which turned out to be a record-breaking negotiating marathon lasting on and off for the next fifteen years.

Despite U.S. stonewalling, the Geneva Conference got over the last hurdle to reach an agreement on the cessation of hostilities in Indochina and provide it with a political settlement.[13] But as events were to prove, the deal came to naught because of Dulles' opposition. The net result over the years was the trauma of U.S. involvement in a no-win war in Vietnam in the 1960s and 1970s.

Although this will-o'-the-wisp goal overshadowed everything else in Geneva, from China's point of view — or, to be more precise, in Zhou Enlai's estimate — the long-drawn-out ambassadorial talks between China and the United States were nevertheless worthwhile, if only because the negotiations in Geneva and later in Warsaw led to the release by the United States of the China-born rocket expert, Professor Qian Xuesen (Chien Hsueh-sen) of the California Institute of Technology, Pasadena, U.S.A.,[14] who had helped build the first American guided missile. Qian Xuesen, a civilian given the rank of colonel in the U.S. army while working on the missile project, was detained for a period of five years merely because it was feared that the ICBM expert might want, which he did, to return to his home country, which had become a Communist-led People's Republic. Eventually Beijing got Washington to agree on releasing Qian, and the professor and his wife Jiang Ying, a German-trained musician, and their two children left American shores for China on board *S.S. President Cleveland* on September 17, 1955.

At a conference years later, Zhou Enlai, speaking of Geneva, stated that it was worth all the trouble of keeping the Americans company at the negotiating table in order to get Qian Xuesen back, although the marathon talks with the United States, he said, had produced little else that could be considered positive.

There were side-shows to the main drama in Geneva. Zhou Enlai carried on talks inside the conference hall and outside with the main cast. Sometimes discussions were held at his lakeside villa, which was also frequented by parliamentarians from other European countries and well-known figures who wished to meet the Chinese statesman. Among them was Charlie Chaplin, the genius of the cinematic world. British Foreign Secretary Anthony Eden got to know the Chinese Premier well in Geneva, and their frequent contact led to an agreement to set up a liaison office at the chargé d'affaires level in each other's capital.

Perhaps of greater significance from a long-term view was Zhou Enlai's journey in June to India and Burma in between sessions of the conference, for the Five Principles of Peaceful Coexistence concluded during his visits was instrumental in broadening what China had championed all along—a united front of Third World countries against imperialism. The Five Principles first initiated by Zhou Enlai are: mutual respect for territorial integrity and sovereignty; mutual non-aggression; mutual non-interference in each other's internal affairs; equality and mutual benefit; and peaceful coexistence. This five-point guide to international conduct underlies the subsequent Ten Principles adopted at the 1955 Bandung Conference in Indonesia—Zhou Enlai's second major international conference.

On his way to the Afro-Asian Conference scheduled for April 18-24 in Indonesia's summer resort city of Bandung, the Chinese Premier narrowly missed an assassination attempt on his life. Though not in the best of health after an appendicitis operation, he deemed the conference so important that he decided to be there at any cost. It was his plan to travel on April 11 with his staff on a chartered Indian airliner, *Princess Kashmir,* which would stop over in Hong Kong to pick up members of the delegation. A time-bomb was planted in the wings of the plane by Kuomintang agents during refuelling at Kaitak Airport, and the plane blew up in the skies just as it was approaching the coastline of North Borneo. Eleven people, not including members of the crew, lost their lives, among them eight from China, and one each from Vietnam, Poland and Austria. An epitaph on the eleven martyrs who died for the cause of peace, independence and freedom is engraved on a mass tombstone erected in the Babaoshan Cemetery of Revolutionaries in Beijing.

By a fluke of luck, Zhou Enlai was not on the flight because a late invitation to be in Rangoon, Burma, to meet with the Burmese, Indian and Egyptian Prime Ministers made a change of plan necessary. It spared China an incalculable catastrophe.

From Geneva to Bandung was a milestone. If Geneva was designed to solve the legacy of colonialism and the problems arising from the Korea and Indochina wars, Bandung was called to discuss how best to preserve the independence, economic as well as political, of the new-born countries in Asia and Africa from predatory imperialist powers. Many of the speeches delivered on April 18, the opening day, set the tone for the conference — to strengthen the ties of solidarity against imperialism and colonialism in Asia and Africa. But the difference in social systems and political ideologies, plus mutual apprehension and misunderstanding, fostered and fuelled by the former colonial powers, tended to drive a wedge between participants. From the start a discordant note jarred on the prevailing theme of unity and common cause. A couple of delegates spouted a welter of rancour — "the menace of communism," "subversive activities," "absence of religious freedom," etc. Such innuendoes had China as their target. Tension gripped the conference. It called for a prompt response.

As China was due to speak the following day, Zhou Enlai decided to distribute his prepared speech rather than deliver it at the afternoon session. In the little time left him after the morning session he drafted a new supplementary speech during the lunch hour to answer the veiled attacks, sending it page by page to the staff for translation. When called upon to address the gathering, the agile and astute diplomat who the year before had produced such a powerful impact on the world in Geneva mounted the rostrum.

"The Chinese delegation," he declared, "has come for the purpose of seeking unity, not of picking quarrels. We Communists never disclaim our belief in communism nor do we deny that socialism is a good system. Nevertheless there is no point for any one to trumpet one's ideology or political system, since such differences do exist among us.

"The Chinese delegation is here to seek a community of views and not to raise points of difference. Is there a basis for finding a community of views among us? I think there is. And that is because most of the countries in Asia and Africa have been through periods of misfortune and suffering, and continue to experience such, thanks to colonialism. This is recognized by us all. If we seek common ground and remove the misfortune and suffering imposed on us by colonialism, then it is easy for us to understand and respect each other, to be sympathetic and helpful to each other...."[15]

After making China's position clear, Zhou Enlai went on to take up the allegations about the absence of religious freedom in China and the bugbear of "subversive activities." He knocked the bottom out of these tales and invited all delegates to the Bandung Conference to visit China at their pleasure and see for themselves what the country was like, especially the coastal and frontier provinces. As if addressing the ill-wishers, he assumed a conciliatory tone to assure them that China did not mind people who knew nothing of the true situation having their share of doubt. We have no bamboo screen (bamboo curtain), he pointed out, but there are people who want to put some smoke screen between us. The Chinese Premier's speech, seeking concurrence while shelving differences, served to get hidden obstacles out of the way and did much to put the conference on the right track.

For the week-long conference Zhou Enlai virtually worked around the clock, getting no more than three hours of sleep each day. It was a worthwhile sacrifice, for the Ten Principles, embodying the Five Principles of Peaceful Coexistence in spirit if not in letter, crowned the Bandung Conference with success and laid the cornerstone of the code by which the countries of Asia and Africa—and later on Latin America—came to guide their bilateral and multilateral relationships. History will certainly not slight his monumental contribution to the people of the vast region that today is called the Third World.

Though not of the Chinese delegation's doing, Taiwan nevertheless cropped up at the conference because there were some hazy ideas floating about on the situation at the time in the Taiwan area. Guided by the principle of seeking a community of views and pigeonholing differences of opinion, Zhou Enlai put China's case before the delegates, though he did not ask that Taiwan be included in the conference's agenda. Outside the conference hall, he held talks with the heads of government of many countries and was closeted specifically with the leaders of the Burmese, Ceylonese, Indian, Indonesian, Pakistani, Philippine and Thai delegations to explain China's position.

There are two sides to the question, the Chinese Premier pointed out. First, Taiwan is Chinese territory. When and how Taiwan is to be liberated by the Chinese people is a matter that is strictly and exclusively China's business. It is an internal affair and brooks no interference by any foreign country. Second, the cause of tension in the Far East, and particularly in the Taiwan area, must be traced to the occupation of China's territory Taiwan by the United States alone. While the Chinese government is willing to hold talks with the United States to settle this side — the international side — of the question, the sovereign right of the Chinese people to liberate Taiwan cannot be prejudiced in the least. Premier Zhou Enlai availed himself of the opportunity presented by the conference to make an announcement which contained an amicable note to Washington: "The Chinese and American people are friendly with one another. The Chinese people do not want war with the United States. The government of China is ready to sit down with the government of the United States to negotiate."

Eventually Chinese and American diplomats held ambassadorial talks in Warsaw, taking the first step in the long journey to Shanghai where the history-making Joint Communique signed by Premier Zhou Enali and President Richard Nixon on February 28, 1972, at the conclusion of the President's visit to China ended two decades of confrontation and began a new period of conciliation between the two countries. The international side of the Taiwan question, in so far as it affects the United States, was thus at last resolved, to the extent that "the United States Government does not challenge" the position held by the people of China, "that all Chinese on either side of the Taiwan Strait maintain there is but one China and that

Taiwan is a part of China." In 1979, a quarter century after the Warsaw talks, China and the United States normalized relations on the understanding that the latter terminate its diplomatic ties with Taiwan, abrogate the U.S.-Taiwan treaty and withdraw U.S. armed forces from the region.

After Bandung Zhou Enlai's next major move in the world arena was a trip in 1956 to broaden China's diplomatic horizons, billed as a tour "in search of friendship, peace and knowledge," which took him to eleven countries in Asia and Europe. It was a time when among other things China was planning to explore and develop its oil industry in a big way. Wherever he went, he took a special interest in visiting factories and refineries and their installations. He thought China could learn from their experiences.

But his longest trip abroad — a record for any prime minister in the world — was made between December 1963 and February 1964, an itinerary which included visits to fourteen countries in Asia, Africa and Europe. He was accompanied by Marshal Chen Yi, Vice-Premier and Foreign Minister, on this seventy-two-day tour. It was during his journey through the African continent that Zhou Enlai enunciated the Eight Principles governing Chinese aid to foreign countries, introducing a new concept in international relations which won immediate favour with Third World countries for the spirit of genuine equality and disinterest underlying these principles.[16]

Zhou Enlai had made an exhaustive study of the question before going on the tour. There was on his desk in Zhongnanhai an updated dossier on China's foreign aid programme filled with marginal notes in his own handwriting. He made a point of inspecting Chinese aid projects in the countries he visited to see how they were being carried out and what problems required further attention. He compared the aid programmes furnished by other countries and found they had something in common in that the aid extended was in most cases profit-motivated, with strings attached and privileges extorted, favouring the donor out of all proportion. Aid under these conditions inevitably made the recipient more and more dependent on the donor.

Zhou Enlai had China's recent past and the colonial history of the Third World countries in mind when he deliberated on China's economic relations with these countries. Since China and all other underdeveloped countries had suffered exploitation by the big powers, he decided that China's aid must be of a different kind, free from any taint of exploitation.

Addressing the CPPCC First Plenary Session in Beijing, 1950.

At the First National People's Congress in Beijing, 1954.

With Chairman Mao and Marshal Zhu De on the Tiananmen rostrum to receive the salutes of the National Day parade, 1954.

With Marshal He Long in Chongqing, 1957.

Pulling his weight at a construction site, 1958.

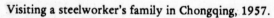

Visiting a steelworker's family in Chongqing, 1957.

Attending a meeting with Soong Ching Ling and Dong
Biwu, Vice-Chairmen of the People's Republic of China.

A get-together just before the
Spring Festival, 1962, with
Zhang Zhizhong, Fu Zuoyi and
Qu Wu (*with spectacles*).

Zhou and Chen Yi at a social gathering in He Xiangning's home (*holding walking-stick*). Her son Liao Chengzhi and daughter-in-law are on far left.

A warm toast to Soong Ching Ling (*fourth from left*) on the twenty-fifth anniversary of the China Welfare Institute, 1963.

Acknowledging greetings with Chairman Mao Zedong, and Vice-Premiers Deng Xiaoping and Li Fuchun.

Visiting the Foreign Languages Press with Chen Yi, 1963.

Celebrating International Women's Day, 1960.

What's the Premier reading?
Ask the flight attendants.

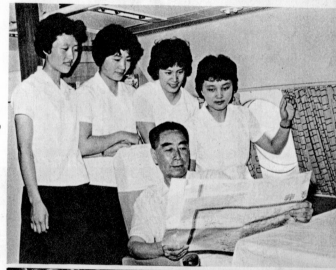

"Well done!" The Premier commends the "Iron Man," Wang Jinxi, from Daqing oilfield, 1966.

Zhou hosts his last National Day reception to mark the People's Republic's silver jubilee.

At his desk in Zhongnanhai.

The Zhous with Edgar Snow, 1938.

Laying a wreath before Lenin Mausoleum in Moscow, 1952.

Zhou's first major international conference in Geneva, 1954.

A photo with Charlie Chaplin autographed by Zhou Enlai in Chinese on left margin, 1954.

Addressing the Afro-Asian Conference in Bandung, Indonesia, 1955.

Zhou Enlai and He Long with Japanese ping-pong players. Kimiyo Matsuzaki, the women's champion, is on the Premier's left.

The Zhous take Edgar Snow (*in shorts*) to see the Miyun reservoir, Beijing, 1960.

On a visit to Burma with He Long, 1957.

"Welcome home!" Mao greets Zhou on his return from Moscow after attending the Twenty-second Soviet Party Congress, 1961.

Vacationing with Anna Louise Strong, 1962.

The Premier and Deng Yingchao with visitors from Japan.

Visiting Sri Lanka (Ceylon) with Soong Ching Ling and Chen Yi, 1964.

Zhou's journey through Africa includes a visit to Tanzania.

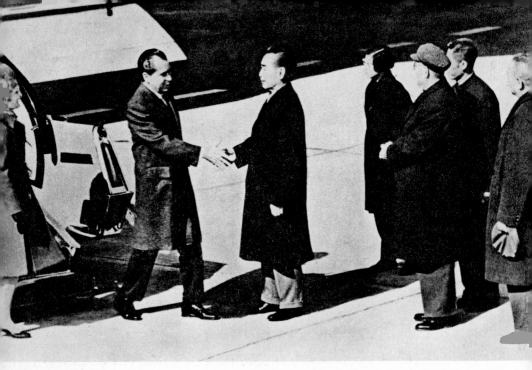

The handshake that melts a quarter century of hostility. The Nixons visit China, 1972.

Zhou watches as Mao Zedong compares notes with Henry Kissinger.

The Premier makes a point during the visit of Japanese Prime Minister Kakuei Tanaka to China, 1972.

The visiting Premier of China calls on Romanian President Nicolae Ceausescu, 1966.

Zhou Enlai and visiting French President Pompidou toast to Sino-French friendship, 1974.

The seriously ill Premier meets with his last foreign visitor from abroad, Ilie Verdet, delegation head from Romania, September 1975.

Sun Weishi, the Zhous' adopted daughter, pins on each a red flower to mark her parents' silver jubilee wedding.

An outing with Deng Yingchao.

The Zhous at the Great Wall.

Photograph of a more formal occasion in Nanjing, 1946.

It's fun to ride on a pedicab to transport rugs to the hostel where they're staying.

清漓满江水，前人已议多，
人在画船里，山川似比胸。

A day off for the Zhous with Chen Y
and his wife in Yangshuo, Guangxi

It's a game each to the Premier and th
Marshal.

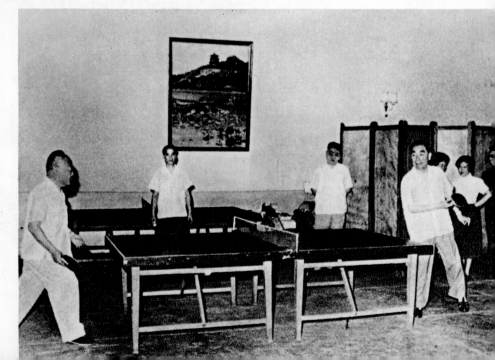

中国人民伟大的无产阶级革命家、杰出的共产主义战士周恩来同志永垂不朽！

All Beijing turns out to pay last respects to the beloved Premier.

The entire length of Chang'an Boulevard to Babaoshan in the west is thronged with people weeping, packed three or four deep, as the hearse moves slowly out of the hospital to the mortuary.

Wreaths to the memory of the departed Premier Zhou Enlai multiply, covering part of the Monument to the People's Heroes.

Thus were formulated his now famous guiding stipulations: To respect strictly the sovereign rights of the recipient country, to attach no strings of any kind, to enable the recipient country to stand on its own feet and develop without outside interference, to require Chinese personnel working on aid projects to share weal and woe and live and work in the same conditions as the local personnel in similar positions. He regarded the last mentioned the most important, a challenging proposition to aid personnel psychologically not quite prepared to put up with harsh conditions in a foreign land.

Sometimes there were conflicts of interest because some aid projects, when completed, would compete with China's traditional export items. But if a country expressed its interest in seeking assistance to build a particular factory, say, a textile mill, sugar refinery, tea plant, cigarettes factory, etc., Zhou Enlai would try to get his government, as far as possible, to extend such aid as requested. In that event, China would not only undertake to build the project in question but also teach and pass on experience, say, of how to grow cotton, sugar cane, tea and tobacco. For the whole idea of disinterested aid, as Zhou put it, is to make it possible for the recipient country to achieve self-reliance in know-how as well as in supply of raw material. He often reminded government departments charged with foreign aid projects to remember that if China had no interest other than just to look after itself that would be selfish nationalism, and if China set itself up haughtily as a benefactor that would be big-nation chauvinism. He never allowed them to forget that, and particularly big-nation chauvinism — for China, he said, is a big country and unless constantly on guard government officials are apt to throw their weight about vis-a-vis countries receiving Chinese aid.[17]

The one aid project undertaken by China that took much of his time and gave him more headaches than others was the construction of the railway which connects Tanzania with Zambia, popularly known as the Tanzam or Friendship Railway. Tenders had been offered to several Western countries when the plan was first broached. All declined. It was clearly not a profitable proposition, and moreover the difficulties and hazards involved in cutting through almost impenetrable jungles to lay tracks seemed insurmountable. The two countries turned to China hopefully, but not very confidently. They knew China was not a rich country either and it had a heavy railway building programme of its own to fulfil. To their gratification Beijing agreed to bankroll and construct the projected trunk line.

It took six years of unremitting effort to complete this 1,800-kilometre railway to link landlocked Zambia with Tanzania on the eastern seaboard. By the time it was ready to be commissioned, in July 1976 to be exact, Zhou Enlai had left this world. It was fitting that the people of Tanzania and Zambia, as they staged festivities to celebrate the opening of their railway to traffic, should pay tribute to the man who had done much to help them turn a dream into reality by observing minutes of silence that day to honour his memory.

Another precept of which Zhou Enlai kept reminding his staff on that tour is that states, big or small, must be treated on an equal footing, and that the smaller the state, the greater the respect must be shown it. One incident speaks volumes for this principle, which he strictly observed throughout his premiership.

A few days before Zhou Enlai's arrival in Accra, the capital of Ghana in West Africa (a country with a population of eight million, roughly the same as Beijing's, and with an area slightly larger than Hebei Province in which Beijing is located) a coup threatened to topple the regime of Dr. Kwame Nkrumah, the President. Nkrumah was then putting the finishing touches on the preparations to welcome the distinguished visitor from China. There was talk among the Chinese staff of postponing or scratching the visit for security's sake. Zhou disagreed. The more the hosts found themselves in trouble, he explained, the more they needed support, and the more we should go as originally planned. He asked the Ghanaian government to dispense with protocol, doing away with the usual welcome and send-off formalities at the airport, in order to ensure President Nkrumah maximum safety. For good measure he suggested that the scheduled talks, the banquet to be given in his honour and other activities, all take place in the castle where the Ghanaian leader was staying. He gave little thought to his own personal safety.

In contrast to Ghana, his visit to the Sudan shed light on this characteristic of his in a different context. Khartoum had proposed that Premier Zhou Enlai and the host ride in an open car from the airport to the guesthouse to allow people in the capital to get a glimpse of their Chinese guest. The situation in the Sudan then being rather fluid, the Chinese delegation staff demurred. When informed of such non-arrangements, the Premier rapped the over-anxious aides and told them to arrange with Sudanese officials an open motorcade from the guesthouse to the airport on the day of departure, in order to make amends. Was this protocol? Superficially, yes, but the decision taken went far beyond that. It was meant to be a gesture of solidarity with the besieged leader of an oppressed nation.

One lasting impression left behind by Zhou Enlai in the countries he visited was his folksy style. He went out of his way to meet ordinary people. When it was time to say goodbye, he would seek out the car drivers, the guesthouse and hotel kitchen staff, the aircraft crew, and the plainclothes security men to thank them all for making his visit a pleasant and enjoyable one. He sprang the biggest surprise on the reporters covering his tour by the unusual kindness he showed to the "untouchables" employed by the Chinese Embassy in New Delhi. He shook hands with them, one and all, pumping sympathy and commiseration into his handshakes. At the bottom of the social ladder, the "untouchables" in India, regarded as following the most degrading occupation, cleaning toilets and sweeping floors, are traditionally outcasts shunned and spurned by all except people within their own caste — a system of exploitation and oppression rather than an attitude to the calling that keeps the harijans in thrall, downtrodden and degraded.

Among China's top leaders Zhou Enlai had more face-to-face dealings than any other with the Kremlin leaders. He negotiated with Stalin at the turn of the 1950s in Moscow, and later maintained that for all his foibles and failings Stalin was a great proletarian revolutionary. He took strong exception to the way the late Soviet leader was reviled by his successors and told them to their face that their policies were deviating from orthodox Marxism. In a Moscow confrontation with Nikita Khrushchev Zhou Enlai challenged his paternalistic claim to speak for the international communist movement and castigated his crass analysis which condemned Stalin for all the things that had gone wrong in the Soviet Union.

In the second half of 1956, two events fraught with peril rocked Moscow-dominated Eastern Europe. One was the outbreak of demonstrations in Poznan, Poland, and the other was the insurrection in Budapest, Hungary. Both came in the wake of the "de-Stalinization" pushed earlier in February by Khrushchev and his collaborators. In Poland it was a domestic uproar because the Poznan workers, fed up with the way things were going in the political and economic spheres, took to the streets to give vent to their discontent, whereas in Hungary it was a different matter, nothing but a counter-revolution, compounded as it was by the intrusion of hostile forces from outside the country. There protest marchers not only opposed the constituted authority but decided to overthrow it and take Hungary out of the Warsaw Pact. In both cases Khrushchev lost his nerve, moving Warsaw Pact armies about to threaten Poland with the use of force, while to deal with Hungary he sent Soviet troops into the country to quell the insurrection without even a fig-leaf in the shape, say, of an "invitation" from the injured country which marked his successor Brezhnev's rape of Czechoslovakia in 1968 and Afghanistan ten years later.

On his visit to Moscow in January 1957 to discuss the East European situation with the Soviet leaders, Zhou Enlai rapped them for interfering in Poland's internal affairs and brandishing the big stick to thwart any line of policy or action that ran counter to the Kremlin's.

From Moscow he journeyed to Poland and Hungary. In Budapest, where the guns had yet to fall silent, he brushed aside risks to speak to a rally of activists at which he hauled the Soviet leadership over the coals for not observing the principles of equality of nations and proletarian internationalism. This stirring speech brought tears to the eyes of veteran Hungarian Communists.

Polemics on tenets of Marxism-Leninism brought the split between Beijing and Moscow into the open in 1960. Under Khrushchev the Soviet Union threw its weight about — not only in relations between states but also in relations between the two Parties. Sino-Soviet relations, which had grown increasingly sour for some time, now reached a new low. Khrushchev put the screws on, fondly hoping that China would be intimidated into hewing to the Soviet line. Without warning he tore to pieces several hundred agreements and contracts with the Chinese government, withdrew en bloc Soviet personnel working on aid projects, and stopped shipping essential equipment to China. What is more, Moscow dunned Beijing for repayment of loans contracted during the Korean war.

The Soviet leader thought he had China by the throat, for in terms of farm production 1960 was a bad year for the country. There had been crop failures, thanks in part to erroneous policies in the rural areas. China indeed went through a very difficult time.

But Zhou Enlai, as head of the government, and as directed by Mao Zedong, responded to the Soviet pressure by stepping up the polemical struggle and organizing the nation in a united effort to offset the havoc wrought by the Soviets and nature. As a result, things began to hum again the following year and in October, when he attended the Twenty-second Soviet Party Congress in Moscow, China had economically turned the corner.

The Twenty-second Party Congress, if noted for nothing else in particular, is remembered for the profanity heaped on Stalin once again. The dead leader not only became the object of abuse at the sessions, his sarcophagus was also defiled and removed from Red Square, with his body reburied elsewhere in an unceremonious manner. Zhou Enlai let Khrushchev and his cronies know where China stood on this matter. He led the Chinese delegation to Red Square and left a wreath before the Lenin mausoleum. Then he searched out Stalin's new resting place and laid before it a bouquet of flowers bearing an inscription — an act of defiance and contempt for his desecrators. "To J.V. Stalin, a great Marxist-Leninist," it said. That done, Zhou walked out on the Soviet Congress without waiting for it to wind up its business and flew home.

When *The Spirit of '76* carrying U.S. President Richard M. Nixon landed on February 21, 1972, at the Beijing airport to begin what Nixon described at the end of his visit as "the week that changed the world," seventy-three-year-old Premier Zhou Enlai stood rod-erect near the ramp to welcome the first American chief executive ever to set foot on Chinese soil. Immaculate in a gray tunic topped by a dark overcoat to brave the inclement February weather, the frail-looking Premier, unbeknownst to the world, was actually a very sick man. He had suffered from heart failure since 1966 and now was cancer-stricken. The tell-tale shadows that etched Zhou Enlai's kind and alert face accentuated his poor health.

But the week from February 21 to 28, 1972, saw him engaged in session after session of talks and negotiations with the American president, showing no signs of fatigue as he accompanied the Nixons to the social events in the evening as well. Nixon noticed his interlocutor taking some pills halfway through their four-hour meetings and thought they were for high blood pressure. But Zhou's ailment was much more serious. Early on at one meeting, according to Nixon's *Memoirs,* while the Chinese Premier expressed hope that the President and his National Security Adviser would continue in office, he intimated that he himself might not be on the scene. "For example, if I should die of a heart attack, you would have to deal with a different counterpart." He was speaking not hypothetically but the plain truth, and only half of the truth at that. Death, kept at bay by sheer will-power, as well as medical treatment, was less than four years away.[18]

In the meantime he soldiered on, as firmly in the driver's seat as ever, first in his Zhongnanhai office and, when no longer able to be there, from a hospital bed. As co-architect with Mao Zedong of the new approach to the United States, he gave his entire attention to Nixon's visit, undertaking to negotiate for his country in matters big and small and orchestrating the activities which climaxed in the signing of the famous Shanghai Communique on the President's last day in China.

Concluded on February 28, 1972, the Joint Communique is a unique document in the annals of international affairs, the outcome of a long and intense negotiating process of give-and-take. It is unique because, unlike most international agreements which employ banalities and platitudes to gloss over differences that cannot be composed in the negotiation process, this joint communique lists and defines the points of difference as well as the concurring opinions between the two countries. The disputes and differences are uniformly prefaced with the formula, "the U.S. side stated" or "the Chinese side stated," by which each party to the communique calls attention to matters where there is no agreement.

All this reminds one of the policy Zhou Enlai adopted back in 1955 in the Indonesian city of Bandung—seeking concurrence and shelving differences. What sets Bandung apart from Shanghai is that while the differences in Bandung were left unrecorded in the Afro-Asian concord of Ten Principles, the Shanghai Communique catalogues and sets forth the discordant points at length. It was Zhou Enlai all over again.

At daggers drawn for two decades, the People's Republic of China and the United States of America had been exchanging venomous invective without cease since the Korean war of the early 1950s. While the People's Republic was pilloried as international "criminals" or "outlaws" in the American media, the United States was cast in the role of "arch imperialist" in the Chinese press. So before that historic handclasp between the American President and the Chinese Premier at noontime on February 21, 1972, could melt all the rigidity and sterility of the hostile years, much had to be done on both sides of the Pacific to defuse the enmity accumulated down the years and explain to the people the need for turning over a new page in Sino-American relations.

On his part Nixon dwelled on the importance of establishing a dialogue with the leaders in Beijing and spoke about "ending the isolation of mainland China from the world community."

Through Edgar Snow, the American writer, Mao Zedong had earlier sent an open and clear signal suggesting that Richard Nixon, if he so wished, would be welcome to visit China either as President or as a private tourist.[19]

The State Council under Zhou Enlai took the opportunity to enlighten all sectors of the people on the changing factors in the international situation that called for exploration of a new avenue to set China on the course of resuming contact with the United States. Reports carrying essential information on the United States were relayed through government channels at all levels, together with explanations as to why President Nixon, hitherto roundly abused in the Chinese press, was invited to China as a guest of the government. For it would be difficult for the man in the street, if not prepared beforehand, to swallow the affront of seeing the "arch imperialist" being dined in the Great Hall of the People.

Indeed, for quite some time before the Sino-American rapprochement actually took place, the triangular relationship of China, the Soviet Union and the United States had undergone some changes. By massing a million hostile troops on its borders with China, the Soviet Union had brought the strained relationships between the two countries to breaking-point. The circamstances of the time made it possible for a change from collision to conciliation in China's relationship with the United States. So the corner was not too difficult to turn. A typical Chinese expression frequently used at the time was *zhuanwanzi,* literally, to turn a corner, in other words, to follow a different tack.

If from the start the reception accorded the American visitors was low-key, merely courteous and correct, that was only to be expected. Twenty years of name-calling hostility could not be transformed overnight. Moreover, the two countries, then without diplomatic relations did not recognize each other officially. But Chairman Mao Zedong's unscheduled meeting with the American President within hours of his arrival was a sure sign that the hosts had a warm welcome in store. The coverage of Nixon's first day and night in Beijing and the make-up of *People's Daily,* the Party organ, with six photographs the following morning, pointed to a more amicable reception than at first envisaged. Zhou Enlai also saw to it that an escalating format of warmth be timed to give expression to these sentiments. It came on the third evening of the Nixons' visit. Zhou Enlai took them to watch a programme of table-tennis exhibition matches and gymnastics in a newly-built stadium. There the capacity crowd frequently burst out clapping, often in unison, as much to cheer the performers as to bid welcome to the Premier's honoured guests. In the eyes of the spectators, the first official U.S. party to the new China had arrived.

Zhou Enlai went out of his way to make his guests feel at home. The negotiations with Nixon were held alternately at the Great Hall of the People and at the Guesthouse in Diaoyutai (The Fishing Terrace) where the American President was installed. Such arrangements gave the distinguished visitor a feeling of staying in an official residence, rather than in a guesthouse, to host the negotiations. Surely President Nixon must have felt that way when he stood at the door of his "official residence" to greet the arrival of Premier Zhou and his party to conduct official business.

As noted before, Zhou Enlai always made sure that none of his guests had cause to complain of "being left out." Secretary of State William P. Rogers was not included in the American party when it met with Mao Zedong, and it was National Security Adviser Henry Kissinger who sat alongside the President at important talks. Near the end of the visit, the Premier paid a special call on Mr. Rogers. It was a touching gesture, vintage Zhou Enlai — the consummate diplomat.

Chapter Eight
Not Gods, But Men

At the south end of Tiananmen Square between the Great Hall of the People and the Museum of the Chinese Revolution stands the Monument to the People's Heroes. Its inscription reads:

> Eternal glory to the people's heroes who laid down their lives in the last three years for the People's War of Liberation and the People's Revolution!
> Eternal glory to the people's heroes who laid down their lives in the last thirty years for the People's War of Liberation and the People's Revolution!
> Eternal glory to the people's heroes who laid down their lives in the period from 1840 to this date for fighting the internal and external enemies and striving to win national independence, freedom and well-being for the people!

> Inaugurated by the First Plenum of the Chinese People's Political Consultative Conference
> September 30, 1949

Ground-breaking for the monument took place just one day before the proclamation of the birth of the People's Republic by Mao Zedong on Tiananmen rostrum. When Zhou Enlai took the microphone to address the assembled dignitaries, Mao Zedong stood near, flanked by Soong Ching Ling and Marshal Zhu De. This solemn ceremony marked the end of one era and the beginning of a new one during which Mao and Zhou were to work in tandem for a quarter century. The Monument to the People's Heroes is symbolic of this partnership. Mao was the author of the monument's inscription, and Zhou the calligrapher who gave it permanent shape.

The relationship of the two men actually dates from the mid-1920s in

119

Guangzhou (Canton) when the Communist Party collaborated with the Kuomintang in launching the Northern Expedition to rid China of the warlord regime in Beijing. But it was not until a few months after the start of the Long March in late autumn of 1934 when the Red Army was forced to give up its base in Jiangxi to move north that the seal was set on their lasting partnership.

An enlarged Politburo meeting was convened in January 1935 at the small town of Zunyi in Guizhou Province to appraise past mistakes and consider the future. Wang Jiaxiang (1906-1974), a top Party leader and Director of the General Political Department, called for the removal of Qin Bangxian (1907-1946), also known as Bo Gu, and Li De (1900-1974), the German national Otto Braun, who represented the Communist International in the Chinese Soviet Area, from the military command and the leadership in general. Zhou Enlai who was partly — though not mainly — responsible for the reverses suffered fo far in the military sphere agreed with Wang and threw his considerable weight and prestige behind Mao Zedong, who emerged from the heated debate to become the Party's new leader.[1]

In the 1920s and early '30s Zhou Enlai was more prominent in the party and a better known Communist than Mao Zedong. But from his long experience of struggle with Chiang Kai-shek, particularly in the campaigns to defend the base areas from Chiang's all-out attempts to destroy them, Zhou Enlai came to realize that Mao Zedong's imaginative formula — to organize rural China in order to lay siege to the urban centres — was just the solution for resuscitating the revolution. He also came to believe that Mao Zedong was the one man who could get the Red Army out of the doldrums and turn the situation around. He was convinced of Mao's exceptional calibre and quite ready to defer to Mao and play second fiddle. From 1935 on, with Zhou's able support, plus the dedicated efforts of scores of tested comrades, Mao led the Chinese Revolution to victory.

Zhou Enlai and Mao Zedong came from very different backgrounds, although by Chinese reckoning both were southerners — i. e., people hailing from south of the Yangtze River. The eldest son of a mandarin family which had come down in the world at the time of his birth, Zhou Enlai claimed Shaoxing in Zhejiang Province as his ancestral home. He studied at a U.S. missionary-supported secondary school in Tianjin and later went abroad, first to Japan and then to France and Germany, where he embraced Marxism in earnest. Thus at an early age Zhou Enlai was exposed to foreign and Western influences.

In contrast, Mao Zedong, born to a better-than-the-average peasant family in the breadbasket province of Hunan, was more at home with the country than the town. He knew the soil and the worth of it from his boyhood. Most Hunanese have a weakness for hot peppers, the more pungent the better, and Mao was no exception. As a boy he had to help his father in the fields and managed to study sporadically under an oil-lamp at home; only much later did he go to a regular school in Changsha, the provincial capital, and then to Beijing University where he became an assistant in the library. His formal education remained somewhat patchy. A voracious reader, Mao Zedong was largely self-educated. In his youth he had never been outside China, and what he knew of the world beyond came from reading about it in newspapers and magazines — first at a Changsha public library and later at the Beijing University library[2] — quite unlike Zhou Enlai, who had direct personal exposure and experience.

Whatever the source of his learning, which was limited to anything his aides could lay their hands on in the way of newspapers and magazines obtained at post offices remote from towns during the war with Chiang Kai-shek, Mao became a brilliant political and military strategist. From the time of the Long March through the Anti-Japanese War and the War of Liberation, his grasp of the overall situation in China and popular sentiment was decisive for the eventual victory of the revolution. He was a leader men followed eagerly, able to explain complex ideas to ordinary people in language they could understand.

Zhou Enlai knew English and French and had a nodding acquaintance with Japanese and German from his student days abroad, while Mao Zedong, who learned his ABC's in English as a high-school student in Changsha, and renewed his interest in the language only when as leader of the country he was obliged to meet visitors from abroad and thought some knowledge of English would be helpful. He kept up with his English lessons till late in life, and even during the Cultural Revolution, with the help of a tutor, because he thought he would thus be able to read some philosophical treatises in the original.

One thing they shared in common in their early career was journalistic experience, both being writers of the first order. In post-liberation China, while Mao continued to write at infrequent intervals for *People's Daily*, the Party organ, Zhou Enlai played the journalistic role mostly in an editorial capacity. When *People's Daily* printed something important, especially a leading article on foreign policy, more often than not it was Zhou Enlai who okayed the page proofs, scanning the headlines and even the make-up. Sometimes an interview with a foreign correspondent had to be interrupted to allow the Premier to give the pages a final going-over to meet the printer's deadline in the wee hours of the morning. Practically all interviews with the Premier took place after nightfall because this was the time Zhou — and Mao too, for that matter — was in his element, a habit picked up in guerrilla days when the Party leaders were busy with the conduct of the war during the day and did their paper work at night. In the last years of the Cultural Revolution ill health and hospitalization forced Zhou Enlai to relinquish much of his oversight role, and Jiang Qing and her accomplices started to use the mass media for their own ends.

No two men sharing power at the pinnacle could be as different in temperament as Mao Zedong and Zhou Enlai. With only five years separating them in age, they were of the same generation, but upbringings in different surroundings gave them different traits. Where Mao was decisive and forceful, Zhou was circumspect and conciliatory. Where Mao was earthy and bluff, Zhou was urbane and subtle. Where Mao was witty and would tell a joke to make his point, Zhou was more matter-of-fact and would marshal his thoughts and arguments to put his views across. Mao was apt to act on the spur of the moment — as in launching the Great Leap Forward in August 1958 — whereas the moderate Zhou constantly counselled caution, the deliberate weighing of the pros and cons before taking action.

Both men believed in and acted on the mass line, which in Marxist terminology means reaching out to the people for opinions. They discountenanced *yiyantang,* or a one-man council of war. While both Mao and Zhou practised as well as preached the mass line with great success in pre-liberation years, Mao tended eventually to forget it, the more so as his prestige soared, and he preferred his own opinions to collegiate views and so allowed the cult of personality surrounding himself to thrive, despite his verbal opposition to its practice. He lapsed into *yiyantang,* again and again in his last years, long before the Cultural Revolution, which was its very child. *Yiyantang,* which finds criticism repugnant and is impervious to reason, is a style of work and a line of action that gnaw at the body politic. There is fertile soil for its growth even in socialist China, for it is congenial with paterfamilias, a patriarchal style of rule which has existed for thousands of years in China as a part of its culture. Coupled with the genuine popular adulation and hero worship of Mao because of his real achievements — which went to his head — this made matters worse. Herein lay the source of much of China's ills in the 1960s and 1970s.

In his later years Mao enjoyed the company of conservatives of his own generation. He counted among his personal friends prominent figures standing to the far right of the political spectrum such as the Kuomintang general Zhang Zhizhong (1890-1969), who represented Chiang Kai-shek at the peace talks with the Communists in 1949 and chose to remain with his hosts when the talks broke down. In his two-volume *Memoirs*, published posthumously in 1985, Zhang Zhizhong made an interesting mention of his wish to join the CPC in 1925 when he was Zhou Enlai's colleague at Whampoa Military Academy. He approached Zhou, who expressed his appreciation but indicated that the matter must be referred to the Party organization. Since there existed a concord between the two Parties that the CPC would not recruit high-ranking KMT officers, the application had to be shelved. But in all the years since the founding of the People's Republic in 1949 the former KMT general had been treated as a socially prominent dignitary whose friendship was valued and cultivated by Mao and other Party leaders.

Zhou Enlai, as Chairman of the Chinese People's Political Consultative Conference, the united front organization, mixed with people of all backgrounds and ages. He enjoyed learning from academics with different specialties as much as he enjoyed the company of people in the arts, sports and entertainment world. It is hard to imagine Mao going out of his way, as Zhou did, to make a friend out of Kimiyo Matsuzaki, the Japanese ping-pong player.

Mao had his decided preferences and made no effort to conceal his likes and dislikes. Of the Politburo members who passed away during his later years Mao put in a personal appearance only at the memorial service in January 1972 for Marshal Chen Yi, with whom he had often compared notes and exchanged letters on the the writing of classical Chinese poetry.[3] Chen Yi had been much abused in the Cultural Revolution despite Zhou Enlai's sustained efforts to protect him, and it was perhaps out of some contrite feeling that the Chairman made the unusual gesture of paying his last respects in person.

In one of his pensive, candid moments Mao Zedong described himself as having a tiger-monkey personality — two thirds tiger and one third monkey. This was in a letter dated July 8, 1966, sent from Wuhan to his wife

Jiang Qing at the beginning of the Cultural Revolution. The letter was circulated among officials and Party members subsequent to Lin Biao's death, but why was never explained. It discussed among other things Lin Biao's obsession with the study of *coups d'état,* in China and other countries, and his inordinate enthusiasm to laud Mao Zedong to the skies.

Mao's assessment of his own personality as a hybrid of tiger and monkey is an interesting diagnosis. By nature the tiger is strong, intrepid, always on the attack, while the monkey is playful, clever, and ever ready to take a chance, according to Chinese folklore. The tiger and the monkey are both popular among Chinese people.

There were times in the history of modern China when the trial of strength between the Communists and the Kuomintang seemed hopelessly unequal for the former — when defeat, writ large, seemed the only, inevitable outcome. It was the fearlessness of the tiger — and the ready-to-take-a-chance pluckiness of the monkey — in Mao Zedong that carried him and his comrades through against formidable odds. In 1927, after the Kuomintang crackdown on the Communists throughout the country, it was Mao Zedong's bold idea to mobilize the peasants and wage armed struggle from the countryside rather than continue to rely on the easily crushed urban uprisings which most Communist leaders still favoured. It was his daring and resourceful strategies during the 1934-35 Long March which saved the Red Army forces and turned what started out as a retreat into an epic of heroism that stirred the world. The decision in 1946 to slug it out with Chiang Kai-shek's armies, which were far superior to the Communist-led forces in equipment and number, was another bold but calculated stroke.

After the nationwide victory the most important instance was of course the decision to send the Chinese People's Volunteers to Korea in 1950 and pit them against the U.S. war machine. It was a decision which hung by a thread. In the wake of more than two decades of civil strife, to take on a superpower must have seemed madness to some. Only the intrepidity of Mao Zedong, who had been proved right again and again over the years, convinced his colleagues in the Politburo and government to go along with the decision.

After the war in Korea had ended in an armistice, and after sharing with his comrades the triumph of bringing about the rehabilitation of the economy within a short space of years, success went to Mao's head. He began to ignore some of the more important of his own precepts that had guided the Chinese Revolution along the road to victory.

One of the first to read these danger signals and try to sound a warning, albeit in an indirect way, was Tian Jiaying (1922-1966), Mao's own secretary who edited the manuscripts and drafted footnotes for the first four volumes of *Selected Works of Mao Tse-tung*.[4]

Chubby, of medium build and a tireless conversationalist like most Sichuanese, Tian Jiaying was orphaned and grew up in Chengdu, the provincial capital. The family was poor, and from childhood Jiaying knew intimately the seamy side of life, having served as an apprentice in a traditional Chinese herbal pharmacy. Self-educated, by fifteen he was conversant with the classics and could write poetry in the classical style. As a teen-ager he threw himself into the political activities organized by the underground Communist Party in Chengdu and during the anti-Japanese struggle went to Yan'an, then a magnet for all revolutionary-minded youth.

In 1948 he was picked to succeed Hu Qiaomu as confidential secretary to Mao Zedong. Down the years from Yan'an to Beijing, Tian had served as the Chairman's eyes and ears by going deep into the rural areas to study conditions at the grassroots in addition to doing his secretarial chores. When Mao set up his office and home in the sanctum of Zhongnanhai following Beijing's liberation in 1949, Tian moved into Zhongnanhai too, in order to be on call at all times.

Zhongnanhai was inhabitated by top-echelon Party and government figures. Unavoidably it was a hunting ground for time-servers. Tian Jiaying hated these types, and in particular, Chen Boda and Jiang Qing, who rubbed him the wrong way. Compared with the high-ranking residents in these cloistered quarters, Tian was after all a middle-level functionary, not entitled to perks but permitted to live and work in Zhongnanhai only because he was Mao's secretary. He had friends outside the walls of Zhongnanhai. One particularly close to him was Li Rui, who worked with the power and energy departments but also occasionally wrote for the press. They had known each other well during the Yan'an days, and had maintained a firm friendship. In the cradle of the Chinese Revolution they had been taught to be honest, to themselves as well as to others, and to despise the fulsome types who tried to advance their careers by watching the political barometer. They were taught to respect the truth and not to open their mouths unless they were sure of the facts, but if they felt they were right they should speak up. That was the tradition Tian Jiaying and Li Rui shared as they got together to talk about old times and the problems that bothered them in the political domain since coming to Beijing.

Chen Boda, Tian told Li Rui, often buttonholed him in the Zhongnanhai compound to fish for information. Tian was embarrassed and revolted to find a man so much his senior in age and Party standing cottoning up to him just because he was Mao's secretary. The man who in the mid 1960s was to become head of the Cultural Revolution Directorate would ask such questions as: "What's the Chairman reading these days?" "What new books are attracting his attention?" "What problems are keeping him busy?" Tian and Li were disgusted with the opportunists who went through contortions to find which way the wind was blowing and trimmed their sails accordingly.[5]

In November 1958 the Great Leap Forward was in full spate and a Party Politburo meeting on the subject was held in Zhengzhou, Henan Province. Obviously bent on going with the tide, Chen Boda came up with a "fantastic" idea: dispense with commodity production and abolish money as a medium of exchange. He formally proposed this at the Party meeting. Mao came down hard on the opportunist and dismissed it as hogwash, for he retained enough sense in those hectic days to repudiate the idea as impossible and dangerous politically. The rebuff curbed but did not cure Chen's opportunism, which surfaced again in the Cultural Revolution.

In less than eight months the deplorable consequences of the Great Leap Forward became increasingly clear to those who monitored the rural scene. Tian Jiaying, who did an in-depth study of the situation in a county of his home province, was told by grassroots cadres that they were forced to lie and pad the production figures, and that quite a number of peasants had actually starved since the Great Leap Forward began.

On the eve of the 1959 Party Central Committee meeting at Lushan, in Jiangxi Province, he reported the rural situation to Mao, while Li Rui, then working in the industrial sector, briefed the leader on the problems facing the factories, mines and transport systems. Mao had three spirited bull sessions (the Chinese term is *shenxianhui,* literally a gathering of sprites, describing such an informal, freewheeling discussion) with Tian, Li and a few others to pick their brains. As Li Rui later recalled, Mao was prepared to correct the "Left" mistakes and listed nineteen questions to be submitted to the Central Committee plenum for discussion.[6]

All set to go into the Party's erroneous ultra-Left policies of the immediate past, the plenum however made a sharp volte-face. For Marshal Peng Dehuai, the Defence Minister and Politburo member, had submitted his famous letter criticizing the Great Leap Forward as "petty-bourgeois hotheadedness." This didn't go down well with Mao, and on July 23 the Central Committee members were asked to sit in judgment on Peng Dehuai's "Right opportunism" and his "anti-Party activities."[7]

Tian Jiaying and Li Rui were struck dumb by the announcement. If the Party was not going to correct its ultra-Left mistakes and instead went for comrades holding moderate views, then may Marx help us, thought the two young men.

As Mao's secretary, Tian knew the Chairman well, and while he revered the great man he could put his finger on his fortes and foibles as few could. If I should ever leave Zhongnanhai to work elsewhere, he once confided to his friend, I would on my departure offer a couple of opinions. What were they? The most important one, he said, was that Chairman Mao should so conduct himself that people wouldn't talk or speak ill of him, "when he has passed his hundredth year," an elegant Chinese circumlocution meaning "after a person's death." Tian, looking far into the future, was thinking about Mao Zedong's place in history. It showed his care for the Party leader's reputation. Unfortunately, Li Rui whispered this into the ear of a close friend in strictest confidence while the Lushan meeting was in progress. Somehow Tian's private conversation went the rounds, and one Central Committee member brought the matter up at a plenary meeting. The well-meant words were twisted out of all proportion. Finally the subject was dropped, and Tian kept his job as Mao's secretary. But things were never the same again for him at Zhongnanhai.

In the next few years Tian Jiaying was hard at work writing the compendious footnotes, 987 items in all, to four volumes of Mao's *Selected Works*. It was a monumental, time-consuming task. Tian every now and then had to consult the Chairman himself, but found him loath to go over his own writings of years past. Mao's interests, said Tian, seemed to change, now taken up entirely with new things, new trends, new problems. Tian had intended to suggest, but stopped short of saying aloud, that the Chairman should relinquish his day-to-day supervision of the affairs of state to concentrate on summing up essential lessons of the Chinese Revolution, and to devote more of his time to theoretical work which, Tian believed, would be of far greater significance to future generations. At the end of 1958, Mao did decide to give up his post as Chairman of the People's Republic (retaining the Party Chairmanship), but did not start any theoretical summing up.[8]

Came the Cultural Revolution. Chen Boda, back in circulation, did not wait to get even with Tian Jiaying. On May 21, 1966, the Cultural Revolution Directorate, of which he was now chief, sent a hireling to Tian's home to read out an indictment: Ganging up with the Director of the Party's General Office now under investigation (meaning Yang Shangkun, who years before had refused to satisfy Chen's request for posher living quarters in Zhongnanhai); consistently holding Right-opportunist views; doctoring the Chairman's writings (meaning that Tian did not approve of putting Peng Dehuai's name in an article concerning Mao's opinion about *Hai Rui Dismissed from Office*).

In summary fashion, Tian Jiaying was sacked and ordered to move out of Zhongnanhai at once, to turn over all classified material in his possession and to own up to his errors. There was little the infuriated Tian could do, since the ultra-Leftists now had Mao's ear.

On May 23, Tian took his own life. Quoting Lu Xun the great writer, Li Rui remarked that suicide was a protest against events of the time. Jiaying's death, his friend lamented, was an act of protest against what was happening all around him.[9]

Tian Jiaying was among the earliest of many victims. The next ten years caused terrible harm to China, this time not just economically, but in every sphere of human endeavour. The Great Leap Forward and the Cultural Revolution were initiated and fuelled by Mao Zedong without making a thorough-going analysis of the situation facing the country — what it could and could not do — and particularly in the latter instance, without drawing a clear distinction between friends and foes — whom to attack and whom to protect. They were mistakes made not by a single individual but by a group of leaders dominated by one man who allowed *yiyantang* and the monkey side of his personality to get the better of him. Unlike the Great Leap mistake, in which Lin Biao and Jiang Qing played no important role, in the Cultural Revolution Mao used these two to spearhead the revolution, and they in turn used his mantle to gain their own ends. For good measure they extolled Mao almost as a god, the better to manipulate him. Since the Chairman was suffering from Parkinson's disease and was very hard of hearing, his aides and interpreters had to watch his lip movements and guess what he wished to say. All this kept him further isolated from what was going on around him or in the country, and Jiang Qing and company made the most of the situation.

Lin Biao's gambit at the outset was to make unscrupulous use of that creation of his — the little red book, *Quotations from Chairman Mao Zedong* — to show that he was more revolutionary-minded, more dedicated, more loyal to Mao, than anyone else in the political firmament. According to Lin Biao, who never tired of singing Mao's praises, "the Chairman's teachings are omnipotent and the gospel truth."

Before Lin Biao was officially designated successor to Mao Zedong, most members of the Politburo, Zhou Enlai included, took exception to Lin Biao's fanaticism in unduly stressing politics at the expense of work performance. Politics, Zhou Enlai maintained, proves its worth only if it leads to good work. Lin Biao, through the print media he managed to keep under his thumb, attacked the Premier — though not naming names — for spreading what he called heresy. But throughout the Cultural Revolution years Zhou Enlai stuck to his guns despite Lin Biao's and then Jiang Qing's wild charges of deviations from the Party line. In the departments under the State Council Zhou enforced the principle that politics must square with creditable work, a principle which helped preserve a measure of sanity and keep the groggy machinery of government running in those topsy-turvy days when politics meant revolution and revolution meant licence.

Twice in his career after 1949, Zhou Enlai found himself in the hapless position of having to clean up the mess created by erroneous policies, during and after the Great Leap Forward and during the Cultural Revolution. With the help of several technically oriented Vice-Premiers, he successfully put the ship of state on an even keel again after the three years of difficulties from 1959 to 1961, brought about by wrong policies, crop failures and Soviet withdrawal of assistance and technicians. Things began to pick up again in 1962, and China would have travelled the road of recovery and development into the 1970s had not subsequent ultra-Left policies and the shattering events of the Cultural Revolution supervened.

It would seem that Zhou Enlai didn't do quite as well in the later period, for after Lin Biao's death Jiang Qing and her gang, entrenched in positions of power, were still able to carry on their wrecking activities. But Zhou Enlai did manage to preserve a large corps of top-level, tested and tempered Party and government leaders, Deng Xiaoping among them.

By comparison no event in Zhou Enlai's twilight years — not even the delicate diplomacy leading to the reopening of Sino-U.S. relations—can be of greater importance from a long-term point of view, than his success in preserving thousands of good people and keeping them out of harm's way. It is an enduring monument to his resourcefulness as a statesman and skill as an infighter in complex and seemingly hopeless circumstances.

In the first five years of the Cultural Revolution, as distinct from the last five, Zhou Enlai was obliged to go along with Mao Zedong, since only retention of the premiership enabled him to hold together the sprawling leviathan of the government. Even so he found himself in an impossible position, for he had to deal with an array of forces that could not be readily categorized as outright foes or as real comrades. But with Lin Biao out of the picture in 1971, and the wings of the Red Guards clipped, Zhou's struggle was made a little less complicated during the second half of the Cultural Revolution. His shrewd handling of the Lin Biao debacle worked to his advantage. The whole Lin Biao affair jolted Mao Zedong, for he never dreamed that his hand-picked successor would turn against him, even to the extent of plotting his murder. So Mao was inclined once again to look to Zhou Enlai as an indispensable comrade and colleague.

Whereas in the first half of the period Zhou Enlai ranked third in the Party hierarchy after Lin Biao, he was now second only to Chairman Mao. All this made a difference. Before his plane crash in 1971, the "crown prince" Lin Biao could, for instance, approach Zhou Enlai with a suggestion dressed up as if it came from Mao, while Zhou could not side-step him or keep him in the dark if there was a matter of importance to take up with the Chairman. Now all this had changed and to a certain extent things were simpler. But only superficially.

In 1976, with Mao's physical infirmities becoming increasingly serious, the Jiang Qing clique hit upon an ingenious stratagem to keep the ailing Chairman under its thumb. Denied direct access to her husband, Jiang Qing got Mao's nephew, Mao Yuanxin, transferred to Beijing from Shenyang, northeast China, and planted him in Zhongnanhai as Mao's liaison officer—an extraordinary arrangement if examined from the Party's or government's point of view. Communications to and from Mao, she made sure, went through the young man, who was at her beck and call. There is no knowing at this remove whether what passed as instructions, orders and directives nominally with Mao's imprimatur were tampered with or falsified.

Never before the Cultural Revolution had Zhou Enlai faced a challenge of such magnitude and complexity, as he must wage warfare with a powerful faction within the Party in order to protect upright and experienced cadres from being destroyed. He laboured on knowing that if he went down, the entire ship of state with many good comrades would go down with him, since his enemies were interested not in laying their hands on just a few ministries but were out to seize total power in the Party and government — a disaster for the Chinese people. As time went on, this became abundantly clear when Jiang Qing and her supporters, in the Chairman's name, launched the incongruous "Criticize Lin Biao, Criticize Confucius" campaign at a mass rally in Beijing in January 1974. For the first time Jiang Qing, who orchestrated the proceedings, publicly blasted the Premier for not moving fast enough to "keep in step with the revolution." As events were to prove, Jiang Qing and her supporters made "Confucius" the code name for Zhou Enlai. Though Mao gave his approval at first to the preposterous campaign launched by Jiang Qing, Wang Hongwen et al, he withdrew it when he realized what they were up to and censured his estranged wife for harbouring ambitions to become the Party Chairman and form a "cabinet" of her own. In this connection Mao branded Jiang Qing and her clique as a "Gang of Four," and the nickname stuck.[10]

Zhou was hospitalized later in the year but retaining Mao's trust, continued to run the day-to-day business of the Party and government as before. The Gang of Four, bent on immediate seizure of power, tried to force the issue. Wang Hongwen, whose meteoric rise in the early days of the Cultural Revolution made him the youngest member of the gang, was dispatched to Changsha in Hunan, where Mao Zedong was staying. This happened shortly before the Second Plenum of the Tenth Party Congress and the Fourth National People's Congress, at which the most important item on the agenda was the formation of the government — the choice of the Premier and the setup of the new State Council, the cabinet. Wang hinted to Mao that it would be a good thing to drop Zhou Enlai in the new government and not name Deng Xiaoping as first Vice-Premier. He made the mistake of saturating his arguments with calumnies, for which he was given a dressing down by the Chairman. Jiang Qing had counted on Wang's journey to secure Mao's approval for organizing the cabinet she had in mind. She lost the gamble.

Some time before Christmas 1974 Zhou Enlai flew to Changsha. The special flight group in charge of the Premier's air trips were overjoyed to have the Premier aboard once again, for he had not been on their plane for well over a year. He must have turned the corner, they thought, otherwise he would not be taking the trip. But in fact he was not well at all and just managed to pull himself together to undertake this mission, for China's future hung in the balance.

On December 23 Zhou Enlai was closeted with Mao Zedong, who at last decided that Zhou, weak as he was, should remain at the helm and select the Vice-Premiers and ministers at his own discretion. The mission completed, the special flight group flew Zhou home to Beijing, back to his hospital bed. As always, before taking leave, the Premier went into the cabin to thank the crew. His gait was not too steady, but with the help of his secretary he made the rounds to shake hands with everyone. "Thanks for everything. It's been a delightful journey," he said. "I'll travel with you again." But it was Zhou Enlai's last flight.

The importance of the decision taken at Changsha cannot be too strongly emphasized. Though the final structure of the State Council as submitted to the Fourth National People's Congress for approval the following January inevitably included some ultra-Leftists, because the astute Zhou Enlai saw fit to make a gesture of conciliation to his detractors, practically all sensitive portfolios remained with officials Zhou could trust to work for the national interest. Thwarted of increased power and given not the plums they had looked for[11], the frustrated Jiang Qing and company stepped up its manoeuvres and concentrated its attacks on Deng Xiaoping, the central figure in the new cabinet and Zhou's closest deputy. Deng eventually was forced out of office for the second time in a space of ten years. But the edifice Zhou Enlai painstakingly built in his last days remained by and large intact despite the turmoils of 1975-76.

Mao Zedong certainly made serious mistakes during the Cultural Revolution, but his decisive support of Zhou Enlai at this decisive juncture was greatly to his credit.[12] Perhaps his unscheduled encounter with Wang Hongwen alerted him to the full dimensions of his wife's sinister ambition and he decided to block her, though stopping short of removing her altogether from the political scene.

In the history of the People's Republic 1975-76 is important for another reason. Many Party veterans who had been calumniated, dismissed, and in some cases clapped in prison were now exonerated and given work again. Their liberation could not have come at a more opportune moment, for the modernization programme first enunciated by Zhou Enlai at the 1975 session of the National People's Congress (his last public act *vis-à-vis* this supreme state organ) needed experienced personnel familiar with the economy and government administration to launch it on course. The fact that thousands of good people persecuted first by Lin Biao and then by Jiang Qing and company were being cleared and returned to active service proved that the tide had turned. For Jiang Qing and her cohorts were now seen more and more as a spent force. Further evidence was provided by their inability to carry the "Criticize Confucius" (really the "Criticize Zhou Enlai") campaign to its conclusion. Their reign of terror was drawing to a close.

The cost in human terms had been enormous. Countless people, high and low, had been falsely accused, subjected to kangaroo courts, interrogated brutally, and imprisoned. Some died prematurely because needed medical care was deliberately withheld. Others committed suicide.

Questions have been asked about Zhou Enlai's actions when all this was happening. Could he not have taken a firmer stand in opposition to this madness? Was there more he could have done to protect and save these people?

These questions can only be answered in the context of Zhou's relationship with Mao. Both were men of thought as well as men of action, but while Mao was more a man of thought than a man of action, Zhou was the opposite. In the quarter of a century since the Communist takeover in 1949 most of the time Mao was the thinker, the theoretician, the man of ideas, while Zhou was the doer, the executive, the administrator. They complemented each other in the halcyon days when Party policies were sound and correct.

Zhou Enlai of course was no mean Marxist thinker in his own right and left many works in the form of speeches and reports on politics, military affairs, culture, education, science, technology, arts and literature and on intellectuals and the united front. He did not permit extensive publication of his writings in his lifetime, a privilege he believed, rightly or wrongly, should be reserved exclusively for Mao Zedong. The two-volume *Selected Works of Zhou Enlai,* published in 1981 and 1984, offers revealing glimpses of Zhou's acute mind, realistic outlook, and emphasis on conciliation and persuasion to resolve contradictions and unite opponents.

Zhou deferred to Mao because he looked upon him as the Party's indisputable leader and theoretician of the Chinese Revolution. He bowed to Mao's judgment on the need to launch the Cultural Revolution, though he was later to doubt the moves and measures taken in that traumatic period ushered in by the "great teacher" to keep China from being adulterated by revisionism.

Mao had been right so many times before. If he decided that the Cultural Revolution was good for the Party and the country — in order, he maintained, to avert the danger of revisionism and a lapse into capitalist ways — Zhou Enlai went along without much question. Zhou had always shown himself to be a model in observing Party discipline and abiding by Party decisions, and the highest Party leaders supported Mao at this time.

If Zhou held an opinion different from the Party decision, he would still carry it out faithfully, allowing his own views to fall into abeyance until an opportunity presented itself to bring the matter up again at the next Party meeting. If he put forward a proposal of his own that was not accepted, Zhou would sink his differences and do his best to implement the Party line.

Such was his attitude towards the Cultural Revolution, at least in its first phase. Zhou Enlai stood with Mao Zedong, for better or worse. Since Lin Biao, Mao's designated successor, supposedly reflected Mao's views, Zhou also went along, though with some reservations.

From the outset Lin Biao ordained that the Cultural Revolution was a movement to fight bureaucracy, to vet all cadres, Party and otherwise, to see if they were politically fit to hold their jobs. Lin Biao cast the net wide, and his men dropped dark hints that very few even of the members of the Politburo would be exempt from the "sanitizing" process. Mao did not challenge let alone repudiate this proposition, and soon himself joined the fray with his "Bombard the Headquarters!" big-character poster, which set the stage for Red Guard campaigns against anyone unfortunate enough to be identified as part of the "bourgeois headquarters."

Himself modest to a fault, Zhou always believed that even basically good officials could improve their performance. He too hated and fought against the bureaucratic style of work. Could he now come forward to block the vetting of his own subordinates who had been criticized? He had not the prescience at this early stage to see the Cultural Revolution as a curse on the nation to be exorcised at all costs. As the cavalcade of struggle rumbled along, and more and more close associates were persecuted, it must have dawned on Zhou that something was terribly wrong with the Cultural Revolution if it made no distinction between friends and foes and was hell-bent on devouring the children of an earlier revolution. And he must at some point have recognized the ulterior motives of such people as

Lin Biao and Jiang Qing.

Perhaps the good Party man in him and his tremendous respect for Mao partially blinded his otherwise sharp judgment on the need to change course and blunted his courage to stand up to Mao for leading the Party and country astray. But he must also have concluded at this critical juncture that it was not in the nation's best interest for him to oppose the course of events too openly. He believed that, all things considered, it was better not to brave the storm but stoop to conquer. So long as he was Premier some rationality might still survive in the day-to-day running of the government and economy. He could offer some measure of protection to threatened cadres at all levels and perhaps alleviate the sufferings of millions across the nation. And by blocking the opportunists' ambitions for supreme, unlimited power, he might preserve the country from even worse tragedy in the long term. It was probably the only prudent course open to him, for if Zhou came out in undisguised opposition it would aggravate the "full-scale civil war" that was in progress.

It was not to play safe that he kept a low profile. Zhou had never been known to flinch from danger in a revolutionary career spanning over half a century; his physical and moral courage were unquestioned. He chose for himself perhaps what was an even more difficult and agonizing role than if he had spoken out openly and become a martyr. Just as the birth of the People's Republic was inconceivable without the guiding hand of Mao Zedong, it was equally inconceivable for the wheels of government to keep turning at this period without the steadying hand of Zhou Enlai. More than anyone else at the top, it was Zhou Enlai who personally and consistently concerned himself with the fate of those who had been disgraced, imprisoned, or sent off to remote parts. He intervened whenever possible to make their lot easier to bear or to effect their release at the first opportunity. If he could not prevent the damage, he did what he could to contain it.

After Lin Biao's death, he worked indefatigably to secure the exoneration of people who had been wronged, and since he saw the Chairman more often than before he would approach him at opportune moments and ask if this or that person might not be exonerated and take up his life and work again. Later on he would submit long lists of cadres, some still in prison, some still under house arrest, some idle, and personally go over them with Mao to secure his approval for their release or reappointment. But Jiang Qing, Kang Sheng and their cohorts used every possible delaying tactic, and sometimes exoneration, when it came at long last, did not mean immediate freedom. Many waited several years for their release, and one of their great regrets in later years was their inability to pay their last respects to the man they considered their saviour — Zhou Enlai — when he passed away in January 1976.

Mao Zedong took an Olympian stance on these matters, understandable in his last years when he was seriously ill much of the time. But before the end there were signs of introspection on Mao's part. Once, when looking back upon the events of the Cultural Revolution, he was obliged to admit there were errors and wrongdoings. He thought the whole business merited a *"san-qi-kai"* (translation: thirty-seventy split) verdict. As to whether it was seventy percent good and thirty percent bad Mao did not say, but it was taken for granted this was what he meant.[13]

Down the years, Zhou Enlai retained Mao's trust, though only to a certain extent. Surrounded by an obsequious group bent on ingratiating themselves through gross flattery, Mao kept increasingly aloof from his associates in the Politburo and divorced himself more and more from reality — an ideal situation for allowing mistakes and excesses to grow more blatant. Even after Lin Biao's death he did not reverse course and disown the ultra-Left measures adopted in his name or pursued by his wife. Instead he carried on as before, letting things drift and allowing his immediate circles to treat him like an oracle. It was a striking example of the tendency to *yiyantang* he himself had so often denounced in his earlier years.

Shortly after the Lin Biao affair Zhou Enlai, who was entrusted with supervision of *People's Daily,* the Party organ, made an attempt to turn things around. It was 1972, and Zhou thought it high time to criticize and repudiate the ultra-Left ideas and practices that plagued the country. Wang Ruoshui, one of the top men on the editorial board and a noted writer on philosophical subjects, couldn't agree more with Zhou's directive, and changes were made accordingly to reflect in the paper revulsion against the extreme radicalism of the Gang of Four. Zhang Chunqiao blew his top, and so did Yao Wenyuan. A meeting of the chief editors was called and a dressing down delivered. But, in the mind of the unrepentant Wang Ruoshui, Zhou Enlai was right, not Jiang Qing's panjandrums.

Taking advantage of Zhang's and Yao's absence from Beijing, Wang had a full page of the paper devoted to criticism of ultra-Leftism. The infuriated Gang of Four came down on the offenders and threatened strong action. Wang appealed directly to the Party Chairman in the hope that a letter setting forth his reasons for criticizing ultra-Leftism would meet with Mao's approval. But Mao set his face against the idea, for he maintained that the task before the country was to go on lashing out at the "ultra-Right."[14]

Wang Ruoshui, Hu Jiwei, the senior editor, and several like-minded colleagues were summoned to the Great Hall of the People. There seated behind a table were Jiang Qing, Zhang Chunqiao, Yao Wenyuan — and Zhou Enlai. On the table was Wang's letter to the Chairman, and at sight of it Wang's heart sank. Zhou Enlai looked embarrassment itself. It was plain that he would have liked to shield Wang, Hu and their comrades under fire, but couldn't. It also seemed obvious that he himself too was a target. For the final arbiter, Mao himself, had made it clear where he stood[15]. In his relations with the Chairman, Zhou deferred to Mao most of the time, and again on this occasion. If fighting ultra-Leftism was what the country then needed most of all, and Zhou's stand could have made a difference, perhaps he gave up too easily, lacking the combativeness to stick to his guns. But then perhaps most of the blame should be apportioned elsewhere. Mao apparently could not understand what was wrong with the country, or with himself, or the harm he was doing to the revolutionary cause he had served so long and so well.

In the closing years of his life Mao Zedong, ill and isolated, became more infatuated with his own wisdom. The sycophants around him played on this fatal weakness of his for all it was worth. If there was one man who could have reminded Mao, even if only in a roundabout way, of how his *yiyantang* had led the country to its sorry plight and of the need to revive democracy in the Party, it was Zhou Enlai. Alas, he was by now critically ill himself. It was out of the question for the sick man, experienced and resourceful as he was, to undertake a task which required delicate handling, consummate tact, infinite patience. At any rate, it was perhaps too late in the day to make Mao see that the people around him were doing him no service by deifying him.

That Mao Zedong was no god but a mortal capable of making mistakes was the theme of the article "To Learn from Mao Zedong" carried by the Chinese press in October 1978. It was taken from a speech made by Zhou Enlai back in May 1949, but which did not see print till thirty years after the event and two years after both men had passed away. In his speech Zhou

had remarked that Mao Zedong, born and bred a peasant, had evolved
from a boyhood permeated with obscurantism and superstition to a
manhood dedicated to progress and revolution. For all his greatness, he
was not infallible. Mao's extraordinary stature, Zhou maintained, lay in his
resolve to break out of the shell of the old, repudiate it, and embrace the
new. This was a timely idea to revive in the wake of the Cultural
Revolution. It was a great tragedy that Mao, the tested revolutionary,
towards the end of his life abandoned this process of constantly testing and
remaking himself.

To the extent that Zhou Enlai had been Mao Zedong's closest associate
for forty years and was well aware of Mao's strengths and weaknesses,
perhaps he too failed, as a comrade and a friend, in being a shade too
anxious to preserve camaraderie at the expense of candour, and in not
being bold enough to risk confrontation. There was perhaps too much of
the suave gentleman and not enough of the candid Marxist in Zhou Enlai.
He was given to too much shadowboxing with Mao Zedong rather than
taking Mao on in a face-to-face contest of wills, as sometimes seemed not
only necessary but imperative. It may be that Zhou gave in too readily to
Mao, whether he believed Mao was right or dead wrong. Nevertheless,
because he had struggled so hard in the Cultural Revolution to keep the
ship of state afloat; because he had done so much to ward off attacks and
cushion blows for victims of that terrible period; because he had succeeded
in holding the Gang of Four at bay and preventing them from seizing
supreme power — all this from a hospital bed in his last two years — the
people of China today are inclined to pass over failings on Zhou Enlai's
part.

Zhou Enlai came from a wine country, Shaoxing in the east China
province of Zhejiang, famous for its mellow and congenial *Shaoxing* wine.
It is quite unlike that other famous Chinese drink, *maotai,* the potent liquor
with a deceptive transparent appearance that Zhou Enlai and his comrades
came upon in Guizhou Province on the Long March. Like *Shaoxing,* Zhou
Enlai the man and the statesman was by nature mild and gentle, full of
charm and grace, conciliatory and free of cantankerousness. Yet he was
also the iron-willed revolutionary fighter. In his complex, charismatic
personality there was both *Shaoxing* and *maotai,* with *Shaoxing*
predominant.

When interviewed by Oriana Fallaci in Beijing's Great Hall of the
People in August 1980, Deng Xiaoping told the Italian journalist what kind

of a man Zhou Enlai was. He spoke affectionately of the late Premier as "my elder brother," a man who "was much respected by his comrades and all the people," and how fortunate it was that Zhou survived the Cultural Revolution, though, Deng pointed out, "he said and did many things that he would have wished not to. But people forgave him because had he not done and said those things, he himself would not have been able to survive and play the neutralizing role he did, which reduced losses. He succeeded in protecting quite a number of people."[16]

In fielding Fallaci's penetrating question, on the subject of the Cultural Revolution in particular, Deng Xiaoping said that while Mao Zedong was primarily responsible for the mistakes made, he himself, Zhou Enlai, and other veteran comrades must in one way or another be held responsible, too. "We should not lay all past mistakes on Chairman Mao." Compared to his signal countributions to the Chinese Revolution and the rejuvenation of China as a nation, Mao's mistakes, he stated, were secondary. The underlying cause, as Deng remarked with some emphasis and the *Resolution on CPC History (1949-81)* expounded at length, must be traced not to personal factors but institutionally to the power structure of the time which allowed democratic centralism to be impaired and collective leadership to be eroded.[17] The tragedy was all the more distressing since to the end of his days, instead of looking back upon the past with a critical eye, Mao Zedong should remain convinced that what he did was for the good of the country and that all his thoughts and actions, in theory and practice, were in accord with the tenets of Marxism and the needs of the dictatorship of the proletariat.

Chapter Nine

Cultural Revolution Madness

Mao Zedong opened Pandora's Box in 1966. Even now, after the lapse of two decades, not all the ills let loose by the innocuously named Cultural Revolution have been brought under control.[1] Mao tragically misjudged the true situation of the country, and his unfounded suspicion that revisionism was breaking out everywhere begot a misguided political movement that Lin Biao, Jiang Qing and their allies almost immediately made part of their own game plan for seizing power.

Chaos ensued — and was encouraged by the opportunists. They perceived that large numbers of their former comrades, particularly those in high places, would have to be cleared from their path. That their avenue to power would be strewn with corpses apparently did not cost them any sleep. Xinhua News Agency, the official clearing house, reported during the November 1980 trial of Jiang Qing and others that 34,274 people had been "persecuted to death" — in other words, died unnaturally — during the ten years of the Cultural Revolution. This is possibly a conservative figure.

According to one survey,[2] in Beijing alone from the last week of August to the end of September 1966, some forty days, more than 1,700 persons were done to death without trial or charge, more than 33,600 homes were raided without search warrants, and more than 84,000 residents lumped together as "undesirables" were kicked out of the city. Not until June 1981 did the Party finally sit in judgment on this lawless decade. Its Central Committee, meeting in plenary session, brought in the verdict "wrong from beginning to end."

The Cultural Revolution started in the spring of 1966 with what was ostensibly an ordinary academic debate in newspapers and magazines about the political and literary worth of a Beijing opera called *Hai Rui Dismissed from Office*. Jiang Qing, reportedly inspired by Mao Zedong, had recruited writers to go for the playwright and his script. One of her tame hacks was a relatively obscure middle-level functionary of the Shanghai Party Committee's Propaganda Department, Yao Wenyuan. This time-server quickly found favour with her group, and began a rapid climb up the political ladder. Eventually he became the press czar. The critiques of *Hai Rui* condemned it as a vicious allegory, the target being the great man himself—Chairman Mao Zedong. The playwright, Wu Han, came under severe fire, but the full range of the vitriol was reserved for the man or faction that allegedly put Wu up to it.

Hai Rui was a Chinese folk hero, an upright official of the Ming Dynasty (1368-1644) admired down the ages as an unusually intrepid, plain-spoken man who did not hesitate to tell the emperor to his face that he was wrong.

To those who sought out ulterior meanings, the historical Hai Rui recalled a modern hero, Marshal Peng Dehuai (1898-1974), another man who never minced his words. Born to a peasant family and largely self-taught, Peng had risen in the KMT army through sheer ability.[3] He had come over to the Communist side because of his basic sense of justice and feeling for the common people. A dedicated Communist, a soldier to his fingertips, Peng had done valiant service to the Chinese Revolution and had a distinguished military record in Korea.

His honesty and bluntness proved his undoing. At the July 1959 Party Central Committee meeting called at Lushan, Jiangxi Province, specifically to criticize the ultra-Leftism of the Great Leap Forward, Peng wrote a private letter to Mao Zedong that set off a conflagration. Apparently touched on the raw by Peng's honest assessment of the situation, Mao turned the meeting around into an attack on Peng for "anti-Party" and "anti-socialist" behaviour. The crusty soldier was stripped of his posts as Minister of Defence and member of the Party Politburo. Peng's criticisms were in fact quite correct. Both agriculture and industry were in serious trouble, and the padded figures and boastful exaggerations only created a false image of success when the truth was exactly opposite. Top Party leaders, who had already discussed the problems of the Great Leap Forward in several meetings and were prepared to lay out plans for correcting them at the Lushan meeting, were shocked to find the old Marshal so harshly penalized merely for speaking his mind.

Did they all agree with the Chairman's change of direction? Did they not agree with Peng Dehuai's estimate of the situation?

Zhou Enlai, for one, had misgivings at least on the reported iron and steel production figures and the value of "backyard steel-making," about which he had gathered information through his own channels. But neither he nor his Politburo colleagues spoke up. No one questioned, much less challenged, Mao's wisdom in taking the conference in an entirely different direction, an attitude that did not redound to their credit.[4]

Mao Zedong had by now become much too independent for the good of the Party or the country. Even in his relations with close colleagues, members of the Politburo, he seemed less than tolerant of opinions which differed from his own. Such an attitude went against his own political philosophy — the mass line. And it grew worse with the passage of time and the great adulation he received. From being too independent was but one step to being too domineering.[5]

Early in 1966, all on his own, the "great teacher" (one of the epithets bestowed on him by Lin Biao) plunged the nation into the catastrophe of the Cultural Revolution. After the 1959 movement against "Right opportunism," associated with Peng Dehuai, many people inside the Party feared to share their thoughts with others, much as it was in the days after the "anti-Rightist movement" of 1957, when people outside the Party thought it best to keep their mouths shut. Democratic centralism within the Party virtually became a dead letter with Peng Dehuai's downfall.

Even in disgrace, Peng himself could not be intimidated. Once, when his niece asked him why he'd stuck his neck out to comment on economic affairs, he said, "Why shouldn't I? I'm a Party man, and a Politburo member. If I'm sure something is wrong, in our economy or any other area, I must raise the matter, or sound a warning. I wouldn't be worthy to be a Communist if I kept my mouth shut."

Chinese Communists owe it to the people, he told her, not only to call attention to mistakes and injustices, but to set them right. For her benefit he spelled out the five "Don't Be Afraids" expected of all good Communists: don't be afraid of being dismissed from office; don't be afraid of being divorced by your wife; don't be afraid of being expelled from the Party; don't be afraid of jail; and don't be afraid of the firing squad. "I have never feared death," said the old soldier. "Why should I fear anything? That's why I stuck my neck out."[6]

His courage was to be tested even more starkly. Arrested early in the Cultural Revolution by forces loyal to Lin Biao, Peng was imprisoned and interrogated again and again. Death claimed him, still in prison, in 1974.

In the late 1970s Peng, along with a host of other well-known figures, was rehabilitated and his honour restored, albeit posthumously. Deng Xiaoping who himself endured humiliations and the loss of freedom during the Cultural Revolution, had this to say in 1980:

> In the first half of 1959 we were correcting "Left" mistakes. And the early stage of the Lushan meeting was devoted to economic work. With the issuance of Comrade Peng Dehuai's letter, however, there was a change of direction. Comrade Peng's views were correct, and it was normal for him as a member of the Political Bureau to write to the Chairman. Although he had his shortcomings, the way his case was handled was totally wrong.[7]

Was the play *Hai Rui Dismissed from Office* meant to refer to Peng Dehuai?

Wu Han (1909-1969), the playwright, strongly denied it. Wu was one of Beijing's Vice-Mayors at the outbreak of the Cultural Revolution. He was not really a political pro, or even playwright, but an academic, a professor of history recognized by his peers as one of the very few experts on Ming Dynasty history. He was happiest when delving into old volumes and archives.

He would have been content to bury himself among old folios but for the 1946 murder by Kuomintang assassins of his colleague Professor Wen Yiduo (1899-1946), a fearless critic of the Chiang Kai-shek regime. Wen's assassination in broad daylight on the streets of Kunming shocked Chinese intellectuals. It shook them out of their routine and turned them into civil rights champions. The struggle waged against the Kuomintang eventually drew Wu Han and others like him to the Chinese Communist Party.[8]

There is some irony in the way Wu Han became involved with the historical figure of Hai Rui. In 1959 it happened that Mao Zedong, just before presiding over an enlarged meething of the Party's Politburo in Shanghai (March 25 to April 4), had seen a native Hunan opera with Hai Rui, the honest man who dared to rebuke an emperor, in the last act. He was intrigued, sent for Hai Rui's biography and told the gathering that they could all learn something from the man.

The Party's top figures had been discussing how best to check the fantastically inflated production figures and the hyperbole about superhuman achievements that accompanied the Great Leap Forward and the birth of people's communes the year before. That's the kind of man and the spirit we need, said Mao of Hai Rui. The call went out after the Party conference to emulate the Hai Rui spirit. Several suggested that Wu Han, the expert on Ming history, write something to popularize the story of Hai Rui. Wu Han produced a short piece called "Hai Rui Berates the Emperor" for *People's Daily* at the urging of Hu Qiaomu, a member of the Party Central Committee and specialist in propaganda work. Hu had attended Qinghua University at the same time as Wu Han, his junior by one year, and later, from the Yan'an days, served as secretary to Mao Zedong.

In a reminiscence published in October 1984, Guo Xinhua, formerly Wu Han's secretary, recalled a conversation with Wu some time after the furore had arisen over the play:

"Comrade Hu Qiaomu came to see me about writing up Hai Rui.... He said it was Chairman Mao who wanted to foster the Hai Rui spirit.... Peng Dehuai is a general who has won his spurs in battle and I have nothing but admiration for the man.... But he had nothing to do with my play *Hai Rui* whatsoever."

Lin Biao, Jiang Qing and their allies soon took aim at more prominent officials of the Beijing Party Committee — Deng Tuo (1912-1966), the man in charge of the arts and education and one-time Editor-in-Chief of *People's Daily*, the Party organ; and Liao Mosha, Director of its United Front Department.

They and Wu Han were branded as "bad elements" guilty of "crimes against the Party, socialism, and Chairman Mao," of peddling "revisionism" in *Notes on the Three Family Village*, a regular column in *Frontline*, the biweekly Beijing Party Committee organ.

The vilification of these intellectuals was a prelude of things to come, though the ultimate aim of their persecutors was to bring down Party and government leaders who were not in their camp. The "anti-Party, anti-socialist, anti-Chairman Mao" counter-revolutionary label was to be pinned on many of the nation's intellectual elite. All so branded were openly maligned by "big-character posters" which were posted not only at their work places but all over town. Most were summarily sacked, bundled off to prison, or sent off to "exile" in the countryside.

Red Guards raided and searched Deng Tuo's home, turned his house upside down and smudged or despoiled his manuscripts. His valuable scrolls, paintings and antique furniture were confiscated. It was the last straw for a man steeped in the culture of the old-style Chinese intelligentsia.

He preferred death to insult and humiliation, and on May 18, 1966, this brilliant writer and journalist took his own life.[9]

Only one of the "Three Family Village" writers survived the horrors of the Cultural Revolution — Liao Mosha, the least known of the trio. For a period of a year or so following Deng Tuo's death, Liao Mosha and Wu Han had been paired off for "struggle meetings" from place to place. They were dragged from one public meeting to another, displayed on the stage like performing animals, their heads bowed down before the audience and their hands twisted and trussed behind their backs by the Red Guards. They were interrogated and ordered to own up to their "crimes." Wu Han, who had long led the sequestered life of an academic, soon perished in prison. Liao Mosha endured eight years of the punishment that was the lot of most jailed intellectuals. Though he emerged from incarceration a physical wreck and was then sent to a labour camp in the south China province of Jiangxi, he lived to see the day of reckoning and was one of the prosecution witnesses at the special tribunal set up in Beijing in November 1980 to try Jiang Qing and her henchmen.

In the eyes of Lin Biao and Jiang Qing, such figures as Wu Han, Deng Tuo, and Liao Mosha were small fry whose elimination was important only in so far as they formed stepping stones to the removal of bigger objects. Four men in particular in the first days of the Cultural Revolution were high on their hit list: Peng Zhen, a Politburo member and the number one man of the Beijing municipal government; Luo Ruiqing, one-time Minister of Public Security, a senior general of the People's Liberation Army and Chief of its General Staff; Lu Dingyi, an alternate Politburo member, Vice-Premier and Director of the Party's Propaganda Department; and Yang Shangkun, a member of the Party Central Committee and its Secretariat and Director of the all-important General Office of the Party Central Committee.

An enlarged Politburo meeting was convened in Beijing from May 4 to May 26, 1966. The session was presided over by Liu Shaoqi, then Vice-Chairman of the Party, in the absence of Mao Zedong, who was on a working holiday away from the capital. But the agenda was determined by Mao before he left, and the meeting to all intents and purposes was dominated by Lin Biao, Kang Sheng, Chen Boda and Zhang Chunqiao.

Peng, Luo, Lu and Yang were charged with organizing an anti-Party bloc and dealt with accordingly — denounced, dismissed and detained without specific charges. The disgrace of the fallen men who each in their own way held important positions of responsibility in Beijing's power structure sent shock waves throughout the country. More important and perhaps ominous as well, the meeting adopted what was called the "May 16th Circular," drafted and made final by Mao himself,[10] who controlled the operations of the burgeoning Cultural Revolution from afar.

In one passage there was mention of a "Khrushchev-type of a person sleeping in our midst." The language used was so circumlocutory, and the meaning so ambiguous that no one, not even Liu Shaoqi, Zhou Enlai or Deng Xiaoping had any idea who or what was meant. They were kept in the dark about much of what was actually going on (for instance the decision to release the first big-character poster put up by Beijing University's lecturers, which sparked off a nationwide campaign of similar big-character posters) since Lin Biao and his set of conspirators, having as they did the Chairman's ear, maintained a direct line of communication with him. It was an impossible situation, and Liu Shaoqi was obliged to ask the Chairman to return to Beijing, which he did on July 18.

Changes pregnant with dire consequences ensued from this extraordinary meeting and Mao's return. First, the removal of the four men without any significant opposition hastened the fall of Liu Shaoqi and Deng Xiaoping, now also accused of heading a "bourgeois" headquarters in rivalry with, if not in opposition to, Mao's "proletarian" headquarters. Second, with the establishment of a task group to be called the Cultural Revolution Directorate, of which Mao's wife Jiang Qing was made deputy chief, she took centre stage instead of waiting in the wings. At the time of the enlarged Politburo meeting she was not even a member of the Party Central Committee and played no official part, but now she called the shots. Third, since this task force was held directly accountable to the small group of the Politburo's Standing Committee, Jiang Qing and her coterie were able to bypass the Party Secretariat and Politburo to do much as they pleased. Fourth, the entry of the Red Guards into the mainstream of political life was a disturbing and disruptive factor which scattered law and order to the winds and plunged China into chaos. More than any other top leader, Zhou Enlai as Premier had to take much of the heat in the criticism of his associates and subordinates, in addition to his usual punishing workload.

The term "Red Guard" entered the English language only with the advent of China's Cultural Revolution. The British *Concise Oxford Dictionary* (seventh edition, 1982) defined a Red Guard as a "young activist in Communist China." The American *Webster's Ninth New Collegiate Dictionary* (1983) called a Red Guard "a member of a teenage activist orgainzation in China serving the Maoist Party." The operative word was "activist." Mostly teenagers, energetic but naive, loyal to what they considered the socialist cause but lacking greatly in political understanding, they were shamelessly manipulated and became the shock troops for Lin Biao and Jiang Qing, who fondly called them her "kid generals." No one can be sure when, where, how it all began, but the Red Guards multiplied in no time, responding to Mao Zedong's words that "to rebel is justified." It was summer vacation time and they roared into rebellion — first against the school authorities, their teachers, and then, socially, against all things in their way.

On August 18 Mao Zedong took the salutes of Beijing's Red Guards convened in Tiananmen Square, an event which conferred on the kids some kind of status. Others in the country asked for the same privilege. In the short span of a month, ten million of them converged on Beijing to receive Mao's "blessings." From all corners of the country their journey to the capital put the transportation departments, especially the train services, under enormous pressure. Premier Zhou Enlai suddenly found millions of young people on his hands — to be lodged, to be fed, and some even to be clothed (for lack of a change of clothes or warmer clothing) all at the same time. A red armband bearing the words "Red Guard" was flaunted as a free pass, and all who had one on his or her arm regarded themselves as Chairman Mao's guests. They got free rides, free accommodation, free food, free entertainment — all, of course, at government expense.

After that there was no stopping these young people. Rebellion was the order of the day, respecting neither person nor place. Excesses were egregious. Mao, who had called on the young to rebel, hastily qualified the slogan to read "to rebel *against reactionaries* is justified." But the damage had been done. Who was to decide what people or things were reactionary was not really defined; many youngsters took the decisions into their own hand. In any case it did not suit Lin Biao and Jiang Qing to hold the Red Guards in check.

One thing that alarmed Zhou Enlai as the Red Guards went on the rampage was the likelihood that many patriots and politically prominent figures with or without political affiliation might be attacked or harmed. These were people the Communist Party had worked over the years to cultivate as part of the united front which had helped the revolution to victory and played an important part in the country's economy, culture, and social life. For Zhou Enlai, who had worked harder and done more than most to bring about the united front, its preservation was second instinct.

Early in the morning of August 30 he received an urgent note from Chairman Mao attached to a report. The note read: "Forward this to the Premier to take action at his discretion. He should be protected." "He" was Zhang Shizhao (1881-1973) of Changsha, Hunan Province, an old lawyer friend of the Chairman's, who had dashed off a letter of the same date, complaining of the search of his home the night before by Red Guards. Acting instantly, the Premier lashed out against those responsible for the transgression, ordered the rare books and valuables confiscated to be restored to their owner, and dispatched PLA soldiers to guard Zhang's home. Zhou also took further precautions. Mao Zedong's note served as a timely catalyst to widen the scope of the people to be protected.[11] He decided then and there to draw up a protection list, which included such distinguished names as Soong Ching Ling (Mme. Sun Yat-sen), poet, historian and writer Guo Moruo, Li Zongren (former Acting President of the Kuomintang regime who had returned to the homeland in the summer of 1965), and many others in different fields.

The Premier's August 30, 1966, protection list was further expanded to include the Vice-Chairmen of the Standing Committee of the National People's Congress, members of the NPC Standing Committee and the Vice-Chairmen of the People's Republic; Ministers and Vice-Ministers of the State Council; Vice-Chairmen of the Chinese People's Political Consultative Conference; Vice-Premiers of the State Council; leaders of the various democratic parties; and the President of the Supreme People's Court and the Chief Procurator of the Supreme People's Procuratorate.

Zhou's attention was drawn to a rumour that the Red Guards were planning to besiege Soong Ching Ling's home and demand, of all things, that she change her hairdo (the three Soong sisters all had long worn their hair done up in buns in deference to their mother's wish). Zhou Enlai immediatly called Beijing's Red Guards together and reasoned with them, though he could simply have issued an order. His talk with the Red Guards is one example of the kind of patient persuasion rather than administrative coercion Zhou Enlai used again and again during the Cultural Revolution:

> Soong Ching Ling — she is Dr. Sun Yat-sen's widow. Dr. Sun Yat-
> sen's signal contribution to the country has been reaffirmed by

Chairman Mao in an important article, *On the People's Democratic Dictatorship*, written after Beijing's liberation. His signal achievement has also been engraved on the Monument to the People's Heroes. Fellow students in Nanjing want to pull down Dr. Sun Yat-sen's bronze statue. Now that isn't right. We're absolutely opposed to it. On May Day and National Day (October 1) every year we put up Dr. Sun Yat-sen's portrait opposite the Tiananmen rostrum — that's Chairman Mao's idea. As a bourgeois revolutionary leader Dr. Sun Yat-sen had achievements to his credit and shortcomings as well.

Ever since his widow began to co-operate with us she has never bowed down to Chiang Kai-shek. After the failure of the Great Revolution she went abroad. She was credited with saving the lives of our underground Party workers. During the war with Japan she worked in league with us. During the War of Liberation her sympathy lay with us. Her co-operation with the Communist Party down the years has been consistent, unfailing from beginning to the end. We must respect her. Now she is advanced in years. We shall be commemorating the centenary of Dr. Sun Yat-sen this year and she is going to write an article on the occasion, which will have great impact internationally. Now to daub her home with big-character posters — that just won't do. Of her family of three brothers and three sisters, none but she took the path of revolution. The fact that her younger sister is married to Chiang Kai-shek is no reason whatsoever to throw her over. The house where she lives was put at her disposal by the state. Some have said: "I'm not afraid to say it, I'm not afraid to do it, and like it or not, I'll go there." That's wrong. At all events we must reason them out of it.[12]

Zhou Enlai's intervention at the right moment averted what could have been an ugly confrontation, putting the long-existing concord with Soong Ching Ling, who stood as a symbol of Dr. Sun Yat-sen's collaboration with the Communist Party, under severe strain. For more than half a century Zhou and his wife had gone to great lengths to strengthen these ties of friendship, contracted partly on a personal basis but mostly in the interests of the Communist Party. This unwritten alliance, unusual in that it linked an individual with an organization, stood the stress of the times, especially in the years following the rupture of the Kuomintang with the

Communists. Chiang Kai-shek's relationship with his sister-in-law, the widow of the founder of the Republic, was touch-and-go, to say the least. A number of ultra-Right members of the Kuomintang considered her a thorn in their side and would have liked to do away with her. Soong Ching Ling's personal safety was therefore never far from the thoughts of Yan'an leaders, and Zhou Enlai in particular, who maintained a line of communication with her through the underground Party in Shanghai, sometimes via Hong Kong.

Held in high esteem by Mao Zedong and Zhou Enlai, indeed by people from all walks of life, Soong Ching Ling played a significant role in the government of the new China she had helped bring into existence. Like every one else, she was surprised by the ferocity of the Cultural Revolution when it burst upon the political horizon. She was unhappy about what was happening to people she knew and respected, but could do little to influence events. While, as usual, Zhou Enlai saw to it that she herself would not be jeopardized, Soong Ching Ling distanced herself from the political upstarts who were arrogating power to themselves and abusing their positions to the detriment of the country. For much of the Cultural Revolution Soong Ching Ling kept herself out of the limelight.

Zhou Enlai had many other occasions during this period to exercise his political skills. In the early days of the Cultural Revolution, for instance, the Beijing Hotel staff, like other units, was divided into two opposing factions. Management slacked off and services were in disarray. Nobody was willing, for instance, to shine the guests' shoes. Rebellion was in the air, and the attendants began to chuck jobs they were loath to do. Shining shoes for guests was considered menial, a service to be done away with. Didn't Jiang Qing and her Cultural Revolution Directorate call on young people to rise and rebel against "bourgeois" practices? Here in this hotel, so the younger people among the staff decided, there was a lot to rebel against. Things were getting out of hand, and the matter came to Zhou Enlai's notice.

He got the hotel staff together and talked to them about proper attitudes towards work and different ways of serving the country. In a socialist society, the Premier maintained, there is a division of labour, just as in a capitalist country. Where the two systems differ is that under socialism everyone is equal and the work each one does is neither particularly ennobling nor particularly demeaning. One should give his all, and if the job entails shining shoes for hotel guests then one must do that, to the best of one's ability. Sink your differences, Zhou Enlai appealed to them. Work together and do what the job requires. If you still do not want to polish shoes for the guests, then I must come to do it for you.

The thrust went home. Services came more or less back to normal, though the two factions, like all such factions in the country, did not compose their differences till much later.

Zhou Enlai was able to keep Soong Ching Ling and others out of harm's way during the Cultural Revolution, but in other cases he was not able to intervene. One such case was that of Ma Sicong, or Sitson Ma, as he is better known in Western music circles. Zhou knew Ma in his Chongqing years of the late 1930s and early 1940s, when he instructed Party members working underground in arts circles to cultivate Ma because he thought the man well worth winning over to the Communist side.

A first-rate violinist and a notable composer, Ma had quite a few options before him in the spring of 1949, when Beijing invited him to take part in the first Chinese People's Political Consultative Conference to be held in liberated north China. He could start afresh in Taiwan, where the authorities offered him the most prestigious musical post. He could return to Europe, where he could take his pick of many jobs. Or he could stay put in Hong Kong, only a short distance from his old home in Haifeng, Guangdong Province. But he and his pianist wife Wang Moli decided to join their Communist friends.

Ma, then only thirty-eight, was made President of the Central Conservatory, the appointment being personally approved by Zhou Enlai. A high salary and certain perquisites went with the position — a spacious house, a chauffeured car and a chef to cook for the family. He was elected to the National People's Congress, he was a Vice-Chairman of the All-China Federation of Literary and Arts Circles and Vice-Chairman of the Association of Chinese Musicians.

All this made him an irresistible target to the Red Guards early in the Cultural Revolution. He was ridiculed and attacked in big-character posters as a "reactionary authority on music," his income was drastically reduced, he was thrown out of his home (which had already been raided and plundered), and sent to a detention centre at the College of Socialism. Ma was hauled to "struggle meetings" before his own students, now drunk with revolution. For, compared with fellow students of the Shanghai Conservatory, where a couple of the teaching staff had reportedly "died from disgrace," they had no great "victories" to show.

According to eyewitness accounts, one of the first things the students did was to have Ma's head shaved like a convict. He was beaten until he bled. The confinement and abuse continued until the noted musician was seriously considering suicide. He was talked out of it by his old chef Jia Junshan, a warm-hearted man with a strong sense of justice.

Jia also kept in touch with Ma's wife Wang Moli, who with her children had gone into hiding with relatives in Guangzhou.

Guangzhou, three or four hours' journey from Hong Kong, the first stop to the outside world, was rife with stories of how people, to escape from the horrors of the Cultural Revolution, could make their getaway by land or sea — for a price. After much soul-searching the family decided to take this chance. Ma himself was able to join them when, in November 1966, he and other faculty members were allowed to return home. With Jia Junshan's help, and some of his savings, Ma and family did make good their escape in a small boat.

Their flight was labeled "treason to the country." The family's personal property was confiscated and all Ma's compositions and scores were banned. Several people were implicated, among them Jia Junshan, who was imprisoned for four years for helping the fugitives.

Zhou Enlai took a very different view, which he revealed in a conversation with a visiting U.S. delegation. "I have two regrets in my long career," he told them. "One concerns Ma Sicong. He was well into his fifties when he had to leave the country and live abroad. It's most regrettable."[13] The victims of persecution reacted in different ways. Some committed suicide like Deng Tuo and Tian Jiaying, Mao's secretary. Others, such as Ma Sicong and his family, fled the country. Most people put up a kind of passive resistance. Then there was Zhang Zhixin, a woman of thirty-nine, an ordinary Party office worker whom no one had ever heard of until her case shocked the conscience of the nation. In a direct and uncomplicated way she stood up to her accusers and fought them to her last breath.

College-educated, the mother of two small children, Zhang was a gentle soul who played the violin. She came from a poor family in Tianjin in north China. She took her Party membership seriously, unlike some who saw it as a path to political advancement. When it came to defending the truth, she was unshakable.

Zhang Zhixin was a low-level functionary of the Liaoning Provincial Party Committee in Shenyang when she was charged with a preposterous "crime of thought" — specifically, "disagreeing with Jiang Qing and distorting Jiang Qing's interpretation of Marxism and Mao Zedong Thought." Zhang did not deny it. She said openly that Jiang Qing was wrong, that her actions went against the grain of Party principles. Her immediate superiors cautioned her; her friends advised her to keep her thoughts to herself. There were warnings from the provincial Party organization that such opposition to Jiang Qing meant opposition to Chairman Mao. But these pressures could not deter Zhang. It was not her views, she replied, but those who twisted them that ran counter to the proletarian headquarters. She challenged Jiang Qing's right to speak for Chairman Mao. The frustrated Party bosses dispatched her to a May 7th Cadres School (essentially a labour camp). But she was also offered leniency if she recanted.

Neither coercion nor cajolery could change her views, and she was dragged before a kangaroo court as an active counter-revolutionary. She was not allowed to speak at the trial, for fear that she might turn the tables on her persecutors.

Zhang was summarily sentenced to death. The capital punishment was carried out on April 5, 1975, without informing her family. The details of her death made the nation shudder when they were disclosed after the downfall of Jiang Qing. Her executioners were so fearful that Zhang would shout her defiance and denounce Jiang Qing at the end that they slit her windpipe minutes before she was hauled in front a firing squad. Her name has since become a household word, glorified as a martyr and remembered as a symbol of resistance.

The opportunists, however, were really after bigger game — such as Liu Shaoqi. Second only to Mao Zedong in Party standing, Liu took precedence over all other member of the Politburo, including Zhou Enlai, and moreover held the position of head of state. He was accused of heading a "bourgeois headquarters," along with Deng Xiaoping, the Party's General Secretary, and of leading China into the quagmire of revisionism and capitalism.

Most of the top figures of the Party hierarchy had their reservations, if not outright disapproval, of the Cultural Revolution. For one thing it was so sudden, so novel, so different from past practice; for another, it seemed directed mostly against their own kind. Though all took part in the rallies held in Tiananmen Square, being required to make a show of Party solidarity, high-ranking participants, including even Liu Shaoqi, each kept their own counsel as to whether they really supported the movement.

Tactful as usual, Zhou Enlai put some respectful distance between himself and the scheming Lin Biao, who was more enthusiatic than anyone else in lauding Mao Zedong and the Cultural Revolution. While the latter called on all to go full steam ahead with the revolution initiated by the Chairman, the astute Zhou Enlai hinted a need for moderation, quoting and expounding some commonplace Party principles in an oblique and unobtrusive way to put a damper on Lin's fiery rhetoric. His speech in mid-September to Red Guards from the Engineering Institute of Harbin, northeast China, who had come to Beijing to present their case, laid stress on the credit as well as debit side of Party and government work. Achievements, he said, outweighed shortcomings in the seventeen years since the founding of the People's Republic. The bottom line was — be analytical and keep a sense of proportion. That was as far as he could go to make his point about avoiding extremes without drawing the fire of Mao and Lin.

Mao Zedong held the compass and supposedly knew where he wanted to direct the movement. But Liu was baffled, and though he had not lost his bearings completely, he was not sure how to proceed. He was candid with himself and his audience when he made his last speech to a large crowd towards the end of July. As to how to proceed with the Cultural Revolution, he told an assembly of cadres in the Great Hall of the People, you have no idea or any understanding. You want me to tell you how to go about this revolution. Frankly I don't know, nor do I think other comrades of the Party Centre have any idea. Exactly a week later, on August 5, Mao Zedong put up his first and only big-character poster "Bombard the Headquarters." The target was unmistakable, it was spearheaded at the "bourgeois" headquarters of which, presumably, Liu Shaoqi was the chief.

In all about a hundred charges were made against Liu. One preposterous accusation was that he and his wife Wang Guangmei led a luxurious life. Taking their cue from Jiang Qing, Qinghua University Red Guards hauled Wang before a "struggle meeting" with a string of ping-pong balls wound around her neck because she had worn a pearl necklace on a state visit with her husband to Indonesia in 1963. Actually, the necklace had been borrowed and some new clothes made only at the urging of the Protocal Department of the Ministry of Foreign Affairs.

Born in the same year (1898) as Zhou Enlai, Liu Shaoqi and his contemporary came into the Communist Party more or less at the same time, one in China and the other in France. Liu too was most of his life a professional revolutionary and shared an exalted status with the other giants — Mao Zedong, Zhou Enlai and Zhu De. An outstanding organizer and the author of many Marxist works, the most celebrated being his *How to Be a Good Communist*, Liu Shaoqi excelled as an underground Party leader in the White (Kuomintang) areas on and off for twenty years.[14] His great forte was his ability to keep his cool and analytical strength and political balance in difficult and dangerous situations. He was appointed Political Commissar to help Acting Commander Chen Yi reorganize the forces of the New Fourth Army that had been treacherously attacked by Chiang Kai-shek in southern Anhui Province in January 1941. He did a good job of expanding the Party's scattered forces in Kuomintang areas far from their Yan'an headquarters. Zhou Enlai once said of him: "In the Party's history Liu Shaoqi has never erred at critical junctures." A high tribute from one great revolutionary to another.

Liu Shaoqi's downfall was swift. By a Party resolution adopted in 1968 Liu Shaoqi was condemned as a "renegade, traitor and scab" and he and his family were driven out of their home in Zhongnanhai. Liu and his wife were incarcerated in separate prisons in Beijing, and denounced *in absentia* in "struggle meetings" at which his close associates, chief among them Deng Xiaoping, sometimes stood in for him.

Then, on October 17, 1969, Liu Shaoqi was secretly flown to Kaifeng, Henan Province, to be kept in solitary confinement at a sequestered government compound. A diabetic who had come down with pneumonia, he was in no fit condition to travel and he was taken on a stretcher. Four weeks later, on November 12, the former head of state died at a quarter to seven on a bleak morning, only his jailer was with him at his last moments. His wife and children were not informed, and had no idea where he was. Not until eleven years after his death was Liu Shaoqi posthumously rehabilitated with full honours and given a state memorial service. Should Mao Zedong be held partly responsible for his old comrade Liu Shaoqi's tragic death? Perhaps yes, in the sense that he set the stage for the persecution of Liu Shaoqi (and Deng Xiaoping) with the "Bombard the Headquarters" big-character poster, and because he approved of the Party's 1968 resolution condemning Liu as a "renegade, traitor and scab." Nevertheless, Mao was of two minds when it came to the question of overthrowing the veteran cadres or only criticizing them.

To quote Deng Xiaoping: "We cannot say that he bore no responsibility for the intensified persecution of veteran cadres that occurred later, but he was not the only one to blame. In some instances, persecutions had already been carried out by Lin Biao and the Gang of Four, while in others they took place behind Comrade Mao's back. This notwithstanding, it must be said that the overthrow of a large number of cadres was one of the biggest tragedies of Comrade Mao Zedong's later years."[15]

The case of Bo Yibo, who used to work closely with Liu Shaoqi in Kuomintang-controlled areas, is another example of how Zhou Enlai used his position to protect comrades in distress.

On August 18, 1966, Mao Zedong and other top leaders were assembled on the rostrum of Tiananmen to review a parade of Red Guards, the first of eight such occasions. Zhou Enlai, apprehensive of the gathering storm, drew Bo Yibo aside and whispered: "Yibo, this will be an ordeal. You must bear up as well as you can." For through the grapevine his aides had received word that Lin Biao, Jiang Qing and Kang Sheng were out to get what they called the "traitors" such as Bo who had emerged alive from Kuomintang prisons.

Bo Yibo and sixty other Communists held for political offences were actually released in 1936 following a compact made with the Kuomintang authorities. The Communist Party Central Committee itself had negotiated their freedom. Yet thirty years later they were pilloried for allegedly winning their freedom by betraying the party.

When the first of these former inmates was seized by Red Guards, Zhou Enlai sent Mao Zedong a note reminding him that both the Seventh and Eighth Party Congresses had reviewed the "case of sixty-one" and given their approval. At the same time he wired the Red Guards in Xi'an, saying that if they were in possesssion of any new evidence they must forward it to the Party Centre in Beijing.[16] But the opportunists were not to be stopped so easily.

As a target, Bo Yibo loomed large. He was then an alternate member of the Party Politburo, a Vice-Premier and Minister in Charge of the State Economic Commission, and a deputy to the National People's Congress. A victim of Ménière's disease, Bo Yibo had a bad fall in his bathroom one morning late that eventful August, and was confined to bed. He asked Premier Zhou for a few weeks' leave of absence, and Zhou noted in the margin of the memo: "Agreed that Bo go on leave for six months." It was meant to get Bo away from the rough-and-tumble struggle that had taken hold in Beijing and from the snares of Lin Biao and Kang Sheng. Bo Yibo and his wife hurriedly left for Guangzhou in the south, which they thought would be their haven.

On New Year's Day 1967 Bo's wife was attending a party given by old friends. Bo himself did not have the heart to face the merriment. Around noon Zhao Ziyang — today China's Premier but at that time Guangdong's First Party Secretary — turned up with grave news. Sixty Red Guards, he told Bo, had arrived from Beijing and were on their way to seize him.

No sooner had Zhao left than Bo Yibo thrust all classified documents and material he had with him into a folder and ran across the courtyard to the bungalow where Dong Biwu, Acting Chairman of the People's Republic, was staying. "Dong Lao! Dong Lao!" Bo Yibo shouted for help. But before he could get the eighty-year-old Dong Biwu to open the door the feisty, blustering youngsters were already upon him. He was knocked to the ground. Dong hobbled over on his walking stick, and knowing there was no point in arguing with the intruders, bent over to take the folder from Bo. "Yibo, go with them," he said. "My son too has been taken into custody. It seems there must be some misunderstanding. Sooner or later, the situation will be cleared up. I can only say this much. You know how things are with me...." The old man, already in tears, didn't finish the sentence. Dong and Mao were then the only two surviving founders of the Chinese Communist Party.

As Bo was about to be hustled into a car, he pleaded with his captors to wait just a while so he could say farewell to his wife. No, they bellowed. He was whisked away to the railway station for a Beijing-bound train. Before they reached the final leg of their journey, Kang Sheng, directing the operation from Beijing, ordered them to alight at Baoding, a junction some three hours from the capital, where two hundred Red Guards were waiting to transfer the prisoner to a truck. Kang wanted to be sure that his prize would reach the destination arranged for him — a prison outside Deshengmen Gate.

Imprisonment was later commuted to detention, which hardly made any difference. But with this change in status Zhou Enlai managed to get word through to put Bo in a hospital for medical treatment, a stratagem to obtain some sort of relief for his suffering associate.[17] After Jiang Qing's downfall Bo told friends that but for Premier Zhou's constant solicitations about his health, a signal to the enemy camp that Bo Yibo's case was not forgotten, he would surely have died.

Zhou Enlai's efforts to protect Party and government cadres extended in many cases to their young children, too. When parents were jailed or detained and their homes broken up, it was always Zhou's intervention that induced their parents' work unit to cough up small sums of money (wages being withheld in all such cases) for the children's upkeep.

Bespectacled, lacklustre, grossly ambitious, Kang Sheng (1898-1975) whose original name was Zhang Shuping, came from a big but impoverished landlord family in Zhucheng county in the coastal province of Shandong, the same county where Jiang Qing was born of more humble antecedents. Kang Sheng won Mao Zedong's ear during the early days of the Cultural Revolution and wielded enormous power, serving outwardly as "adviser" to the Cultural Revolution Directorate, but mostly operating viciously from behind the scenes. Although he held no office in the administrative branch of the government, by the 1970s he had become a member of the Party Politburo Standing Committee. Practically all the frame-ups of Party veterans could be traced to Kang Sheng, even though they appeared on the surface to be the work of the Lin Biao and Jiang Qing groups.

A calculating careerist from the time he joined the Party in the 1920s, he did not hesitate to ride to the top on the backs of others. He built up a power base among fellow provincials of the same stripe to form a "Shandong gang" in the 1940s when he was sent to work as an underground Party leader in his home province. The circumstances in which he and Jiang Qing first came to know each other in the 1930s can be described, charitably, as arcane, for their relationship in that period, which blossomed into political collaboration, raised the eyebrows of many straitlaced comrades. But for Kang Sheng the sometime movie actress would never have made the ranks of the Communist Party, let alone have married the Party Chairman.

Until his death in 1975 Kang Sheng was *de facto* head of the Party's security apparatus, known simply as the Social Department, whose function was to provide security for the Party hierarchy and prevent undesirables from infiltrating into its ranks. In Yan'an Kang used his position to persecute hundreds of innocent Party cadres as Kuomintang spies. There were such excesses that both Liu Shaoqi and Zhou Enlai proposed that Kang Sheng be removed from this sensitive department. But it was wartime, and most Central Committee members were preoccupied in other Liberated Areas. The slippery Kang Sheng managed to keep his job, though only after owning up to his mistakes and making some kind of self-criticism.

The matter was brought up again in 1966 by Liu Shaoqi, who spoke to Chairman Mao of the need to review the so-called case of "spies working for the Soviets" and to look into Kang Sheng's personal history and records. The Cultural Revolution intervened and, once set in motion, put everything else in abeyance. The first major political figure to pay for the Party's negligence was none other than Liu Shaoqi himself.

Another victim was Li Lisan of Liling, Hunan Province (1899-1967), one of the top Party leaders in the 1920s, who married a Soviet woman during his extended stay in the Soviet Union. He was accused by Kang Sheng of heading a "Soviet spy ring" involving several hundred people. Though the charges were never proved, Li Lisan and his comrades were left to rot and die in prison. It was no accident that Kang Sheng picked on Li Lisan, for at the Seventh Party Congress held in Yan'an in 1945, Li Lisan had trodden on Kang's toes when, in speaking of his own mistakes, he brought some of the skeletons in the cupboard of the secret police chief out into the open. Kang Sheng was not one to forgive and forget.

The first big-character poster that incited similar action throughout the country, ushering in the Cultural Revolution in a big way, was instigated by Kang Sheng and his wife Cao Yiou, who inspired the joint writers, a Beijing University woman lecturer and her colleagues, to produce it. Kang then got the nod from Mao Zedong to splash the poster on the front pages of newspapers and blare it over the radio day and night. The poster called for the overthrow of all "capitalist roaders" — which came to mean anybody in a position of authority. In no time China's officialdom, from top to bottom, was rocked by waves of attacks and leading officials and cadres were being accused of every crime under the sun.

As the movement rumbled on and many Party veterans fell by the wayside, Kang Sheng grew increasingly powerful, especially after Lin Biao's death in a plane crash. He was supposed to report the findings of a probe into Lin Biao's case to Zhou Enlai, who headed the investigation group, but instead saw fit to conceal documents and materials seized from the clandestine offices set up by Lin Biao in various cities. He also took key Lin Biao allies from these places under his wing. He put the lid on evidence that might incriminate the Jiang Qing gang, as well as strengthened his own power base. His bloated staff grew to such an extent that Kang Sheng was the only top leader to have more than one office in Beijing. He boasted three separate ones in 1974, in addition to the offices set up in fifty-four cities around the country to do his murky chores.

True to form, he bugged the official residences of Mao Zedong, Zhou Enlai, Zhu De. This came to Mao's knowledge in September 1972 and he rapped Kang Sheng over the knuckles. Kang categorically denied any knowledge. However, three months later, when the Chairman was rearranging his study, he came upon listening devices. He demanded an explanation. Kang Sheng swore vigorously he knew nothing about the gadgets, but before he answered the Chairman's summons he had the three technicians who actually installed them silenced forever. Dead men do not talk.

Zhou Enlai, admitted to hospital in the summer of 1974, one day phoned Ye Jianying, one of the four surviving PLA Marshals, and joked about his hospitalization. "You see," the Premier quipped, "I've sought a hideout here because I can no longer carry on as usual in Zhongnanhai. In the hospital I say what I please." The old Marshal knew what he meant.

Not until the Gang of Four fell from power was Kang Sheng exposed in some detail as the *eminence grise* of the Cultural Revolution, the villain pulling the wires from behind the scenes, the ulcer gnawing at the body politic of the Chinese Communist Party for many years. Repudiated and stripped of all honours in death, Kang Sheng was read out of the Party posthumously in October 1980 with all the ignominy he deserved.

In the latter half of 1966 and early 1967, practically all of China's ambassadors were called home to take part in the Cultural Revolution. Some were subjected to questioning and harassment by the Red Guards the moment they got off the plane. An enraged Chen Yi, the Foreign Minister, demanded an explanation from Chen Boda and Jiang Qing, chief and deputy chief of the Cultural Revolution Directorate, but they refused to see him or give any reason why foreign service officials were being roughed up at the airport. Only Zhou Enlai's direct intervention stopped these antics.

One ambassador of senior rank, Liu Xiao, one-time Vice-Minister of Foreign Affairs, was not seen again after having been invited to dinner with Kang Sheng. Chen Yi called Kang Sheng to ask what had happened. Kang said: "Liu Xiao has admitted that he is a double agent and is now writing a statement to expose the Party's East China Bureau and the Shanghai Bureau, too." He added an oblique hint: "I just don't know who else is involved in this case." Chen Yi, who had been head of both bureaus in post-liberation Shanghai, shouted into the phone: "Kang Sheng, why don't you come and arrest me, too?" Always a slick operator who knew when a man's patience had been tried too far, Kang hung up. Then he complained to Chairman Mao that Chen Yi was interfering with his work. A seed of suspicion planted in time, he calculated, would eventually bear fruit.

Liu Xiao had of course not "confessed" anything. After some verbal sparring with Kang Sheng over the dinner table, he had been seized by Kang Sheng's men as he left the house to return home. Liu remained behind bars without trial or investigation, Chen Yi's protests notwithstanding.

Kang Sheng's threats made no impression on the intrepid and outspoken Chen Yi, who continued to speak up for his comrades and what he perceived to be the correct Party line. He was at his most impassioned and vehement at one February 1967 meeting, presided over by Zhou Enlai and attended by Vice-Premiers and Marshals of the People's Liberation Army. The army veterans confronted the firebrands of the Cultural Revolution Directorate, (Chen Boda, Jiang Qing, Kang Sheng *et al*) with considerable heat.[18]

Chen Yi shook with anger and pounded the table to make his point. Party veterans, he said, were being tormented and even tortured by bands of irresponsible persons. Why, he asked his adversaries pointblank, should comrades who have given their all and have been with the Party so long be so persecuted? "In the Party's history there have been people who used their position to frame Party veterans and abuse them in the most abominable way," the Marshal bellowed. "But in later years these types ended up going over to the counter-revolutionary camp. Here are people trying to do the same thing. Let me tell you they will come to no good."

The affable and well-liked soldier-poet was Premier Zhou Enlai's close associate and friend, the Vice-Premier chosen to serve as his Foreign Minister. Therefore he was high on Lin Biao's and Jiang Qing's hit list. Addressing a large gathering of cadres early in the Cultural Revolution, Chen had set forth his views on this extraordinary political movement, when perhaps silence was the better part of valour. He publicly said that he had made mistakes before and could do the same again, and that in the long history of the Chinese Revolution he had not always been on Chairman Mao's side. He gave no guarantee that he would not oppose Mao again.[19]

Lin Biao, Jiang Qing and the Red Guards were outraged by the old warhorse's blunt talk. In their minds Chairman Mao's every word or phrase was gospel truth. Chen Yi was taken to task for his outspoken views, but he won the respect and affection of many for sticking by what he thought was right.

One day the Marshal was summoned to the Beijing Institute of Foreign Languages to account for his "reactionary views" before a student body meeting. He arrived in his limousine at the appointed time and as he entered the hall was handed a dunce cap to wear. Chen did not lose his sense of humour. He stood erect like the soldier, every now and then adjusting the high paper headgear. Then he was asked, as was usual in these cases, to recite a quotation from Chairman Mao, a ritual which always began "Chairman Mao says," and followed with a quotation from the little red book. After clearing his throat, Marshal Chen Yi intoned: "Chairman Mao says: 'Comrade Chen Yi is a fine comrade.'"

The startled Red Guards on the platform looked at each other in bewilderment. Some quickly leafed through the little red book but could find no such quotation.

Chen Yi had of course made it up on the spur of the moment. He smiled wryly as he was pressed for the source of the quote.

Zhou Enlai's right-hand man was excoriated now not only for his unrepentant "reactionary" views but also for falsification of the sacrosanct little red book. His choicest comments, all taken out of context, had been collected and printed in book form under the title *Chen Yi's Malice,* and these were ticked off one by one before the meeting was adjourned and he was dismissed. He was escorted to his car by several Red Guards and as he was about to hop in, he doffed his dunce cap and handed it to one of them. "Please take good care of it, will you? I'll need it at the next meeting."

Mao Zedong himself took with a grain of salt the lurid stories put out by the Red Guards about Chen Yi. Mao's comment on the book brought out by the Red Guards to defame the Marshal was a terse one-liner: *"Chen Yi's Malice* is not malicious." The Chairman said that Chen Yi, though under fire, should keep his job. But in the few years left to him the old warrior remained on the sidelines despite Zhou Enlai's efforts to clear his friend and close associate.

Three years Zhou Enlai's junior, Chen Yi had been in France on the work-study programme at more or less the same time with his friend. He did not stay long. In a demonstration organized by Chinese students to protest the high-handed measures of Lyons University, Chen Yi, an active student leader, was expelled from the country in October 1921 and returned to China. Later he played a prominent part in the 1927 Nanchang Uprising under Zhou Enlai's leadership and had since spent a lifetime in uniform.

Chen Yi's straightforward record from his student days to the birth of the People's Republic gave his enemies no opening to get him by blowing up any incident in his personal history. But he was a thorn in their flesh as part of Zhou Enlai's inner circle, so they attacked his stewardship of the Foreign Ministry, accusing him of carrying out a revisionist foreign policy which capitulated to the forces of imperialism.

Chen Yi counterattacked with vigour. In the seventeen years since the People's Republic came into existence, he said, China's foreign policy had been formulated by Chairman Mao and the Party Politburo and its execution guided by the Chairman and the Premier at every juncture. Errors and flaws there might be in the day-to-day performance — and he was ready to assume responsibility for that — but by no stretch of imagination could anyone accuse the government of following a "revisionist" foreign policy. Privately, he told comrades in his office that "those who talk big in revolutionary jargon are nothing but phrasemongers. They haven't done an honest day's work in their lives." His aides pleaded with him: "Marshal, the least said the better."

"Oh, no, I'm not going to let them gag me," he said. "I may step on somebody's toes and it's possible I may get into trouble for that, or even get done in, but if for fear of this I shrink from saying what I think ought to be said, then as a Communist I am not worth a penny."

To put pressure on Chen Yi the Red Guards, instigated by Lin Biao and Jiang Qing, laid siege to the Foreign Ministry building by putting up dozens of tents around its premises and kept a sharp watch for a chance to grab the man in charge. Minister of Public Security Xie Fuzhi, who was then high on the Lin Biao-Jiang Qing totem pole and the number one man in Beijing's municipal government, gave the young rioters all the assistance they needed. They were provided with loudspeakers through which they chanted, "Get Chen Yi! Get Chen Yi!" "Down with Chen Yi!"

Graffiti were splashed at street corners and on the walls of the capital everywhere calling for his outster. Eventually permission was given for a meeting to be held in the Great Hall of the People to "criticize" Marshal Chen Yi. Zhou Enlai as Premier agreed to be present on the understanding that the proceedings were confined strictly to "criticism." He refused to mount the platform until a huge banner inscribed with the legend "Down with Chen Yi!" hanging from the balcony was removed. After that the Premier sat alongside his colleague, apparently to express sympathy with his ordeal, and heard out his accusers.

Suddenly several burly Red Guards sprang from their seats in the front rows and forced their way up to the platform. Zhou Enlai ordered the proceedings to stop at once. He reprimanded those presiding over the meeting for breaking their promise and warned them that he was not going to tolerate violence. Then he walked out on the meeting, but not before ordering the security staff he had brought along to protect the Vice-Premier and see him safely home afterwards.

Zhou Enlai took painstaking care to see that every measure was adopted to foil attempts to kidnap the Marshal. The Premier had to make the protection measures foolproof, for Lin Biao and Jiang Qing had a secret ally in the Minister of Public Security, a man officially accountable to himself in the State Council but with a foot in the enemy's camp.

Of the ten Marshals of the People's Liberation Army, Lin Biao and Jiang Qing calculated, four still stood in their way in 1967. They were Chen Yi, Ye Jianying, Xu Xiangqian and Nie Rongzhen. Excluding Lin Biao himself, of the remaining five, Zhu De, well into his eighties, was considered too old to interfere with their plot to seize power; He Long and Peng Dehuai had already been downed; Luo Ronghuan was already dead; and Liu Bocheng, the commanding general of the Second Field Army with his close friend Deng Xiaoping as Political Commissar, was considered *hors de combat* in any political struggle since he had been incapacitated and bed-ridden for many years.

In this scenario Chen Yi stood out among the four to be eliminated — first of all, because like Ye, Xu, Nie, he was Zhou Enlai's right-hand man. Second, he was a favourite of Mao Zedong's sharing a common interest with the Chairman in classical Chinese poetry. Third, he was outspoken and no respecter of persons; he must be gagged and made an example of to warn others that defiance meant trouble. Fourth, among the four Marshals, Chen Yi was best known abroad. Lin Biao and Jiang Qing at last succeeded in manoeuvring their foe out of Beijing, ostensibly to carry out Chairman Mao's directive to make a study of local conditions in a factory at the grassroots. It was a brief stint and the Marshal returned to the capital, but never again to resume his regular role as Vice-Premier and Foreign Minister.

His health was failing and he discovered, perhaps too late, that he had cancer. Usually a lively and witty conversationalist, Chen Yi for a time kept much to himself. Then an event of enormous portent shattered the calm all around him and broke his silence — the Lin Biao affair.

The would-be power usurper, unmasked in a plot to kill Chairman Mao, fled the country with his family and co-conspirators and died in a plane crash over China's border with Mongolia on September 13, 1971. This extraordinary incident stirred Chen Yi's blood. While Zhou Enlai was in continuous conference with Mao Zedong to deal with its aftermath, the ailing Marshal closeted himself with army colleagues to discuss and expose all they knew about the arch criminal.

Ill as he was, Chen Yi spent much time preparing an indictment. But he collapsed from exhaustion in the midst of delivering a speech of stinging attack.

He was rushed to hospital and underwent surgery, but remained delirious most of the time. The Premier, who left instructions to the doctors to report at once when the patient became conscious, turned up at midnight of January 2, but Chen quickly lapsed into a coma again. On January 6 the old warrior breathed his last.

Zhou Enlai's unfailing endeavours to come to the aid of comrades in distress in the Cultural Revolution have become legend. Except for his intervention, many of China's top leaders today would have remained in political limbo or faced even worse fates. When the chips were down, but not before — because premature exertions on his part would harm rather than help — they could count on his being in the right place at the right moment to give them succour. When his position or prestige was not sufficient to achieve the desired result, when everything else failed, the astute Premier would appeal to Mao Zedong, a tactic he could use only sparingly.

His intervention on behalf of Xu Xiangqian of Hubei Province, one of the four active Marshals mentioned above, is a case in point.

August 1, 1967 was the fortieth birthday of the People's Liberation Army, a special, red-letter day for men and women in uniform. As a rule a list of all who attended the reception would be reported in full. *People's Daily,* the party organ, would be scanned the next morning by watchers of the political scene. A prominent figure absent from the name list meant that the person concerned had been purged, fallen out of favour, or was too controversial to be invited. After the so-called "rebellion of February 1967," an incident which put a host of top army officers on the spot, no one except those close to Lin Biao knew for sure twenty-four hours before the event whether he would be at the Great Hall of the People to celebrate the occasion.

Marshal Xu Xiangqian, Vice-Chairman of the Party's Military Commission, found himself left high and dry on the morning of July 31 of that year.

In ordinary or quieter times, Xu would have been among those who made the decision on the invitations instead of being left out himself. Still, he was not precisely relieved of his post, though that was what Lin Biao planned. At five p.m., two hours before the reception, his colleague Ye Jianying unexpectedly turned up at his home to pass on Premier Zhou's word: Get ready for the reception. There had been differences of opinion on whether Xu Xiangqian should be allowed to be present — which meant that Lin Biao and company were opposed. Ye said that the matter was being taken up by the Premier with Chairman Mao. He had been thoughtful enough to bring along a barber, just in case his old colleague, inhibited as he was at the time, should need a haircut.

An hour later, Zhou Enlai called to say that the matter had been cleared with Chairman Mao. Xu was to attend along with several high-ranking officers who were also under attack. Zhou Enlai, always the master tactician in such a situation, alerted trusted security units along the route Xu was to take to the Great Hall. He didn't want the Marshal to fall into unauthorized hands on his way to the reception, since Xie Fuzhi, his ostensible Minister of Public Security, was at the same time serving another master.[20]

Xu Xiangqian had known Zhou Enlai since 1924, when he became a cadet at the Whampoa Military Academy, of which Zhou was then Director of the Political Department.

When the Cultural Revolution began to involve the People's Liberation Army — not the rank and file but its administrative offices and non-combatant units — Xu Xiangqian was head of the armed forces' directing group. He and Lin Biao did not see eye to eye on many matters, and it was on Zhou Enlai that he leaned for advice.

One of Xu's great concerns was to contain the damage done by the Red Guards in Beijing and elsewhere in the country, to make the youngsters see that "enough is enough" without seeming to douse their heads in cold water. He was concerned about their being manipulated by the Lin Biao-Jiang Qing opportunists. He came up with a set of "Don'ts" based in spirit on the *Sixteen Points — Decision of the Central Committee of the Chinese*

Communist Party Concerning the Great Proletarian Cultural Revolution.

A meeting was called to discuss these "Don'ts": Don't make unwarranted arrests, don't make unwarranted searches, don't administer corporal punishment, don't slap heavily-loaded dunce caps on the accused, don't pillory them with defamatory boards on their necks, don't parade them through the streets, etc.

The meeting was chaired by Zhou Enlai, who endorsed all these restrictions. But Jiang Qing and Chen Boda hedged and prevaricated, neither accepting nor rejecting them. Their attitude was a signal, and the result was greater chaos.

Troubled by the turn of events, Mao Zedong decided on January 23, 1968 to call up the army, the navy and air force to help restore stability. He sent officers of the three services as "work teams" into government offices, schools, universities and other establishments, first to guide and advise and then to take charge. Xu Xiangqian's office again drew up the ground rules.

Formulated with the help of Ye Jianying, Chen Yi and Nie Rongzhen, plus several of the top brass from the Party's Military Commission, Xu Xiangqian submitted the regulations to a meeting convened by Zhou Enlai. Again, Jiang Qing and her friends hemmed and hawed, but in vain. For Mao Zedong, when consulted, gave his approval.

The PLA men and women, in their unfamiliar role as civilian administrators, solved some problems and created quite a few as well. Some who private ends in mind took advantage of the power in their hands. Nevertheless, the regulations did serve as a check on the Young Turks in the three services who were exercising authority for the first time in the civil realm. Lin Biao and company regarded these regulations with distaste, and exaggerated out of all proportion faults arising from their enforcement. They blamed those who had had a hand in drafting and implementing them, and began to point their finger at Zhou Enlai, now more and more a roadblock in their struggle for power.

When the grumbling reached Mao Zedong's ears, he said apropos of the use of the military that the situation had been handled fairly well, and that the critics were only wise after the event. Zhou Enlai took such carping criticism in his stride. His main concern was to preserve some measure of stability, particularly in the armed forces.

In addition to his full-time job of running the State Council, with its sprawling administration, the Premier was frequently called to meetings to deal with pressing problems thrown up by the factional fighting between

Red Guard groups. By this time Mao Zedong had designated Zhou Enlai to take part in deliberations of the Cultural Revolution Directorate under Chen Boda and Jiang Qing, and in the Military Commission's Cultural Revolution Group (PLA), headed by Xu Xiangqian, as well as liaison sessions between the two. It was a role well suited to the Premier's ability as a diplomat and negotiator skilled in reconciling opposing points of view. But the situation did not suit Lin Biao, who had an axe of his own to grind.

Lin countered Mao's decision by defining afresh the chain of command: Xu Xiangqian's Military Commission's Cultural Revolution Group must come under the dual leadership of the Military Commission itself, of which he was actual, if not nominal head, and the Cultural Revolution Directorate, but primarily under the latter, to which all matters of importance must be referred for decision.

This move was designed to cut the ground from under Xu Xiangqian's feet and take matters out of Zhou Enlai's hands. When Xu Xiangqian tried to contact the Jiang Qing group, nine times out of ten neither she nor Chen Boda could be reached. And if they were available, all he got was an ambiguous answer or a brush-off. It was an impossible situation. Some PLA units were in a chaotic state because of struggles between rival groups of Red Guards. Xu was disgusted with these developments and spoke of resigning, but was dissuaded by Zhou Enlai.

Also high on Lin Biao's hit list was Luo Ruiqing (1906-1978) of Nanchong, Sichuan Province, one of the ten senior generals of the PLA. Tall for a Sichuanese and robust in build, Luo Ruiqing, nicknamed "the tall one" in army circles, came out of the Cultural Revolution minus the function of a leg, allegedly the result of being pushed over the porch of a house in the summer of 1966 when he was detained for questioning by Red Guards.

Shortly before the Cultural Revolution was to thunder through China, Lin Biao, presiding over a restricted session of Politburo members in Shanghai, had manoeuvred to have Luo Ruiqing stripped of all his Party and government posts. As a senior general, one rank below that of a marshal and one above that of a full general, Luo held far too many sensitive positions for the ambitious Lin Biao. And Luo had been in charge of security matters since the Long March days, and Zhou Enlai's close aide since working under him during the Xi'an Incident of 1936.[21] Lin Biao wanted to get rid of Luo because he stood in his way to "politicize" the army. Jiang Qing's chief objection to Luo was that the general had publicly—and warmly— praised Mao Zedong's first wife Yang Kaihui, who had been executed in 1930 for her revolutionary activities. This did not sit well with the Chairman's third wife.

During the 1960s Lin Biao and Luo Ruiqing were the key figures in China's military power structure. Lin was Defence Minister and sat on the Party Military Commission as an *ex officio* member. Luo was Chief of the General Staff and concurrently Secretary General of the Military Commission, a position entailing supervision of its day-to-day business. While Lin Biao did his best to politicize the army, Luo stressed rigorous professional standards and balanced military and political training.

In December 1965 Luo Ruiqing was relieved of all his posts and his name vanished completely from the news media the following spring. When it reappeared, it was only to be lumped with three others—Peng Zhen, Lu Dingyi and Yang Shangkun—and the "quartet" was accused of forming "an anti-Party faction." A year later, with the Red Guards making wanton arrests and grilling the victims at will, word reached the Premier that Jiang Qing's "kid generals" were out to seize Luo Ruiqing, then receiving hospital treatment for his broken leg. The Beijing Garrison Commander was instructed by the Premier's office to get ready to accommodate Luo and his wife at his barracks. Nevertheless, the Lin Biao and Jiang Qing crowd took advantage of the turmoil and the considerable power in their hands to spirit Luo away to a spot where they could do what they liked with him.

In the face of flagrant violations of law and order — abducting leading cadres, military or otherwise, searching homes of those in important positions and seizing confidential documents in their possession—Zhou Enlai took two specific measures. One was to order the Beijing Garrison to redouble its efforts to provide top officials with more effective protection. The other was to face up to the various factions of the Red Guards himself, meeting with them as often as possible and appealing to their sense of fairness with his usual persuasiveness.

Sometimes they took heed, sometimes they didn't. Interminable meetings and time-consuming, nerve-racking bull sessions with the Red Guards took much out of Zhou Enlai. His health was impaired. And sometimes all this effort was unavailing, as in the case of Luo Ruiqing. In the course of putting pressure on Luo to confess his "wrongdoing," Lin Biao and company not only threatened to terminate therapy for his badly broken leg, but also, when he remained adamant, had it forcibly amputated.

Luo Ruiqing and his wife spent seven years in prison and denied visits by their children. Their son Luo Yu spent four years in solitary confinement. Thanks to Zhou Enlai's unremitting efforts, Luo Ruiqing was finally released in November 1973, and his wife two months later. She knew nothing about the amputation and was crying like a child when husband and wife were reunited in an army hospital ward in a Beijing suburb. The Premier sent regards and words of encouragement, reminding them that there were plenty of opportunities to work for the country again but the important thing for both of them was to get well first.

Of the thirty or so women who survived the Long March ordeal to reach Yan'an in 1935, no more than a dozen are still living today, the most prominent one being of course the still active Deng Yingchao. The least known is probably Wang Dingguo.[22]

Barely twenty when she went on the Long March, Wang Dingguo, serving as a propaganda worker, met quite a few of the Party's high officials in the course of her work, including her future husband, Xie Juezai, many years her senior, a poet in classical Chinese and a great diarist. Her political commissar brought her along when he went to see the ailing Zhou Enlai, then down with typhoid fever, one June afternoon in 1935. After Yan'an Wang spent some years in Lanzhou, Gansu Province, where her husband was head of the Communist Eighth Route Army office.

Zhou Enlai and Deng Yingchao passed through Lanzhou in summer 1939 en route to the Soviet Union for surgical treatment of his dislocated elbow, and stayed with Xie and his wife. On their return the following spring they again stopped over in this northwest China transport centre. By then Xie Juezai had been transferred back to Yan'an, and his family was waiting for transportation, a problem in those wartime days. Although there was room enough on Zhou Enlai's lorry to take a few extra passengers, Mrs. Xie didn't feel like imposing on the Yan'an-bound travellers with two small children. No trouble at all, said Zhou Enlai, and they could help look after the little ones on the trip. The younger of the two kids, only a few months old, would gnaw toothlessly on anyone trying to touch him, including Zhou Enlai; Zhou gave him the nickname puppy. On reaching Yan'an Zhou Enlai brought mother and children to the Party School, and seeing Xie Juezai he joked: "Here you are. I'm turning over your wife and children. Mission completed."

Xie became the People's Republic's first Minister of the Interior and then President of the Supreme People's Court. He did much of the spade work to codify the country's new laws before nationwide victory brought him and his family to Beijing. The impeccable political credentials of such a couple as Xie Juezai and Wang Dingguo should not have aroused suspicions of any kind in any quarter. But things went berserk in the Cultural Revolution.

With the storm breaking all over China, even a veteran Long Marcher like Wang Dingguo was accused as a "traitor" by Lin Biao, Jiang Qing and their adviser Kang Sheng. On February 6, 1969, she was taken into custody and forbidden even to call her husband at home to tell him she was being bundled off to jail. The new power wielders were anxious to eliminate people considered close to Zhou Enlai, and Xie and his family had never made any secret of where they stood with the Premier.

For more than a month the holder of the highest judicial office, who had been paralysed from 1963 on, lost track of his wife. Perquisites due to his position were withdrawn and the cook provided by the government was sent away, though meals were provided everyday from the common mess hall. He had difficulty looking after himself, and helpless as he was, it was his wife's personal safety that worried the old man most of all. In his darkest moment he thought of Zhou Enlai. He knew the Premier had a hard time himself, being assailed with problems thrown at him by the common enemy. Still, he scrawled a letter and had it sent to Zhongnanhai. It was the cry of a sick and desperate man. Three days later, his wife was set free, in consequence of Zhou's intervention. But the prison authorities, acting on the instructions of their masters, set three conditions on her freedom. First, she must report to her workplace at eight every morning and remain there for all working hours; second, she must abstain from all outside contacts; and third, she could not breathe a word about the questioning and investigation she had been through, not even to her husband. Wang Dingguo agreed and hurried home.

She was struck by the sight of a pale, haggard Xie Juezai lying on the sofa. She wanted to know what her husband had been through. She wanted to know how her release had come about, who had rescued her from the jaws of hell. Then suddenly she remembered something and began fumbling around the corners and seat of the sofa. Xie muttered weakly: "They are all here." He even managed a smile. "Don't worry. Every one of them."

When rumours had gone the rounds that the homes of many Party veterans were being searched, Wang Dingguo had taken the precaution of stuffing all Xie Juezai's diaries under the sofa seat and sewing them up. These diaries, kept for over sixty years and running to a million words, contained entries on the times before and after the birth of the Chinese Communist Party and were thus of immense value to students of modern Chinese history. As a teacher-turned-Communist and confidential secretary to Mao Zedong before the Long March in the Jiangxi base area he had recorded not only his own commentaries on political and social events but also conversations and sayings of Mao Zedong, Zhou Enlai, Liu Shaoqi, Zhu De, Ren Bishi[23] and many other prominent figures.

As Wang Dingguo patted the sofa with a deep sense of relief, the telephone rang. She was trembling all over, afraid to lift the receiver. After a minute or so she answered the phone. The voice at the other end said, "Hello, hello. Who's there? Who's speaking? Hello there."

She listened in tremulous silence. Then, in a flash, she recognized the familiar voice.

"It's me…it's me," Wang Dingguo broke down but tried to check herself. "Oh, Premier…I'm home. Thank you, thank you. I'm home now."

"How's Xie Lao? You must take good care of him, very good care." The Premier's voice came over with a tinge of anxiety.

When she put down the receiver, Xie told her about that letter to Zhou Enlai. Had it not been for the Premier, he wondered if his wife would ever have seen him again. Two years later, in June 1971, Xie died. In normal times a man of his status would rate an eye-catching obituary notice in the news media. But the Gang of Four and its adviser Kang Sheng ruled that there would be no obituary notice, no condolences, no wreathes, no rites of any kind to mark his passing. Funerals, they said, were part of the old customs that must be done away with. Zhou Enlai countermanded the order.

Hardly had the tears of the bereft dried than the Jiang Qing gang began harassing the Xie family. First they disconnected the telephone, in an attempt to make life miserable for Wang Dingguo and keep her isolated. Informed about this, Zhou Enlai instructed an aide to have the telephone restored at once and do what needed to be done for the family. This man with awesome national responsibilities still concerned himself with such trivial matters. He even reminded his aide to make sure that in winter the Xie family got a big enough ration of coal and briquettes to keep warm.

Outside Zhou Enlai's immediate circles in Zhongnanhai, Fu Chongbi, Beijing's Garrison Commander, had the most day-to-day contact with the Premier in the first years of the Cultural Revolution. Silver-haired and sixty-seven today, Fu was only a lad when he joined the Red Army to go on the Long March and had risen from the ranks to become the general responsible for the capital's security matters. His job exposed him to constant conflicts with Jiang Qing's crusading Red Guards and thrust him into many face-to-face confrontations with the virago herself.

Fu's first unpleasant contact with Mao's wife came in December 1966 when the Cultural Revolution was moving into high gear. The Red Guards had abducted Peng Zhen, Mayor of Beijing, and his top associates in the dead of night. Zhou Enlai ordered Fu to take measures to free the men and find safe quarters for them. Jiang Qing, delighted with the youngsters' daring feat, taunted the frustrated Garrison Commander when they met face to face.

"How about it? What a wonderful job the kid generals have done! What about you, general, you haven't been able to protect your men, have you?"

Her jubilation was shortlived. Fu found the place where the Mayor and his colleagues were detained and moved them to the garrison headquarters according to the Premier's instructions.

Meanwhile, the Red Guards, emboldened by Jiang Qing and Lin Biao and revelling in their first adventure, began to compete among themselves in doing the "boldest", or "most revolutionary" feats. Rival groups tried to outdo each other in defying law and order and in kidnapping highly-placed officials, especially those who had been blacklisted by Lin Biao and Jiang Qing. Fu Chongbi's Garrison Command personnel, numerically no match for the hordes of young people, were hard pressed to cope with the abductions.

Song Renqiong, First Party Secretary of the Northeast China Bureau and a veteran armyman, had come on official business to Beijing and was staying at the army high-rise hotel a few miles west of Tiananmen Square. He was no friend of Lin Biao, who with Jiang Qing conspired with agents sent from Liaoning Province to seize Song first and frame him later.[24]

Red Guards who monitored Song's movements at the hotel sneaked into the building after nightfall and headed straight for his suite on the top floor. Since they could not carry off their man by force down the elevator or the staircase without attracting undue attention, as the hotel was full of sentries from Fu's Garrison, they decided to tie their captive up and lower him to the ground by a knotted rope. The unusual commotion alerted the soldiers, who rushed to the scene just in time to rescue Song.

When informed of what the Red Guards had intended to do, Zhou Enlai heaved a sigh of relief, for the crazy descent from such a height might have meant instant death to a man of Song's age. To guard against such recurring raids, the Premier told Fu to redouble the sentries at the army hotel.

Lin Biao and Jiang Qing also drew a lesson from their botched abduction of Song Renqiong, and nearly pulled off their plan to kidnap Chen Zaidao and Zhong Hanhua, top brass from PLA's Wuhan Command in central China, who were staying at the hotel at the same time. This time the Lin and Jiang cliques mustered seven thousand Red Guards to storm the hotel, and Fu's security forces were greatly outnumbered. Several hundred youngsters succeeded in breaking through and were dashing up the staircase. It was a touch-and-go situation. The Garrison Commander, who was on the spot, communicated with Zhou Enlai and received instructions to hide the two generals in an unused elevator and leave them at a point in between the eighth and ninth floor. At the same time the Premier phoned Jiang Qing's surrogate, who was directing operations at the hotel, and demanded that he and his besiegers withdraw instantly. The man dilly-dallied. Zhou made the consequences very plain. Either he complied or else he would be referred to Chairman Mao for disciplinary action. The ultimatum worked.

Despite all obstacles and difficulties, Fu Chongbi was commended for doing a good job, among his notable successes the measures taken at certain points to provide protection for Marshal Chen Yi and Marshal Xu Xiangqian. Fu, who worked directly under the Premier in these matters was not only given specific tasks to perform but also suggestions on how to carry them out. Zhou Enlai even went along with Fu on night inspection tours to see if the security precautions for high-ranking PLA officers were tight enough.

On one occasion Zhou Enlai instructed this loyal officer to deploy his men, spread out cars with their engines running, and keep a helicopter hovering nearby in the event that Party veterans being grilled at inquisitorial sessions faced physical danger. They must be rescued at all costs, he said. Fu grew in his job and became bolder and more confident in his encounters with Jiang Qing and her fanatic supporters. At the height of the chaos resulting from the mounting cases of abductions, Fu Chongbi had the satisfaction of upstaging Jiang Qing and making her look foolish in public.

In the summer of 1967, Li Jingquan, First Party Secretary of the Southwest China Bureau and former Political Commissar to Marshal He Long, along with several other Party elders, waited for their fate to be decided while staying in a Party hostel in west Beijing. Most in their sixties, some in ill health, they were pilloried and paraded through the streets of the capital with sandwich-boards hanging from their necks which identified their names and "crimes." Once the number one man of China's most populous province, Sichuan, and He Long's Political Commissar during the War of Liberation, Li Jingquan was a chronic hypertension invalid who should have been put up in a hospital ward instead of a hotel room. There were also scores of high-level but younger cadres at the hostel. If nothing was done to contain the plague of abductions, their turn would come next.

The Premier told Fu Chongbi to take immediate steps to move all these comrades quietly to the garrison headquarters. When Jiang Qing and her hirelings descended on the hostel and found not a trace of the men they had come to get, she flew off the handle. At a meeting later in the day, Jiang Qing glowered at Fu.

"Where are they?" she confronted the Garrison Commander.

Fu played dumb. He looked at the Premier, who kept a straight face. To Jiang Qing's rattling, insistent interrogation he simply shrugged his shoulders. Pressed to the wall, he finally answered, "The higher-ups, they know." The next day he happened to see Chairman Mao and reported to him about the Premier's instructions to protect the besieged cadres. He didn't mention the pressure Jiang Qing was putting on him.

"The Premier has done well. The Garrison Command's doing its duties in protecting these comrades," the Chairman commented. Fu felt reassured.

Regular daily briefings were held in those days, usually with Zhou Enlai in the chair. These were time-consuming affairs attended by leaders of the Cultural Revolution Directorate, chiefly Jiang Qing, Chen Boda and Kang Sheng. The Garrison Command's ranking officers sat in. The day following Fu's meeting with the Chairman, Jiang Qing, on encountering the Garrison Commander, again pressed him for the whereabouts of the missing cadres. She was extremely annoyed and was not going to tolerate further equivocation. She bawled at Fu Chongbi, who remained calm and composed.

"Now where are they?"

"Go and ask the Chairman!"

"...why didn't you say so in the first place?"

"I did. I said the higher-ups knew about it, didn't I?"

Fu reported to Zhou Enlai about seeing Chairman Mao and his reaction, and they had a good laugh together.

In two instances, however, Jiang Qing and company outmanoeuvred him. One concerned Marshal He Long, and the other Senior General Luo Ruiqing. For once a decision had been taken to set up an investigation group to probe the record of an official, however flimsy the charges might be, Fu Chongbi as Garrison Commander had no say in the matter and must surrender the accused under investigation. So he was compelled to turn over these two men when they were in his safe-keeping.

Ultimately, charges were trumped up against Fu Chongbi, and he spent some years in prison in Shenyang in northeast China. Zhou Enlai tipped him off beforehand that Lin Biao was moving against him and that, regretfully, the Premier could not head it off. He told Fu never to give up hope, that things would come right in the end. On March 22, two days before Fu was to be sent out of Beijing, Premier Zhou gave him a send-off dinner in full public glare at the Great Hall of the People. It was a gesture of open support for a devoted and steadfast comrade who had been wrongly accused. Zhou's parting words were: Be ready to answer the call to service again, and in the meantime keep fit and stand firm.

The Premier then tried every means to clear Fu's name, though at every turn Zhou Enlai was blocked by Jiang Qing and company, even after Lin Biao's death. At the end of 1973, however, Mao Zedong approved the dismissal of the case and Fu Chongbi came back to Beijing, absolved of all charges.[25]

It is perhaps fitting to conclude this chapter with an account, however sketchy, of the man who, as far as character assassination was concerned, was abused the most and the longest, not excepting Liu Shaoqi. He was battered and bruised almost to the end of the lawless decade of 1966-76 but emerged unembittered to become China's most prestigious leader.

While Liu Shaoqi was branded China's "number one capitalist-roader," Deng Xiaoping was called the "number two capitalist-roader" with all the consequences of retribution for "treachery" to the Party. Both lost their freedom in the turbulent 1966, and after two years of incarceration in Beijing were bundled away to their separate limbos, one to Kaifeng in Henan Province, central China, and the other to Nanchang in Jiangxi Province in the south. Liu Shaoqi, the older man, ailing and sinking fast, died within weeks of his imprisonment, while Deng Xiaoping survived.

Born on August 24, 1904, Deng Xiaoping of Guang'an County, Sichuan Province, enjoys the reputation for being the most resilient figure in Chinese politics, having gone down thrice in the Communist Party's rough-and-tumble infighting, once before 1949 and twice in the course of the Cultural Revolution. He was one of the first top leaders to be toppled from power and one of the last finally to regain his prominent position, in the summer of 1977.

Like his mentor Zhou Enlai, Deng went to France on a work-study programme in 1920, moved among the progressive circles of Chinese students abroad, and joined the Communist Party. From France he proceeded to the Soviet Union for further studies and returned to China in early 1927 to find the partnership brought about by Dr. Sun Yat-sen between the Kuomintang and the Communists hanging by a thread, if not already breaking up.

Deng's first big job back home was in Guangxi Province (today the Guangxi Zhuang Autonomous Region) in south China, where he helped carve out an armed revolutionary base. His first "downgrading" came in 1933, when he was sacked by the Party's radical Left-wingers for siding with Mao Zedong in disputes over lines of policy.

Deng Xiaoping was no doctrinaire or armchair theorist like so many of his fellow students who returned from the Soviet Union in the 1920s. They kowtowed to everything Soviet since in their eyes the big northern neighbour was the first, and therefore the model, socialist country in the world. Like Zhou Enlai again, Deng put great emphasis on practice and performance, which he regarded as the litmus test of truth and excellence. One of his most famous saying, which later got him into trouble, was a homely metaphor about cats, perhaps from childhood memories of his native Sichuan, then a rodent-infested province. It doesn't matter whether a cat is black or white, Deng said, it is a good cat if it catches mice. Who could object to that? Lin Biao and Jiang Qing, of course, who insisted he was ignoring the political distinctions they were so fond of (including family "class background,") in favour of pragmatic considerations.

A whole exhibition of "Deng Xiaoping's Revisionist and Capitalist

Sayings," an itemized catalogue of one hundred such examples, was held at Qinghua University to demonstrate what a rotten "capitalist-roader" Deng Xiaoping was. Delegations from schools, factories, and government offices were brought in to view this brainchild of Jiang Qing's.

But things stranger than fiction did happen in China's Cultural Revolution. Juggling with the list of figures attending public functions was used by the new power manipulators to show who were in the ascendant and who were in disgrace or on the way out. The list, made up primarily by Lin Biao, Jiang Qing and their supporters, acquired such importance that it came to be looked upon as a political barometer. In August 1966 Liu Shaoqi officially ranked second only to Mao Zedong in the Party and first in the government, and yet the news report in *People's Daily* following the review of the Red Guards by Mao Zedong on August 18, 1966, relegated Liu to eighth place. So everyone knew that Liu was in trouble. Deng Xiaoping was way down the list. Eventually his name appeared only occasionally and then vanished completely except as a target of criticism.

In 1969 Deng and his family were "sent down" from Beijing. This experience was described by his daughter Maomao in an article written for *People's Daily* two days before her father's eightieth birthday in 1984.[26] Entitled "Days in Jiangxi," the article recalled her parents' exile and life as condemned prisoners in a forlorn, completely abandoned infantry school under the watchful eyes of guards sent to keep the "number two capitalist roader" from making his escape. There were in the whole school only three inmates: her father, her mother and her grandmother (Deng Xiaoping's stepmother), whose combined age totalled well over two hundred. Maomao wrote with great warmth of feeling and respect for the history of the period.

As in the cases of other top officials under fire, the alleged guilt of parents rubbed off on other members of the family, irrespective of age. While many school-age children had to go to the countryside for a spell of farm work in pursuance of Mao's teaching, generally lasting for an indefinite period, many kept a low profile or went into hiding to escape detention. Homes were broken up as the younger people were scattered to all corners of the country. Deng Xiaoping's case was no exception. Deng's family was widely scattered even before the three oldest members were sent to Jiangxi Province on October 20, 1969.

Hardly had they settled down to their unfamiliar surroundings in Nanchang, the provincial capital, than Lin Biao's panjandrum in Jiangxi's

PLA Command turned up at their hostel and began to give the new arrivals a tongue-lashing. Deng Xiaoping was warned to "behave himself and submit quietly to reform through labour." Then they were moved to a "home" in the desolate, unused infantry school not far from Nanchang, where Deng Xiaoping and his family dragged out a wretched existence for the next three years. Deng and his wife, who had lost their positions in the government, received only a fraction of their former salaries, the total of which did not go far even in paying their grocery bills. They did all their own cooking, washing, and cleaning.

Of the three, Deng Xiaoping, though already sixty-five, was the most able-bodied. His wife Zhuo Lin had chronic, serious hypertension and his mother was much too old to take on much of the household work. According to daughter Maomao, her father took on the heaviest burdens. When her mother was too ill to get out of bed, Deng would take on nursing duties as well, serving her meals and brewing traditional Chinese medicine. Grandma did some cooking and lighter chores. Maomao's father cut firewood, hauled water, broke up large lumps of coal for their stove, and so on.

The family skimped on bare necessities to put aside a little every month to pay for train fares when Maomao and her younger brother got permission to visit them. Deng and his family cultivated the spaces beside the house for a kitchen garden, partly to supplement their diet and partly to cut down expenses on food.

Acting on instructions from Lin Biao's surrogate, the gaggle of guards detailed to watch them did not allow the three to leave the premises without permission or have any outside contact. Deng and his wife worked half the day in a tractor factory within a twenty-minute walking distance; in the afternoon, together with Deng's stepmother, they took turns working in their vegetable plot; and in the evening Deng and Zhuo Lin spent their time reading while grandma sewed. Deng had asked permission to take along much of the family's library when they were whisked off to Jiangxi, apparently expecting a long confinement. He and Zhuo Lin were thankful for all the books they had brought with them, as the evenings grew longer and longer in the winter months.

In private, according to Maomao, her father was introspective, not really taciturn but a man of few words. Tempered in the crucible of struggle for over half a century, he had turned into an optimist at peace with himself. He was not upset by adversity, nor did he gloat when things were going well. The whirligig of time, with three ups-and-downs in a political career spanning over fifty years, spoke much for this important trait in Deng Xiaoping's character.

Living in isolation as they did in an out-of-the-way town, Deng and his family, compelled to keep to themselves, were starved of news, especially news about the political situation. True, they had *People's Daily* to read and listened to the radio, but that made them none the wiser. In late 1971 they were intrigued in particular by the absence of anything about Lin Biao, "second in command" to Chairman Mao, who did not seem to have taken part in the National Day reception that October 1. Lin Biao absenting himself from this all-important public function? What's up in Beijing? Then on November 5, to their surprise, Deng and his wife were told early in the morning to be sure to get to the factory as soon as they could. There would be a meeting to hear a report on a document from the Party Centre.

This was the first time the Dengs had been asked to a political meeting of any sort since their arrival in Jiangxi two years before. What did it portend? Maomao didn't know what to make of the summons and was glad to have someone to discuss it with (she and her eldest brother Deng Pufang, paralysed from the waist down in consequence of persecution by Kang Sheng's agents at Beijing University, had by now joined the family). Pufang's father had petitioned the Party Centre to let his son join them in Jiangxi, since as a cripple he was unable to support himself with what he earned from making waste-paper baskets in a Beijing reformatory. Brother and sister discussed the sudden turn of events, but became worried when, as lunchtime approached, there was no sign of their parents.

By noontime Deng and his wife returned, but neither said a word because the guards were about. Zhuo Lin nudged her daughter, and when they got to the kitchen, she traced with her forefinger in Maomao's palm four characters: "Lin Biao is dead."

The moment the guards left the house and were out of earshot, the family fell to discussing this event of enormous import. Zhuo Lin recounted in great detail the report given at the factory, about how Lin Biao and wife Ye Qun and son Lin Liguo had plotted to kill Chairman Mao, how they had been exposed and fled the country, and had been killed in a plane crash. Her husband, flushed with emotion and pensive, said little. Deng Xiaoping's one-liner was typical of the man: "There would be no justice in the world if Lin Biao didn't end up the way he did."

From that day on things began to change for the better. Lin Biao's blustering surrogate was ousted. A change in the power elite in Jiangxi brought two leading officials to Deng's door; they called with their compliments and asked if there was anything they could do to make life a little less austere. As a result of their visit, a couple of the nastiest security guards got their marching orders. Then, at the end of 1972, they arranged for Deng and his wife to go on a pilgrimage to the Jinggang Mountains, the fastness from which Mao Zedong and Zhu De set out to carve an independent regime by force of arms in the surrounding areas, and also to revisit an old haunt, Ruijin, capital of the Chinese Soviet in the early 1930s.

In February 1973, the Party Centre notified Deng and his wife that they could return to Beijing. On the 20th, after spending well over three years of enforced inactivity in the south China province, Deng and family began their journey by rail back to Beijing. Two weeks later, on International Women's Day, March 8, Deng Xiaoping made a discreet appearance at the reception given by Zhou Enlai at the Great Hall of the People. He resumed control of the reins of government as the Premier's first lieutenant and took over the premiership, in fact if not in name, when the condition of the hospitalized Zhou Enlai became critical.

Although Deng Xiaoping knew all the time that Jiang Qing and her band of conspirators were pulling out all stops to topple him once again, there was so much to do in the concluding months of 1975 that he ignored the question of his personal welfare. For one thing there was the visit of U.S. President Gerald Ford, Richard Nixon's sucessor in the White House. Deng well knew that China's position in the Sino-Soviet-U.S. triangle of forces was much too important to be rocked by the distractions of domestic politics. Zhou Enlai's stand-in therefore addressed himself entirely to the delicate handling of the diplomatic complexities. Yet the danger signals lurking about him — the stepping up of the "Criticize Deng" campaign triggered by Mao Zedong being the most obvious — were growing more and more ominous.[27]

In the quickening pace of the struggle for supremacy following Zhou Enlai's death, Jiang Qing and her cohorts worked overtime to have their chief enemy knocked from the pinnacle of power. They thought their chance had come when, during *Qingming* Festival in early April, hundreds of thousands of people, poured into Tiananmen Square day after day to express their sorrow over Zhou Enlai's passing three months before — and their simmering discontent with the reign of the Gang of Four. Jiang Qing and her cohorts struck back with vitriolic articles in the media accusing Deng Xiaoping of instigating the people to rise against the Party and Chairman Mao. This was followed by an attempt to manoeuvre the Politburo into adopting two resolutions condemning Deng Xiaoping and stripping him of all posts in both Party and government.[28]

It was clear to most people at the time that such charges were groundless from beginning to end. After Jiang Qing's downfall, the verdict was reversed and Deng Xiaoping was restored to all his positions. He enjoyed greater popularity than ever before and his influence in the Party was reaffirmed when the Third Plenum of the Eleventh Party Central Committee, meeting at the end of 1978, repudiated the "whateverism" pushed by Hua Guofeng, the "dark-horse" successor to Mao Zedong in 1976, and reversed the erroneous resolutions adopted a year before. No other political figure in contemporary China has demonstrated greater resilience than Deng Xiaoping, Zhou Enlai's choice to guide China along the road to modernization blue-printed by Mao and Zhou himself.

And Zhou couldn't have picked a better man for the job — to clear up the Cultural Revolution mess and aftermath, to chart the course of change and reform to meet the needs of modernization, and to revitalize the leadership at all levels with young, dynamic people who are professionally qualified, dedicated to socialism and unafraid of challenge and even opposition. By temperament, by experience and determination, Deng Xiaoping was the man for the job, a man for all seasons like his mentor Zhou Enlai. The reforms he has helped push through have already transformed many areas of Chinese life and laid the groundwork for economic, political, social and cultural advances that will extend well into the next century. The aim is to turn China into a developed, prosperous nation with a high living standard and cultural level, and a democratic, socialist system.

Will mistakes be made and setbacks encountered along the way? Of course. But Deng Xiaoping and those who think like him are confident that such mistakes must be allowed for but can be corrected in the process of reform. Deng Xiaoping, who is notably short, makes a joke in this connection at his own expense. Even if the skies fall, he says, there's no need to worry. After all, it's the tall guys who'd get hit first and bear the brunt.

Chapter Ten

Stewardship from a Hospital Bed

"A man should not be afraid of death. In the event of war, I think the best way to die is on the battlefield. You fight the enemy to the finish, and if you are hit by a bullet, that's it. If there is no war, you work hard, very hard, until you are drained of your last ounce of strength and drop dead."

These words were spoken by Zhou Enlai during the 1966 Chinese Spring Festival in Tianjin, where nearly fifty years ago he had first met Deng Yingchao, his wife. They were taking a rare holiday, and Zhou was in a philosophical mood in response to a suggestion that it was time to slow down. He was speaking to Yang Zhengmin, the son of General Yang Hucheng (one of the two KMT generals who kidnapped Chiang Kai-shek in the 1936 Xi'an Incident). The elder Yang had been executed by the Kuomintang regime in its last days on the mainland, and Yang junior had become one of the Zhou family's unofficially adopted sons.[1]

The Spring Festival is an occasion for family reunions in China and the young man, then doing a tour of army duty in the south, came to Tianjin to see Zhou Enlai and Deng Yingchao. After lunch they had a game of ping-pong. Yang thought the Premier looked thinner than usual and wondered if he was really in good health. Zhou told him he took regular exercises and in the winter could even do without an overcoat. There was nothing the matter with him, he reassured the young man, no reason why he should not carry on as before. But in a few months the tumultuous Cultural Revolution broke out, and no one was able to "carry on as before."

More than any other top leader, Zhou Enlai was obliged to shoulder crushing burdens. His heart trouble, hitherto undetected, began to wear him down and yet the load, instead of being lightened, grew heavier and heavier as the months went by. Many of his right-hand men such as Deng Xiaoping, He Long, Chen Yi, Luo Ruiqing, Bo Yibo, and Lu Dingyi were driven from their jobs. Zhou was left to carry on the normal affairs of state — and the taxing new demand of the Cultural Revolution — with a

183

skeleton staff. In 1972 Zhou Enlai was discovered to have cancer. Only when his condition worsened beyond doubt would he consent to undergo proper treatment. But the work went on. He merely transferred his office from Zhongnanhai to Beijing Hospital.

With Mao's concurrence Deng Xiaoping was brought back as Vice-Premier, taking over the State Council's day-to-day chores, although from his hospital bed Zhou Enlai continued to be concerned with important state matters and to receive prominent visitors from overseas. At seventy-six, Zhou Enlai was determined to die in harness.

By the fall of 1975 he knew he had little time left. One September day he went to the Beijing Hotel for a haircut, and as usual Zhu Dianhua, the oldest and his favourite barber at the shop, attended him. Zhu had cut his hair for well over twenty years and the two had struck up a friendship.[2] Mostly the Premier dropped by the hotel in the evenings. When there were more customers than the barbers could serve, hotel guests would offer to give up their place in line, but Zhou always declined. He would sit reading newspapers until his turn came.

When hard pressed for time, such as when urgent work kept him in Zhongnanhai or when he must keep an appointment with foreign visitors, he would send for Zhu. Often on such occasions the barber would be asked to stay for a quick lunch or supper with the Premier and his wife. Once, while having a shave, the Premier couldn't suppress a cough and Zhu left a small cut on his chin.

Zhu apologized profusely. "It's my fault. Don't blame yourself. I should have said something before I coughed," the Premier tried to put Zhu at ease. "Thank goodness, Lao Zhu, your razor made an expert dodge!"

On that September visit, which turned out to be his last, the Premier suggested that a group photograph be taken as a souvenir. Zhu was delighted with the idea, but since some of the staff were not in that day he wondered if it could be put off for another time. He believed the Premier would be around again soon. Later Zhu deeply regretted this lost opportunity, that he had not recognized the Premier's clear hint, for the photograph was never taken. For the next three months Zhou Enlai was very ill. In December Zhu Dianhua called the hospital several times, offering to come and cut the Premier's hair. When told of Zhu's message, the Premier said to the nurses attending him: "Zhu has been my barber for so many years. He would be heartbroken to see me in this condition. It's better that he does not come."

From the time he checked into the hospital, Zhou Enlai continued to perform tasks and favours that were way beyond the normal scope of his duties. In the summer of 1975, a year after he was hospitalized, he concerned himself with the manuscript of the revised *Xinhua Zidian* (*New China Dictionary*), a popular Chinese reference work for everyday use. The lexicographers, who had consulted with him often over the years, were now ready to send the manuscript to the printer. However, they would like to get the Premier's views on their final product. After all, it was in a way almost as much his baby as theirs. He had supported the project and personally attended several forums to discuss ways and means of bringing out a really good new edition.

They nevertheless entertained no high hopes of hearing from him, knowing that his condition was uncertain and that so many more important matters claimed his attention.

The publishing house was all astir when the memorandum submitted to the State Council was returned from the hospital with Zhou Enlai's unmistakable signature, complete with marginal comments. The staff working on the dictionary were elated because the Premier was well enough to read through their memorandum, and saddened because his writing was shaky. Zhou Enlai scribbled at the end these words: "Sorry to have sat on this because of ill health." The apology left a lump in everyone's throat.[3]

Zhou Enlai had up to fourteen operations during his extended stay in the hospital. Even so, he ventured out, not always with the ready approval of the doctors, to perform several public acts which he thought should not be delegated to anybody else.

The first was the National Day reception held on the eve of the twenty-fifth anniversary of the birth of the People's Republic, which he had fought as hard as anyone else to bring into existence. On the evening of September 30, 1974, to the surprise and joy of those gathered in the Great Hall of the People, Premier Zhou appeared to preside over the silver jubilee. All heads turned as he walked into the banqueting chamber. For the Premier had not been seen in public for more than two months, and word had got round that he had had surgery, the nature of which had not been disclosed. His health had been a matter of public concern and now, seeing him in their midst, people were overjoyed at what they thought was his recovery.

Members of the diplomatic corps, throwing etiquette overboard, craned their necks and even stood on chairs like everybody else, vying to catch a glimpse of the Premier. Then he began to address the gathering. Though he gestured time and again for the applause to end, this clear expression of relief took a long time to quiet down. His brief speech, frequently punctuated by applause, was the last he ever made to an audience with such a large representation of Beijing's foreign community. Dapper as always, he nevertheless looked pallid. But the courtesy, the courtly manners wrapped in smiles, and the familiar jaunty tilt of the head to make a point were the same as ever. Few among the crowd guessed that Zhou had been ill with cancer for more than two years, and none suspected that they would never see him again.

Zhou Enlai also addressed the Fourth National People's Congress, which convened in January 1975. The convocation was a sure indication that the Party's old guard were impatient to get things back to normal again. At any rate, a session of the Congress had long been overdue, the last one having been held before the Cultural Revolution. Just a year previously, Jiang Qing and company had tried their utmost to topple Zhou Enlai from his premiership with the absurd "Criticize Lin Biao, Criticize Confucius" campaign. Despite their blustering, the Premier and his loyal associates remained firmly in the saddle.

Apart from his address to the Fourth National People's Congress, Zhou Enlai presided over the Second Plenum of the Tenth Party Central Committee, which decided on the former's agenda and the composition of the new government. The two months from December 1974 to January 1975 were a period of intense infighting which took much out of the already exhausted and fatally ill Zhou Enlai.

Yet, aware of the precarious state of the nation at this critical juncture, he brushed aside all appeals to go slow. For weeks he worked without let-up to prepare for the two meetings, to weigh the choices for the principal government posts, and to give the finishing touches to his speech before the Congress. Mao was apprehensive. He sent word to Zhou's aides to keep the speech as short as possible so that it could be delivered at one go.[4]

It was indeed Zhou Enlai's shortest speech at a National People's Congress. The deputies listened with rapt attention. For one thing, it was the first Congress after a ten-year interregnum and, for another, the speech sounded the keynote theme of launching China's modernization in the spheres of agriculture, industry, national defence, science and technology. This was the Premier's last speech on the country's future.

His third and last public act took place six months later in June — to officiate at the funeral rites for Marshal He Long. Comrades had tried in vain to prevail upon him not to tempt Beijing's searing hot weather to go to the Babaoshan Cemetery of Revolutionaries for the memorial service, which had been held up for quite some time by the obstruction of Jiang Qing and her cohorts. Zhou was really in no condition to leave the hospital, but he insisted.

The service was not reported in the press the next day. Jiang Qing and her gang saw to that. They did not want the public to know that He Long had been rehabilitated, much less that Premier Zhou Enlai had wrenched himself from the hospital to honour the memory of the man they persecuted to death.

A month later in July, perhaps out of nostalgia, Zhou Enlai ventured from his hospital to the Great Hall of the People, his old stamping ground. He sprang a surprise on the attendants, many of whom he knew by name through his frequent entertainment of state guests there. None dreamed of seeing the ailing Premier in their midst again. They begged him to rest as much as possible.

He smiled and remarked, half in earnest and half in jest: "Can a revolutionary do that?" He walked around, and as he came to the reception hall near the southern entrance, he pointed to a Chinese painting with a pine tree, the famous "All guests welcome" painting on the wall. Here at this spot, he reminisced aloud to the attendants and the staff accompanying him, he had received times without number government leaders from friendly countries. This was the favourite spot for taking group photographs of host and guests.

Two months before his death, Zhou Enlai sent his secretary to see Wang Yeqiu, the Curator of the Chinese Museum, about an event going back some fifty years. He happened to remember it and thought it should be recorded as a matter of history. It was about Yang Du's membership in the Chinese Communist Party.[5]

Little known outside China, Yang Du (1874-1931) who hailed from Hunan Province, was a seasoned wire-puller in the hurly-burly of political life in Beijing during World War I and the leader of a coterie known for short as the Club of Six Gentlemen. Among the six was Yan Fu (1854-1921) of Fujian Province who had studied in England and introduced Western ideas into China with his translations of Thomas Henry Huxley, John

Stuart Mill and Montesquieu. A dyed-in-the-wool conservative, Yang Du thought that China should be ruled by an emperor. More than any one else he was active in urging Yuan Shikai (1859-1916), then President of the Republic, to throw overboard the republican form of government and ascend the throne. It was he who prepared the political climate for the ambitious warlord of Henan Province to crown himself emperor in 1916. As Emperor, Yuan lasted only eighty-three days, but the debacle did not dampen Yang Du's zeal as a power broker. He carried on until the late 1920s, when he became completely disillusioned with his former ideals. He shed his monarchism, and for him the political pendulum now began to swing from the extreme right to the left.

Communism attracted him. Through the good offices of mutual friends he made the acquaintance of Shanghai Party members. He decided to become one himself, and applied for membership. But since he was such a well-known political figure Zhou Enlai, who finally approved the application, thought Yang could do more good as a secret, underground member. He designated Xia Yan, who moved in Shanghai's cultural and movie circles, to maintain a single-track, bilateral connection with the neophyte Communist. Yang took no part in cell activities, but kept in touch with the Party through Xia Yan.[6]

Yang had many friends in the metropolis, among whom was Du Yuesheng, the "Al Capone" of pre-liberation China, who put funds and a fine house at his disposal. It was useful for the Communist Party to have around a man like Yang Du, with so many varied connections, in the days when Shanghai groaned under the Kuomintang reign of terror. Upon admission into the Party, Yang sold his property, donated the proceeds as Party dues, and worked in earnest for his new beliefs. Yet, still much the old pol in manner and habit, Yang could never bring himself to address comrades as such, and though an admirer of Zhou Enlai he invariably addressed him as "Brother Xiangyu," Zhou's courtesy name, or "Mr. Wu Hao," his nom de guerre.

Hobnobbing with warlords and politicians of various hue, Yang Du was regarded by many as a man who chopped and changed politically. When the secret of his Communist Party membership could no longer be kept, some questioned his motive and wondered if he was not an opportunist after all. He was annoyed by such innuendoes, and confided to Xia Yan: "I came into the Party when the reign of white terror was at its worst. If it was opportunism, then it was opportunism at the risk of my own life and family."

. As he lay dying in the hospital, this extraordinary figure from the past came flashing into Zhou's mind. He wanted to be sure that the services Yang Du had rendered the revolution were properly recognized. He asked the Curator of the Chinese Museum to see if the editors compiling *Cihai,* a voluminous reference work which eventually came out in 1979, had an entry on Yang Du. If so they should mention in this revised version of the dictionary that in name and fact Yang Du was a member of the Chinese Communist Party.

Zhou wanted posterity to know that while Yang Du had been part of the most conservative forces in his middle age, and an incorrigible monarchist to boot, he finally saw the light and embraced the doctrines of Communism. Yang Du had done good deeds late in life and, Zhou Enlai thought, he should be remembered.

Zhou Enlai, admired always for his grasp of international affairs, did not lessen his life-long interest even when hospitalized. Retaining a keen desire to be kept posted on what was happening in the world, he got his aides to brief him thoroughly. "I can hear," he told them, "and my mind still functions." In his hospital ward he also continued to see foreign visitors.

The late Henry M. Jackson, then an influential Democratic U.S. senator and his wife were among the first to be received by the Premier on July 5, 1974. The report carried in the Chinese media the following day was the first piece of news that Zhou Enlai was hospitalized, for the Chinese were not in the habit of issuing medical bulletins. This press coverage broke precedent. Xinhua News Agency went out of its way to show that the Jacksons, friends of China, had received VIP treatment, and, more importantly, that the stories going the rounds in Beijing about the Premier falling victim to a serious though unspecified disease were true enough. In the first nine months of 1975, Zhou Enlai granted thirty-two interviews to visitors from abroad, on average nearly one a week, which must be a record for a world statesman of his age (seventy-seven) with terminal cancer.

While losing considerable weight, what bothered Zhou Enlai perhaps more than anything else was the fact that his feet began to swell. He could no longer get into leather shoes to greet guests. Before his old friend, the Korean leader Kim Il Sung, was scheduled to arrive, Zhou Enlai had a pair of loose-fitting cloth shoes made specially for the occasion. Though very ill at the time, he insisted on getting out of bed to welcome the visitor from

Pyongyang. Kim was no stranger to Beijing, and on most of his trips to China it had been Zhou who accompanied him across the country. Kim could speak Mandarin Chinese and this made it easier for them to become fast friends, talking to each other without an interpreter on informal occasions. This April visit was their last meeting.

Ilie Verdet, later Romanian Prime Minister, was the last foreign visitor to be received by Zhou Enlai in hospital, in September 1975. On his arrival in Beijing Verdet expressed a wish to call on the Chinese Premier, but doubted whether it would be possible. Just in case Zhou could manage to spare a few minutes, Verdet indicated he would like to convey in person Romanian leader Nicolae Ceausescu's best wishes for the Premier's speedy recovery. He was in the midst of touring a factory in the capital when he got word that Zhou Enlai would be glad to receive him at the hospital at one o'clock the same day, September 7. At the appointed hour, Zhou emerged from his ward to greet Verdet and members of his delegation in the lobby.

The call was to have been a short one, allowing just enough time for a brief conversation and a photograph to be taken. Zhou asked the guests to step into the reception room, he himself walking alongside them with great difficulty. He declined the offer of help, and the guests were pained to see the strenuous effort it took him to complete the few paces from the lobby to the reception room.

After the usual pleasantries Verdet turned the conversation delicately to the Premier's health. Zhou joked mordantly that he had received Karl Marx's summons to join him, which it was impossible not to accept. Then he recalled his visit to Bucharest ten years before, in 1965, to attend the funeral of Gheorghe Gheorghiu-Dej, Romania's post-war leader. It was March and yet, he told his guests, even without an overcoat he was not a bit bothered by the cold weather. On that visit to Romania he had walked four hours in the funeral procession, but now he couldn't even walk four minutes. He retained fond memories of Bucharest, the Premier said, and felt sad he could not see that beautiful city again.

The conversation was going far beyond the time the doctors allowed, but Zhou Enlai had some words that he would like the delegation head to take back to Ceausescu — a message that the Romanian comrades need not fear for the Chinese Party despite, as he alluded subtly to the Gang of Four, the difficult times it was passing through. Please let Comrade Ceaucescu know, and he implored the delegation head to mark his words, that the Chinese Party, tempered in the cauldron of struggle for over half a century, had a corps of leaders ready to step into the void. Now, he said, the Vice-Premier had assumed overall charge of the government. Someone on the Chinese side interposed at this point to make it clear that the Premier was referring to Deng Xiaoping, who was seated next to Verdet. When the chips are down, Zhou Enlai emphasized, these tested leaders can be expected to take up the reins.

To the very last Zhou was the skilled diplomat concerned with strenghthening China's bonds with friendly countries.

Two regions of China had always been close to the Premier's heart — Taiwan and Tibet — and even as he lay in his hospital bed they were not far from his thoughts. The tenth anniversary of the inauguration of Tibet Autonomous Region came in September 1975 and Hua Guofeng, then Vice-Premier in charge of Public Security, was chosen to lead the delegation to Lhasa, the capital city, for the anniversary celebrations.[7] Before leaving he went to the hospital to see if the Premier had any message for the people of Tibet. Zhou saw him at midnight and suggested that he take as a gift to the Tibetans a couple of documentary films about bee-keeping to boost farming in the region. Ever reluctant to take credit for deeds done to benefit others, Zhou exhorted Hua not to mention that films came from him. In 1951 he had taken personal charge of the negotiations to arrange for the peaceful liberation of Tibet, and had since kept an eye on the progress of this far-off part of the country.

About twice the size of the U.S. state of Texas, with parallel rich natural resources but a tiny population of two million, Tibet was China's least developed area with no industry to speak of at the time of its liberation. Zhou Enlai was astounded by its poverty and backwardness. Such ordinary merchandise as nails, screws and matches had to be imported or shipped overland from Sichuan Province. Before the construction of two highways over treacherous terrain in the early 1950s to connect it with Sichuan and Qinghai Provinces, it was easier to travel to Tibet by way of India.[8]

Liberation meant a new lease of life for the serfs that formed the bulk of the population. Technicians and engineers of all kinds, and teachers as well, were sorely needed, and Zhou Enlai saw to it that Tibet got them. The construction of the Sichuan-Tibet and Qinghai-Tibet highways, which represented extraordinary feats of engineering, in days when China's air transport was still in its infancy, helped considerably to improve conditions in Tibet. In time the region saw the building of its first factories, power stations, modern housing and eventually the inauguration of regular air flights between Lhasa and Chengdu, Sichuan's capital.

To promote national unity, Zhou Enlai urged officials of Han origin and officials of Tibetan origin to learn to speak each other's languages. He often questioned Han cadres back in Beijing on leave or to report on their work to see how well they identified themselves with the local people among whom they had come to live and work. He laid down a hard and fast rule that all Mandarin-speaking government functionaries under fifty years of age appointed to work in Tibet must learn to speak Tibetan well. For those under fifty it was obligatory, he said, and for those above that it was desirable. The directive pleased the Tibetans.

Hua Guofeng was the second high-ranking official Zhou Enlai had sent on an inspection tour of the southwest highland, the first being Marshal Chen Yi before the Cultural Revolution. Although he himself had been to most parts of China over the years, and some places several times, he never got round to visiting what was once known as the land of the lamas. He knew what sacrifices all those from other parts of the country must make to acclimatize to the rarefied atmosphere of Tibet, and he asked Hua to extend on his behalf a word of encouragement and appreciation to these hard-working cadres.

As he sat on his hospital couch ticking off the things uppermost in his mind, he thought it important for cadres of Tibetan origin to be trained to take the place of their Han counterparts, as in all nationality areas where the dominant ethnic group must in time form the core of the administration. He wanted Hua to remind the Han cadres in charge to stress quality rather than quantity in the training of Tibetan functionaries. If the policy towards the nationalities was carried out well, if the training of Tibetan cadres was conducted in a satisfactory manner, if the people of different national groupings lived and worked amicably together, if production rose and livelihood improved, in short, if all this scenario worked out, then all would be well and the future progress of the Tibet Autonomous Region would be assured. That was the bottom line of Zhou's instructions when he bade Hua Guofeng a happy landing in Lhasa.

Will there be a cure for cancer? Zhou Enlai, himself a victim, believed there would and should be one before too long. He was optimistic that by drawing upon the rich store of experience and knowledge of traditional Chinese medicine, China stood a good chance of coming up with a way of conquering this terrible killer. Before he died he expressed the fervent wish that the present generation of Chinese doctors, the traditional and the Western-trained working together, should aim high to make such a breakthrough. His interest did not just begin when he himself contracted the disease. Years and years before, when he was hundred percent fit, he had in his Zhongnanhai office a wall chart showing those parts of the country that have the highest incidence of esophagal cancer. He gave unstinted support to research in this field.

Then in November 1969, without either approval by Mao Zedong or concurrence by Zhou Enlai, the military command issued in Lin Biao's name a "war alert" to disperse all so-called non-essential institutions and personnel to the countryside. Designed as a move by Lin Biao and his henchmen to facilitate their plan to seize power, it was a convenient pretext to banish to the rural areas people and organizations whose presence in the capital they found standing in their way. But the manoeuvre, carried out indiscriminately, hit quite a few establishments that should not have been disbanded in any circumstances.

One of these was the Beijing Tumour Hospital, which had come into being only a few years earlier. Zhou Enlai was outraged by the irresponsible attitude and stupidity of the Lin Biao crowd. Cancer research, he protested, must continue and the attempt to dismantle the hospital must stop. He called on medical and research workers throughout the country to carry on their good work in this field.

In February 1975, some time before he was due for surgery, he summoned to his side the Party Secretary of Ritan Hospital,[9] where Marshal Chen Yi had been laid up in his last days. It was nothing to do with his own case; he had been informed that the rate of lung cancer was rising among the tin-mine workers in the southwest province of Yunnan. The Premier asked the Party secretary whether she was aware of this and asked her to send a medical team there at once to see what could be done to check its growth. He recalled how cancer had taken the life of the Marshal and many others, and hoped that all in the field would work hard in the quest for an answer.

Very little is known about Zhou Enlai's interest in traditional Chinese medicine. He attached much importance to acupuncture and was particularly delighted that acupuncture anesthesia had made great strides in the post-liberation period. He took all eventualities into consideration.

What if war should break out? In that case, acupuncture anesthesia would have a distinct advantage in emergency surgery. While anesthetics may not be always available, a surgeon can take care of that by carrying acupuncture needles in his field kit, which take up hardly any space and cost practically nothing. He implored surgeons in army and other hospitals to master the technique of acupuncture anesthesia. In October 1975 there was news of a breakthrough in theoretical studies of the subject by the Chinese Academy of Medical Sciences. Though then very ill, Zhou Enlai asked the academy to prepare a report on the subject for him. He never lived to read it.

Zhou believed that the integration of traditional Chinese medicine with Western medicine would yield many effective new therapies. He urged widespread dissemination of knowledge of traditional Chinese medicine and the conducting of joint research by traditional Chinese and Western-trained doctors. Publication of diagnoses and prescriptions, he believed, would go a long way towards bringing the essence of traditional Chinese medicine to the knowledge of Western-trained doctors.

Before he checked into the hospital, Zhou Enlai asked one Gao Huiyuan, a disciple of Pu Fuzhou (1888-1975),[10] the well-known physician of traditional Chinese medicine, whether his master, then Vice-President of the Academy of Traditional Chinese Medicine, had left anything in writing about his long experience. He did, Gao said, in fact there was a manuscript written by his master with his assistance and submitted for publication. But bureaucracy had left it lying in some obscure corner to gather dust. Luckily, he told the Premier, he had retrieved the manuscript, which was in his safe-keeping. Send it to me at once, Zhou told Gao. At night the Premier read these documents with great interest and was impressed. He wrote a note urging its immediate publication. *Pu Fuzhou's Diagnoses and Prescriptions* has gained a wide readership in Chinese medical circles.

Convinced that future generations would benefit from the best medical minds of the past, Zhou Enlai seized every opportunity to stress the importance of getting specialists in the field, traditional Chinese doctors and Western-trained doctors alike, to put their distilled wisdom into writing while this was still possible. What he feared most was that effective traditional remedies, often guarded as treasured secrets by families which inherited them, might be lost to posterity forever. Such cures, generally handed down from father to son, could best be preserved in print, he said.

In the fall of 1975 Luo Ruiqing, the former Chief of the General Staff, was undergoing treatment by a traditional orthopedist in Fuzhou, Fujian Province. He was so impressed by his experience that he told Deng Yingchao in great detail about the octagenarian practitioner's treatment. It was a pity, Luo said, that the doctor received no due recognition and that he had no one to pass on his extraordinary knowledge and skill.

When Zhou Enlai was well enough after an operation to be told about what was happening around him, his wife mentioned Luo Ruiqing's call and, of course, the story of the Fuzhou orthopedist. The reaction of the Premier was predictable. He instructed the Fujian provincial government to make immediate arrangements for qualified medics to assist the old bone manipulator in summing up his lifelong experience and getting it down on paper for publication. It would be an invaluable legacy for future students of orthopedics, he said. Zhou was in addition ever in search of ways to put China's large population within reach of medical facilities at the least cost to them in terms of agony and expense. One concrete case concerned women who suffered ectopic pregnancies.

In 1972 the Premier sat in on a medical conference. Seated next to him was Dr. Lin Qiaozhi (1901-1983) of Fujian Province, China's foremost gynecologist. Dr. Lin Qiaozhi (also spelt as Lim Kha-ti), then Vice-President of the Chinese Academy of Medical Sciences, had graduated from the Peking Union Medical College, an institution financed before 1949 by the Rockefeller Foundation, and did postgraduate work abroad. She was a member of the first Chinese delegation of doctors to visit the United States following Richard Nixon's historic journey to China. Zhou Enlai, who had received a report on a possible treatment for ectopic pregnancies using herbal medicine, wondered aloud how Dr. Lin and Western-trained doctors like her treated such patients. In most cases, she answered, we operate.[11]

Zhou Enlai went on to discuss with her the importance of non-surgical remedies for all kinds of complaints. Most of China's population, he explained, is in the countryside, where many peasants are afraid of operations and facilities are poor and limited. He wanted her to try using herbs instead of the scalpel for ectopic pregnancies, and also impressed on her the need to learn and profit from the rich store of traditional Chinese therapies.

When his cancer was first diagnosed in 1972, Zhou Enlai should have stopped all work to go into hospital for treatment. But no amount of persuasion — not even Mao Zedong's — could induce him to leave his Zhongnanhai office in a hurry. Not that Zhou Enlai clung to power. So much needed to be done, he protested, domestically and in the international arena. So many of the "disgraced" cadres needed to be liberated and put to work again. And what efforts were needed to get the dislocated economy rolling again! All too soon his illness, exacerbated by exhaustion from overwork and the harassment of the ultra-Leftists, made hospitalization necessary.

Once admitted to the hospital, the Party Central Committee made all decisions on the medical attention required — a practice it followed for all top leaders. This gave the Gang of Four an opening. In the name of the Central Committee, and not infrequently on Mao's putative authority, Jiang Qing and her cohorts engaged in an incredible spate of petty harassments which hampered the work of the doctors and nurses detailed to look after the Premier.

Mao's wife would call or show up in person and insist that some treatment or other be postponed while she talked over important matters with the Premier. Then she would rattle on about nothing for an hour or so. Once Wang Hongwen had Zhou called to the phone in the middle of blood transfusion. After some argument the medical staff gave in to Wang's flaunting of his authority. With a gown thrown over the Premier's shoulders by a nurse, the hardly ambulatory invalid trudged over to reach for the receiver. The matter, of course, turned out to be of no urgency at all. On at least three occasions the chief attending doctors assigned to the Premier were peremptorily called away to attend to Jiang Qing.

Then there was the matter of the tapes. In the 1960s Zhou Enlai had helped supervise and even suggested lyrics for the "Songs of the Long March" segment of *The East Is Red,* an epic song and dance drama of the Chinese Revolution. All the best films and stage productions made before the Cultural Revolution for which Jiang Qing could claim no credit, including *The East Is Red,* had long since been put in mothballs.

Zhou Enlai had always loved "Songs of the Long March," which reminded him of that heroic episode he had shared with his wife and many old comrades. He asked for tapes of this music to while away the long hours in his hospital bed — a simple request, but one he was denied.

Jiang Qing's surrogate in the Ministry of Culture, who had control over the tapes, made sure that the particular ones asked for never reached the Premier. It was a shabby, heartless act perpetrated against a dying man.

Premier of the People's Republic for over a quarter of a century and one of the supreme leaders of the Chinese Revolution, Zhou Enlai breathed his last at three minutes to ten on the morning of January 8, 1976.

Before the end came, at eleven the previous night, Zhou Enlai half opened his eyes for a last time and whispered weakly to the doctors and nurses around him: "There's little you can do for me here. Go and look after the others who need you more...."

A little later Zhu Dianhua, Zhou's faithful barber, was summoned to help prepare the body for the Premier's lying-in-state. Tears streamed down his cheeks as he bent over to look at his friend, at the beard grown long and unkempt and the familiar sparkling eyes now closed forever. It tugged at his heart to perform this last service for the Premier.

And the news spread, and all across China tears grew to a flood.

Notes

Chapter One

[1] He Long started life as a bush-fighter in rural Hunan where, according to revolutionary folklore, he and his sister brandished a pair of cleavers to strike terror into the local gentry. What he robbed from the rich he gave to the poor, and this episode was used by Lin Biao to defame He Long as a "big bandit" at the beginning of the Cultural Revolution.

[2] At the Eleventh Plenary Session of the Eighth Central Committee of the Communist Party of China (CPC), held during August 1-12, the membership of the Politburo Standing Committee was increased from seven to eleven. The new list included Mao Zedong, Lin Biao, Zhou Enlai, Tao Zhu, Chen Boda, Deng Xiaoping, Kang Sheng, Liu Shaoqi, Zhu De, Li Fuchun, and Chen Yun. Liu Shaoqi, who had ranked next to Party Chairman Mao Zedong before the meeting, was relegated to eighth place, while Lin Biao was pitchforked into Liu's old slot. After the meeting Lin Biao became, and was referred to, as the one and only Vice-Chairman, but it was not until the Party's Ninth Congress in 1969 that he was officially made successor to Chairman Mao Zedong in the Party Constitution — a move without precedent in the history of the international communist movement.

[3] "Uncle Zhou Always Lives in My Heart" by He Xiaoming, He Long's elder daughter, in *Workers Daily*, Beijing, January 6, 1979.

[4] The CPC's Central Committee, which held a plenary session in the second week of January 1975, elected Deng Xiaoping as one of the Party's Vice-Chairmen and a Politburo Standing Committee member. As stand-in for the bed-ridden Zhou Enlai, he had become the chief target of Jiang Qing and her clique of conspirators.

[5] Jiang Qing and her cohorts, who still held considerable power at the time of Zhou Enlai's death, decreed that mourning for the Premier must be reduced to a minimum. Government offices and other establishments were told "not to allow the dead to bear down hard on the living."

[6] No count was kept of the number of poems that appeared in Tiananmen Square during the *Qingming* Festival. The first collection, put together by teachers and students of Beijing's Second Foreign Languages Institute under the homonym "Tong Huai Zhou" (All Cherish Zhou), ran to several hundred. These became known as *The Tiananmen Poems*. Foreign Languages Press (FLP) printed a slender volume of thirty of these poems in 1979.

[7] By CPC Central Committee decision dated April 7, 1976, Deng Xiaoping was relieved of the following posts: Vice-Chairman of the CPC Central Committee, Vice-Premier of the State Council, Vice-Chairman of the Military Commission of the CPC Central Committee, and Chief of the General Staff of the People's Liberation Army.

[8] On February 7, 1977, *People's Daily, Liberation Army Daily* and the journal *Red Flag* jointly ran an editorial advocating the two "whatevers": "Whatever is decided on by Chairman Mao we must resolutely carry out without fail, and whatever instruction is handed

199

down by Chairman Mao we must always obey." Deng Xiaoping pricked the bubble of "whateverism" in his *Selected Works,* p. 51, FLP, Beijing.

⁹"Practice Is the Sole Criterion of Truth," May 11, 1978.

¹⁰"Resolution on Certain Questions in the History of Our Party Since the Founding of the People's Republic of China," known for short as Resolution on CPC History (1949-81), was drafted by a panel of writers under Politburo member Hu Qiaomu, with Deng Xiaoping and Hu Yaobang acting as supervisors. The document, consisting of thirty-eight sections, sums up the history of modern China after the birth of the People's Republic in 1949 with a political balance-sheet of achievements and failures.

¹¹"The Present Situation and the Tasks Before Us" in *Selected Works of Deng Xiaoping,* p. 224.

Chapter Two

¹Lu Xun (1881-1936), though not a member of the Communist Party, was acclaimed by Mao Zedong as "not only a great man of letters but a great thinker and revolutionary." *Selected Works of Mao Tse-tung,* Vol. II, p. 372, FLP, Beijing.

²"Comrade Zhou Enlai's School Days in Shenyang" by Lu Zhong in *Renmin De Haozongli* (*The People's Beloved Premier*), p. 58, People's Publishing House, Shanghai.

³*Ibid.,* p. 57.

⁴*Minquan Bao* (*People's Rights Journal*) and *Minli Bao* (*National Independence Journal*) published in Shanghai. *Da Gong Bao* (*L'Impartial*), published in Tianjin, was also part of Zhou Enlai's daily reading.

⁵"Nankai School Days with Zhou Enlai" by Zhang Honggao in *Renmin De Haozongli,* p. 66.

⁶*Ibid.,* p. 67.

⁷Zhou Enlai's first exposure to Marxism in a serious way was through reading *Studies of Social Problems,* a journal edited and published in Tokyo by Professor Kawakami Hajime of the Imperial University, who first introduced the doctrines of Marxism to Japan.

⁸The warlords who dominated the government in Beijing at the time, better known as the Beiyang (northern) warlords, were divided into three factions—from Hebei, Anhui or Liaoning—all claiming allegiance to Yuan Shikai (1859-1916), the head of this loose-knit junta. Duan Qirui belonged to the Anhui faction.

⁹Beijing's protest marchers, prevented from demonstrating before the diplomatic missions in what was then known as the "legation quarter," headed for the home of Cao Rulin, Minister of Communications, at Zhaojialou. Cao and two colleagues, Zhang Zongxiang and Lu Zongyu, were being denounced in the popular press as "traitors" because of their close involvement in the government's sell-out to Japan since the days of Yuan Shikai. Cao was not home, but the students beat Zhang, who happened to be there, and subsequently burned down the house. See *From the Opium War to the May 4th Movement* by Hu Sheng, Vol. II, p. 960, People's Publishing House, Beijing.

¹⁰Guo Longzhen (1893-1930), also known as Guo Linyi, joined the CPC in 1922. In 1930 she was arrested by the Kuomintang in Qingdao, Shandong Province, and executed in Jinan.

¹¹On the third and last day of the trial, July 8, 1920, Zhou rose from the dock to present the case for the imprisoned students. In a thoroughly prepared brief, he turned their defence into

an indictment of the persecutor and those sitting on the bench. A week later, he and his comrades were freed. See *Comrade Zhou Enlai — His Childhood and Youth* by Hu Hua, p. 70, China Youth Publishing House, Beijing.

¹²Li Dazhao of Hebei Province, after three years of graduate studies in Japan, returned to China in 1916 as a committed Marxist. Apart from teaching at Beijing University, he wrote profusely to popularize socialist and Marxist ideas. He was a principal leader of the May 4th Movement of 1919 and two years later became, along with Mao Zedong, a founder of the Chinese Communist Party.

¹³"Marx to J. Weydemeyer, March 5, 1852" in *Selected Correspondence of Marx and Engels.* p. 86, Foreign Languages Publishing House, Moscow. See also *Comrade Zhou Enlai — His Childhood and Youth,* p. 95.

¹⁴Liu Qingyang (1894-1977) and Zhang Shenfu (born 1893), fellow work-study trainees, stood as sponsors for Zhou Enlai's admission to the CPC. *Selected Works of Zhou Enlai*, Vol. II, p. 357, People's Publishing House, Beijing.

¹⁵Zhu De, a brigadier-general of the old army in Yunnan, turned down an invitation from fellow Sichuanese general Yang Sen to command a division. Instead, he left for Shanghai in search of the Communist Party, determined to enrol in its ranks. Chen Duxiu, the Party's General Secretary, gave him the brush-off. In disgust, Zhu sailed for Europe. His destination was Germany, which he called the "home of Marxism." There he met Zhou Enlai for the first time. He was admitted into the Communist Party under Zhou's sponsorship. See *Comrade Zhou Enlai — His Childhood and Youth,* p. 100, and *Zhou Enlai — the Times of His Youth* by Wang Jingru, p. 339, People's Publishing House, Henan.

Chapter Three

¹During his visit to China in 1922 Viscount Northcliffe, publisher of *The Times* of London, was so impressed with *Shen Bao* that he called it *"The Times* of Shanghai." The owner of China's most prestigious newspaper, Shi Liangcai (1878-1934) has since been compared favourably to his British counterpart. In addition to publishing *Shen Bao,* he made a fortune through other enterprises. He supported Chiang Kai-shek in the late 1920s, but became disillusioned as the Kuomintang leader began making shady deals with Japan, then encroaching more and more openly on China's territory. Shi consequently withheld his support and contributed instead to anti-Japanese causes. He was murdered by Chiang Kai-shek's secret police on November 13, 1934, on the Shanghai-Hangzhou highway. Zhou Enlai, in a report to the CPC Congress on March 3, 1944, reviewing the domestic scene of years past, described Shi Liangcai as a representative figure of "an opposing force within the camp of the ruling classes." *Selected Works of Zhou Enlai,* Vol. I, p. 185. Also *Stories of Modern China's Patriots,* p. 180, People's Publishing House, Shanghai.

²*Shen Bao* was chosen by CPC's Shanghai underground leaders as the vehicle to refute the "Wu Hao renouncing the Party" fabrication not only because it was the most widely read daily, but because progressive writers such as Lu Xun, Ba Jin and Mao Dun, regular contributors to its columns, would make Left-leaning readers ponder over the novel letter to "Mr. Wu Hao" inserted in the paper's advertising section.

³The plane carrying Zhou Enlai and other members of the CPC delegation to the political consultative conference with their Kuomintang counterparts took off from Xi'an in perfect weather on the morning of January 30, 1946, but ran into a hailstorm over the Qinling Mountains. Ye Yangmei, youngest of the dozen or so passengers, was excited because she was

about to be reunited with her father and mother — just released from a KMT prison after five years — and to see her kid brother, born in captivity, for the first time. Two months later, General Ye Ting and his whole family, including Yangmei, died in a plane crash on their return to Yan'an. See *Remembering Premier Zhou Enlai,* Vol. II, p. 116, People's Publishing House, Beijing and *Eventful Years* by Liu Jiuzhou, Peng Haigui and He Qian, p. 99, People's Publishing House, Tianjin.

[4]One of the twelve founding members of the Chinese Communist Party, Chen Duxiu (1879-1942) of Huaining County, Anhui Province, was a professor at Beijing University and made a name as the editor of *Xin Qing Nian* (*New Youth*). He later joined with Li Dazhao, his colleague at Beijing University, to found *Meizhou Pinglun* (*Weekly Review*) to spread what was then called "new culture" and to disseminate Marxist ideas. He was one of the chief activists of the May 4th Movement of 1919 and after the birth of the CPC was one of its top leaders for six years. But at the end of the First Revolutionary Civil War (1925-27) Chen became disillusioned and caved in under Kuomintang repression. He operated as a Trotskyist inside the Party and was expelled in November 1929.

[5]Zhang Guotao (1897-1979) of Pingxiang County, Jiangxi Province, though a CPC founding member, earned notoriety for his shiftiness and right-wing opportunism. In 1935 he endangered the Long March to Shaanxi Province by withdrawing the Fourth Front Army under his command from the prescribed route and setting up an illegitimate Party centre in opposition to Mao Zedong's leadership, as established at the Zunyi Conference. During the Xi'an Incident of 1936 he proposed that Chiang Kai-shek be killed, while Mao Zedong, Zhou Enlai, Zhu De and other top leaders, under the circumstances of Japanese aggression and the necessity to unite the country, believed that national interests required negotiations with the kidnapped Kuomintang leader. In 1938 Zhang secretly left Yan'an, linked himself with the Kuomintang, and was put on its secret police payroll. He was expelled from the CPC. In 1979 he died in Canada.

[6]Son of a famous turn-of-the-century political reformer and prolific writer, Liang Sicheng, studied architecture at Qinghua in Beijing and later did graduate work on a scholarship in the United States. At one time he taught architecture at his Alma Mater. He had a soft spot for traditional Chinese architecture and was criticized for preferring "big top roofs" for the buildings going up in the capital in the late 1950s.

[7]Zhang Honggao was a college student in Japan at the same time as Zhou Enlai. After Zhou's death Zhang published an article in remembrance of his friend from Huaian, recalling their days in Tokyo. He had asked Zhou Enlai's advice on whether he should risk losing his stipend by trying to apply for admission to another college. See "Nankai School Days with Zhou Enlai" in *Renmin De Haozongli* (*The People's Beloved Premier*), Vol. II, p. 67.

[8]It was not plain sailing for Li Lin when she enrolled for graduate studies in Great Britain. In August 1946, after she arrived at Birmingham University, the registrar sent her to the physics department to do research in "plasticity" instead of "elasticity" because an error had been made in one letter in filling out the form at the British Council office in Chongqing. Li survived the mishap and proceeded from Birmingham to Cambridge, where she completed her education and also met her future husband, biochemist Zou Chenglu. She is today one of China's fifteen women academicians of the Chinese Academy of Natural Sciences.

[9]Chen Yuan, also known as Chen Xiying, who joined the teaching staff of Beijing University after studying in Britain, became widely known in China's literary circles in the late 1920s and early 1930s for his polemical articles aimed at Lu Xun, the progressive writer. At the time of the birth of the People's Republic Chen Yuan, based in London, was the KMT representative to UNESCO.

[10]See *People's Daily*, January 9, 1977.

[11] The CPC had called a meeting in Beijing early in 1962 to sum up the work and experience of the years following the founding of the People's Republic, especially the four years since the Great Leap Forward of 1958. It was an enlarged CPC meeting and so was also known popularly as the "Meeting of Seven Thousand People." Mao Zedong criticized himself before the central and local Party cadres for not being modest enough and making decisions that went against the grain of Party traditions — being realistic and following the mass line. Eight months later, at the Tenth Plenum held in Beijing from September 24 to 27, the CPC, following Mao's proposal, stressed class struggle out of all proportion. One of the things which came under fire was the novel *Liu Zhidan*. Liu Zhidan (1903-1936) of Shaanxi Province was a brave and capable Party leader who with the help of his comrades had carved out a base area in northern Shaanxi. His moderate views on how to fight the KMT forces irked the ultra-Leftists. Liu Zhidan fell in battle in 1936. The novel, written by Li Jiantong, his sister-in-law, sought to show the hero in a proper light.

[12] At the end of the Twenty-sixth World Table Tennis Championships of 1961, held in Beijing, Premier Zhou Enlai invited the players to a simple dinner. He took personal charge of the menu — four main dishes and one soup, but no dessert or fruits. He made a point of reminding the guests — bring your own food coupons.

[13] Of the ten "big buildings" constructed in Beijing proper to commemorate the tenth anniversary of China's liberation, the best-known ones include the Great Hall of the People, China Art Gallery and the Railway Station with its twin clock towers.

[14] Du Yuming, released from Gongdelin Prison outside the capital in 1959, was not reunited with his wife Cao Xiuqing until 1963, when she returned from the United States (where she had been living with her daughter and son-in-law Yang Chen Ning, the Nobel Prize physics winner). In 1958 Cao had been given special permission to visit the United States by the Taiwan authorities on condition that she would bring the Nobel Prize winner back to Taiwan within a period of twelve months, but she chose to remain with her daughter's family in Princeton. When she heard of Du Yuming's release, contrary to the Kuomintang's allegation that he had been executed by the Communists, she headed home and was received by Zhou Enlai soon after her arrival. The Premier urged both husband and wife to rebuild a happy home life. Turning to Cao Xiuqing, who had had a hard time earning a living for a family of seven during her enforced stay in Taiwan, he said, "Mrs. Du, you need not worry about family expenses. The government will take care of that." When the Cultural Revolution came, Zhou Enlai thought of the Dus, since such a prominent ex-KMT general could invite unwelcome attention. He had a notice put outside their house: "Inside these premises are important government property and assets. All unauthorized persons keep out." Du Yuming died in May 1981, but his children in Taiwan were not permitted to come to Beijing to attend his funeral.

Chapter Four

[1] Deng Yingchao, whose ancestrol home was in Henan Province, was born in Guangxi Province (today the Guangxi Zhuang Autonomous Region) in south China on February 4, 1904. Her father died when she was a child and her mother moved the family to Tianjin, north China, where she earned her living as a practitioner of traditional Chinese medicine. *People's Daily*, July 22, 1981, p. 8, about Deng Yingchao's marriage to Zhou Enlai.

[2] The Indemnity Fund of 1900 was extorted from the Chinese government following the expedition by the "allied armies" (U.K., U.S.A., Russia, Germany, Japan, France, Austria, Italy, Spain, Holland and Belgium) which overran Beijing and the following year forced the

Manchu rulers to pay an indemnity of 450 million taels of silver. The French Work-Study Programme was financed out of portions of the indemnity funds.

[3]See *Liaowang* (*Outlook*) weekly, March 4, 1985, p. 20.

[4]The Great Strike of Guangzhou and Hong Kong workers which began on June 19, 1925, lasted well over a year. It was a demonstration of solidarity with their Shanghai brothers who had walked out on the owners of a Japanese cotton mill for firing on protest marchers, killing one and wounding many others. The British authorities in Hong Kong declared martial law and cordoned off the colony, but in the end caved in to the strikers. It was the longest strike ever recorded in the history of the world's labour movement.

[5]Chen Tiejun, a Sun Yat-sen University student active in the revolutionary movement in Guangzhou, was on the black list when Chiang Kai-shek turned against the Communists and began arresting and killing CPC members on April 12, 1927. She was warned to flee through the Party underground organization but, knowing that Deng Yingchao was hospitalized, Chen disguised herself as a society lady and went to the hospital to help Zhou Enlai's wife escape. She herself remained behind to assist Party leader Zhou Wenyong with liaison work, and rented rooms for a home as if they were man and wife. Arrested by KMT police, as they were escorted to the execution ground they announced their intention to marry. This episode is known in Chinese revolutionary literature as a "Wedding Before the Firing Squad."

[6]The death of Li Shaoshi shocked Chongqing, then in a hectic state of expectancy since many of its wartime residents were preparing to leave for Shanghai, Nanjing and other parts of the eastern seaboard. Most believed the shooting to be a political assassination.

[7]Dr. Sun Yat-sen brought the Whampoa Military Academy into being with the assistance of the CPC and the Soviet Union. The CPC sent some of its top-level cadres, including Zhou Enlai and Nie Rongzhen, (today one of four surviving PLA Marshals), to help run the academy. Until Chiang Kai-shek turned against the revolution in 1927, the Whampoa Military Academy remained an outstanding example of Kuomintang-Communist collaboration.

[8]According to his bodyguard Liu Jiuzhou, Zhou Enlai's right elbow was so badly dislocated that he had to be helped into his clothes and with his morning toilet and use his left hand to hold the documents that required his attention. *Eventful Years*, p. 31.

[9]"Model Couple — Zhou Enlai and Deng Yingchao" in *Liaowang* (*Outlook*) weekly, p. 18, March 25, 1985.

[10]After his release from prison following the downfall of the Gang of Four, Weishi's husband wrote a long article in her memory, telling the story of one of the worst periods of the Cultural Revolution. It was entitled "Let Not Autumn Winds Carry Away the Hatred in Our Hearts," a line taken from a poem written by Weishi's mother, and has been collected in *Unforgettable Memoirs* published by the printing press of *People's Daily*, p. 221.

[11]Apart from Li Peng, half a dozen or so younger people were inducted into the twenty-two-member Politburo and the eleven-member Secretariat of the CPC Central Committee, thus replacing part of the old guard with young blood and removing to a certain extent the stigma of domination of the Party's sensitive organs by gerontocracy. The youngest two are Hao Jianxiu, a woman just turned fifty, from Shandong Province and Wang Zhaoguo, barely on the shady side of forty, from Hebei Province. Unlike most of their predecessors, both are college-educated.

[12]"On Li Peng" in *Liaowang* (*Outlook*) weekly, p. 6, November 20, 1983.

[13]*Ibid.*, p. 8.

[14]See *China Youth Journal*, p. 1, March 6, 1979.

[15]This long-established habit was continued even after Zhou Enlai's death. On April 11, 1983, all who had worked for some time in Xihuating, Zhou's office in Zhongnanhai — including secretaries, security guards, doctors, nurses and cooks — received an invitation to Xihuating on April 17, beginning from seven in the morning, to have tea with "big sister" Deng Yingchao and see the crabapple trees blossoming in the garden. Crabapple was Zhou Enlai's favourite. On greeting the ninety or so invitees, Deng Yingchao said that most of them who were transferred to other posts in the latter half of 1957 had seen little of each other since then. During the Cultural Revolution, except for official business, she and the Premier abided by a "three-No" guideline to avoid unpleasantness — "No" to receiving visitors; "No" to answering letters; and "No" to making calls. Now, she said, it's time to get together again. *Wen Hui Bao*, Shanghai, May 12, 1983.

[16]*Eventful Years*, p. 80.

Chapter Five

[1]"Guidelines for Myself" in *Selected Works of Zhou Enlai*, Vol. I, p. 144.

[2]The political movements of 1957 and 1959 were both directed against "Rightists." During the former people were accused of attacking the Party and the socialist system, and during the latter of attacking Chairman Mao Zedong. The first campaign had the effect of silencing people outside the Party, the intellectuals in particular, and the second frightened people inside the Party into keeping mum. In the minds of many the 1957 political movement was a terrible blot on the history of the People's Republic. "What, then, was wrong with the anti-rightist struggle?" asked Deng Xiaoping. He answered: "The problem was that, as it developed, the scope and targets of the attack were unduly broadened, and the blows were much too heavy. Large numbers of people were punished inappropriately or too severely." "The Present Situation and the Tasks Before Us" in *Selected Works of Deng Xiaoping*, p. 228.

[3]Following its aggression in 1931, Japan carved out part of northeast China to set up a so-called "State of Manchukuo" with Pu Yi installed as "emperor" in 1934. After Japan's defeat in 1945, the puppet emperor and his close family fled, including brother Pu Jie, his aide-de-camp. They were taken prisoner by the advancing Soviet Red Army. In 1950 Pu Yi and Pu Jie were turned over to the Chinese government. They were kept behind bars at a war criminal detention camp at Fushun, Liaoning Province, until released in December 1959.

[4]"Premier Zhou Enlai and Lao She" by Hu Jieqing (Mrs. Lao She) in *Zuojia De Huainian* (*In Remembrance of Fellow Writers*), People's Publishing House, Sichuan.

[5]On June 10, 1961, the eve of the departure of Hiroko Saga's mother from China, Premier Zhou granted an audience to Pu Jie's mother-in-law, a Japanese noblewoman, at which Pu Yi, Lao She the writer and his wife Hu Jieqing, and the widow of Cheng Yanqiu, the famous Beijing opera female impersonator — all of Manchu origin — were present. It was a large gathering of Manchu ethnics which included members of the former monarch's family. Seen at his best on such occasions — free of official airs, warm and outgoing, considerate without being condescending — the Premier conducted a wide-ranging discussion with his guests on subjects such as equality between fellow Chinese (between Hans and the other national groupings) and between fellow Asians, a topic which had the effect of putting Pu Jie's wife and mother-in-law at ease and reassuring both, especially Mrs. Naoko, that she need not worry about her daughter being discriminated against in China. Zhou told the Japanese noblewoman that allowances would be made for Hiroko Saga in case she found living

conditions austere in Beijing as compared to what she was used to in Japan, and that Mrs. Pu Jie was at liberty to reside in China or in Japan and to travel between the two countries as often as she pleased. Pu Jie and his wife had had two daughters, Huisheng and Husheng, who lived with her maternal grandmother in Japan before Pu Jie gained his freedom. Unbeknownst to anyone in the family, Huisheng, the elder daughter, took an unusual step in writing a letter in Chinese to Premier Zhou Enlai to ask if she could correspond with her father in the detention camp. Permission was given. In prison, Pu Jie was kept informed of his family in Japan by Huisheng. Then the letters stopped completely. Huisheng, a college girl, had been denied approval by her mother to marry to the man she loved. As an act of protest she and the young man blew their brains out together near Tokyo in 1957. It became a sensational story in the Japanese press at the time. Referring to the unhappy incident in his conversation, the Premier asked if he could be favoured with a photograph of Huisheng because he had thought of her as being a very courageous girl. "Conversation with Hiroko Saga, Pu Jie, Pu Yi and Others" in *Selected Works of Zhou Enlai*, Vol. II, p. 316.

[6]After *Teahouse*, a 1985 TV series based on Lao She's *Four Generations Under One Roof* (also known, in the translation by Ida Pruitt, as *The Yellow Storm*) became a hit in Beijing and won a special award.

[7]The 1952 mass movement against capitalist bribery of government officials, tax evasion, cheating on government contracts, theft of state property, and stealing of economic information from government sources.

[8]"Comrade Lao She: In Memorium" in *Remembrances* by Ba Jin, p. 184, People's Publishing House, Ningxia.

[9]"Five Unforgettable Evenings" by the Beijing Institute of Foreign Languages in *Renmin De Haozongli* (*The People's Beloved Premier*), p. 370. "Great Encouragement and Unforgettable Instruction" by the Department of Western Languages of Beijing University, collected in *Beloved Premier Zhou Enlai*, Vol. III, p. 367.

[10]*Reference Material* and *Reference News* are the two main daily internal publications of monitored news reports and magazine articles prepared, translated into Chinese, printed and distributed by Xinhua News Agency. While the four-page *Reference News* has a huge circulation and accepts subscriptions by individuals, *Reference Material* is restricted with circulation only among Party and government offices.

Chapter Six

[1]Hirobumi Daimatsu came to China on Premier Zhou Enlai's invitation in 1965 to help train the country's women volleyball team. Very good at his job, he put the Chinese squad through their paces in the short time he had at his disposal. He was satisfied with the exacting performance he demanded of the Chinese girls and predicted that one day they would become world champions. They proved equal to his expectations, but Daimatsu died of a heart attack in 1978 and so did not live to see it. When they won their first trophy in 1981 they remembered the man who had taught them so much on the court and went to pay their respects at his grave.

[2]Following its first success in 1981, the Chinese women's volleyball team won three additional world championships in a row.

[3]"Luncheon at Premier Zhou Enlai's Home" by Zhou Bin, *People's Daily*, November 3, 1985.

[4]Anna Louise Strong's fifth visit to China in 1946 and her stay in Yan'an was dramatized

and shown on CCTV to mark her centenary on November 24, 1985. The Beijing Film Studio also produced a film, *The Uncrowned Queen*, commemorating the event, with her old friend Dr. Ma Haide (George Hatem) as adviser and Su Fei (Mrs. Ma Haide) as director.

[5]"Remembering Premier Zhou" by Liu Liangmo, *Wen Hui Bao*, March 7, 1979, Shanghai.

[6]On January 4, 1941, six regiments totalling close to ten thousand men of the New Fourth Army were ordered by Chiang Kai-shek's headquarters to move north out of southern Anhui (Anhwei). On January 7 they were encircled and attacked by seven divisions of the Kuomintang forces. While a thousand or so managed to break through, most of the contingent fell in battle or were taken prisoner, including the army's high-ranking officers. By January 17 Chiang was ready to push his anti-Communist campaign as far as he could — declaring the New Fourth Army guilty of mutiny, abolishing its designation, and ordering Ye Ting, the captive army commander, court-martialled. At the same time he hurled 200,000 of his troops against the anti-Japanese base areas south of the Yellow River. This was the peak of Chiang Kai-shek's second anti-Communist campaign. *History of the Communist Party of China*, p. 248, China Youth Publishing House, Beijing. Also see "Order and Statement on the Southern Anhwei Incident" in *Selected Works of Mao Tse-tung*, Vol. II, p. 451.

[7]"Zhou Enlai's Diplomatic Battles in Pre-liberation China Remembered" in *Remembering Premier Zhou Enlai*, Vol. II, p. 99.

[8]"Talk with the American Correspondent Anna Louise Strong," in *Selected Works of Mao Tse-tung*, Vol. IV, p. 97.

[9]"Premier Zhou Enlai's Visit to Liaoning" in *Remembering Premier Zhou Enlai*, Vol. II, p. 148.

[10]Henry Kissinger gives an account of his "Journey to Peking" in *White House Years*, p. 733, Little, Brown and Company, Boston.

Chapter Seven

[1]Zhou Enlai's diplomatic career, in so far as it concerned contact with foreign nationals, may be traced back to his first encounter with the American writer Edgar Snow on the Shaanxi Province front in the summer of 1936 ("The Road to the Red Capital" in *Red Star Over China*). Or earlier still to the 1920s, when he had dealings with representatives of the Communist International sent from Moscow, including Mikhail Markovich Borodin and B. Lominadze.

[2]James Bertram later interviewed Mao Zedong on the role of the Chinese Communist Party and the War of Resistance Against Japan. "Interview with the British Journalist James Bertram" in *Selected Works of Mao Tse-tung*, Vol. II, p. 47.

[3]On September 20, 1984, the Smedley-Strong-Snow Society of China (the SSS Society for short) was founded in Beijing to pay tribute to these staunch friends of the Chinese people for their great contributions to journalism, particularly their unprejudiced, truthful reporting on the struggle between the Kuomintang and the Communists. The society brought out a book to commemorate Anna Louise Strong's centenary and the birthdays of her two compatriots in 1985.

[4]A famed surgeon who had already served against the fascists in the Spanish Civil War, Norman Bethune came to China in the spring of 1938 as the head of a medical team. He died of blood poisoning on November 12, 1939, in north China while operating on wounded soldiers. "In Memory of Norman Bethune" in *Selected Works of Mao Tse-tung*, Vol. II, p. 337.

[5]D. S. Kotnis, the young surgeon of the Indian Medical Aid Team to China, had met Zhou Enlai before arriving in Yan'an and helped treat Zhou's dislocated elbow. He worked most of the time in the Shanxi-Chahar-Hebei Military Area's Norman Bethune International Peace Hospital, of which he became director in January 1941. He married a Chinese woman, his colleague, and joined the CPC. An epileptic, he died of severe convulsions on December 9, 1942, at his post. *Renwu (People)* bimonthly, 1982, No. 6, Beijing.

[6]"Zhou Enlai's Diplomatic Battles in Pre-liberation China Remembered" in *Remembering Premier Zhou Enlai*, Vol. II, p. 97.

[7]Chen Yi took over from Zhou Enlai at the foreign office right after the Eighth Party Congress held in September 1956.

[8]Richard Nixon was impressed with Zhou Enlai's "brilliance and dynamism" and "the combination of elegance and toughness, a very unusual one in the world today" (*The Memoirs of Richard Nixon*, Vol. II, pp. 49 and 101). His National Security Adviser (later Secretary of State) Henry Kissinger found Zhou "one of the two or three most impressive men" he had ever met. To quote Kissinger: "Urbane, infinitely patient, extraordinarily intelligent, subtle, he moved through our discussions with an easy grace that penetrated to the essence of our new relationship as if there were no sensible alternative." (*White House Years*, p. 745).

[9]The Chinese expression used here by Zhou is *ling-qi-lu-zao*, which literally means to build a new kitchen — in plain English, to make a fresh start. *Selected Works of Zhou Enlai*, Vol. II, p. 85.

[10]The Geneva Conference held during April 26-July 21, 1954, settled nothing on the Korea question but reached agreement on a ceasefire in Indochina. *Ibid.*, pp. 146, 236, and 274.

[11]*The Memoirs of Richard Nixon*, Vol. II, p. 26. *White House Years*, p. 742.

[12]It is worth quoting in full Zhou Enlai's remarks on the relationship between "players and the team": "Stick to the team-spirit, and combat self-esteem. Work in foreign affairs is done in the name of the country, and the collective must be borne in mind at all times; if one is prompted by private considerations, this can lead to very serious trouble. It is the triumph of Mao Zedong Thought and the exertions of the people that win us laurels, and such should go to the country. Serving private ends is not permitted in performing duties in the sphere of foreign affairs. Do not gloat when others praise you, for whatever honour comes your way should be regarded as belonging to the people. If others speak ill of you, then examine your work and see if there is anything wrong; in short, put yourself in the team." From "Our Foreign Policy and Tasks" in *Selected Works of Zhou Enlai*, Vol. II, p. 91.

[13]"Speech to the Afro-Asian Conference," *Ibid.*, p. 148.

[14]"Qian Xuesen in USA" by Wen Xiang, *Renwu (People)* bimonthly, 1982, No. 6, p. 20, Beijing.

[15]"Supplementary Speech," *Selected Works of Zhou Enlai*, Vol. II, p. 153.

[16]"Learn from Premier Zhou Enlai and Carry Out the Revolutionary Line in Foreign Policy" in *Remembering Premier Zhou Enlai*, Vol. I, p. 157.

[17]"Great Champion of Internationalism" by the Ministry of Foreign Affairs Study Group in *Renmin De Haozongli (The People's Beloved Premier)*, p. 163.

[18]*The Memoirs of Richard Nixon*, Vol. II, p. 50.

[19]"Learn from Premier Zhou Enlai and Carry Out the Revolutionary Line in Foreign Policy" in *Remembering Premier Zhou Enlai*, Vol. I, p. 170. "A Conversation with Mao Tse-tung" by Edgar Snow, *Life*, April 30, 1971.

Chapter Eight

[1] Wang Jiaxiang, also a Vice-Chairman of the Party's Military Commission, recognized early on the mistakes made by Otto Braun and others in the military sphere. He had been severely wounded during the fourth "encirclement and suppression" campaign launched by Chiang Kai-shek and was on a stretcher part of the time on the Long March. It happened that Mao Zedong was taken ill at the same time and had to be carried on a litter. The two kept company with each other, and Wang confided to Mao that things could not go on like this and that Otto Braun and those who thought and acted like him should be removed from the leadership. Mao, who agreed with him, stressed the importance of integrating the universal truth of Marxism-Leninism with the reality of the Chinese revolution. They began discussing the idea of calling a meeting of the Politburo. Another Vice-Chairman of the Military Commission, Zhou Enlai, who had frequent contact with Braun and abhorred his arbitrary way of handling the military situation. He often challenged Braun's views and decisions, and had heated arguments with the German during the fifth "encirclement and suppression" campaign and on the Long March. According to Wu Xiuquan (one-time Vice-Minister of Foreign Affairs and Ambassador to Yugoslavia) whose part-time duty was interpreter on the Long March, Zhou Enlai at times exchanged strong words directly with Braun in English. "Reminiscences of the Zunyi Conference" in *Records of the Zunyi Conference*, p. 112, People's Publishing House, 1985, Beijing.

[2] On the recommendation of Professor Yang Changji, who later became his father-in-law, Mao Zedong joined the staff of the university library in October 1918. He was made an assistant to the chief librarian, Professor Li Dazhao, one of China's earliest Marxist scholars and with Mao Zedong a founding member of the CPC in 1921. Li Dazhao was arrested by the northern warlord regime for his political beliefs and executed on April 28, 1927. Mao Zedong stayed with the Beijing University library until March 1919.

[3] On December 31, 1977, *People's Daily* used its entire front page to reproduce Mao Zedong's letter, dated July 21, 1965, to Chen Yi in which the Party Chairman discussed poetry with the PLA Marshal. The letter was reproduced in facsimile at the same time.

[4] As an editor of Mao's *Selected Works* and several books of history for the Chinese Academy of Sciences, Tian Jiaying left little behind in the way of writing except a slender volume *Study "Serve the People"*, a collection of articles expounding Mao Zedong Thought in popular language. For a period before nationwide victory in 1949, Tian tutored Mao Anqing, Mao Zedong's elder son, in Chinese language and history.

[5] *Ten Remembrances* by Li Rui, p. 53, People's Publishing House, Beijing.

[6] *Ibid.*, p. 54.

[7] *Memoirs of Peng Dehuai*, p. 276, People's Publishing House, Beijing. *Resolution on CPC History (1949-81)*, p. 28, FLP, Beijing.

[8] *Ten Remembrances*, p. 55.

[9] *Ibid.*, p. 59.

[10] *Resolution on CPC History (1949-81)*, p. 39.

[11] Though Zhang Chunqiao, the so-called "brain" of the Gang of Four, retained the post of Vice-Premier, sensitive portfolios such as Defence and Foreign Affairs remained in the hands of Zhou Enlai's trusted associates.

[12] *Resolution on CPC History (1949-81)*, Section 22.

[13] According to Deng Xiaoping, "Comrade Mao Zedong said that he too had made

mistakes and that there had never been a person whose statements were all correct or who was always absolutely right. He said that if one's work could be rated as seventy percent of achievements and thirty percent mistakes, that would be quite all right, and that he himself would be very happy and satisfied if future generations could give him this seventy-thirty rating after his death." *Selected Works of Deng Xiaoping*, p. 51.

[14] *Resolution on CPC History (1949-81)*, Section 21.

[15] "The Agony of Intelligence" by Wang Ruoshui in *Youth Forum*, 1985, No. 2, later collected in *Xinhua Wenzhai (New China Digest)* monthly, 1985, No. 5, Beijing.

[16] *Selected Works of Deng Xiaoping*, p. 329.

[17] *Resolution on CPC History (1949-81)*, Section 22.

Chapter Nine

[1] Writing in *Red Flag* (1983, No. 6) in the article "Marxism and Conditions in China," historian Hu Sheng had this to say about the Cultural Revolution: "The Cultural Revolution made an erroneous estimate of prevailing conditions (as if bourgeois reactionary forces were making themselves felt everywhere) and at the same time believed that a couple of onslaughts mounted by masses of people would transform prevailing conditions out of all recognition and create the 'purest' and 'most ideal' socialist society. That's just daydreaming and can do nothing but harm." Hu Sheng is today President of the Chinese Academy of Social Sciences.

[2] "Commentary on the First Stage of the Cultural Revolution" by Wang Nianyi in *Research on Party History*, a journal published at irregular intervals by the Party History Research Office of the Museum of the Chinese Revolution, October 20, 1984, Beijing.

[3] *Memoirs of Peng Dehuai*, Chapter 1, People's Publishing House, Beijing.

[4] *Resolution on CPC History (1949-81)*, Section 17.

[5] *Ibid.*, Section 18.

[6] "Remembering Uncle Peng Dehuai" by Peng Gang, *People's Daily*, October 26, 1984.

[7] *Selected Works of Deng Xiaoping*, p. 280.

[8] "I Wept for Yiduo" by Wu Han in *To the Memory of Wen Yiduo: An Anthology*, p. 59, San Lian Publishing House, Beijing.

[9] "Deng Tuo Remembered" by Ding Yilan (his widow) in *News Front*, 1979, No. 1.

[10] The CPC Politburo met May 4-26, 1966, in Beijing. On May 16, it adopted the Circular of the CPC Central Committee (generally known as the "May 16th Circular") which comprises three sections: a preamble announcing the establishment of a Cultural Revolution directorate accountable directly to the Politburo Standing Committee; the announcement of a series of what were, in retrospect, ultra-Left policies and measures to promote the campaign; and a conclusion calling on all in the Party, government, army, education, and culture to "storm the citadels" of bourgeois forces, their representatives and practices. Two days later, on May 18, Lin Biao made his notorious speech about *coups d'etat* and attacked Peng Zhen, Luo Ruiqing, Lu Dingyi and Yang Shangkun for having formed an "anti-Party" clique.

[11] *Selected Works of Zhou Enlai*, p. 450.

[12] *Ibid.*, p. 451.

[13] "Nostalgia — A Short Biography of Sitson Ma" by Ye Yonglie published in *Wenhui Yuekan (Wenhui Monthly)*, 1985, No. 5, Shanghai.

[14]From "Resolution on Certain Questions in the History of Our Party (1945)": "Comrade Liu Shaoqi's ideas on tactics for work in the White areas are likewise a model. Correctly taking into account the glaring disparity between the enemy's strength and our own in the White areas, and particularly in the cities, after the defeat of the revolution in 1927, Comrade Liu Shaoqi advocated systematic organization of our retreat and defence and 'the avoidance of decisive engagements with the enemy for the time being, while the situation and conditions are unfavourable to us,' in order 'to prepare for revolutionary attacks and decisive engagements in the future.'" *Selected Works of Mao Tse-tung*, Vol. III, p. 202.

[15]*Selected Works of Deng Xiaoping*, p. 287.

[16]*Selected Works of Zhou Enlai*, Vol. II, p. 452. In fact Kang Sheng, Jiang Qing's adviser in the Cultural Revolution Directorate, was behind the manoeuvres to "unmask" so-called "traitors" hidden in the Party and re-open the "case of sixty-one." As a result Bo Yibo, An Ziwen, Head of the CPC Organization Department, and many others soon fell victim to false charges made by Kang Sheng and the Red Guards under his thumb. Liu Lantao, First Secretary of the Shaanxi Provincial Party Committee and mentioned in Zhou Enlai's telegram to the Red Guards in Xi'an, was one of the very first to be vilified and manhandled.

[17]Hospitalization was one of the measures taken by Zhou Enlai to protect associates. In a report sent to Mao Zedong he proposed that "confidential medical treatment" at Number 302 Hospital be given to Tao Zhu, then number four in the Party hierarchy, because Lin Biao, Jiang Qing and their supporters were closing in on him early in 1969. *Selected Works of Zhou Enlai*, Vol. II, p. 454.

[18]*Resolution on CPC History (1949-81)*, Section 21.

[19]Speech to the staff of the Foreign Languages Press, August 1966.

[20]"Reminiscences of Premier Zhou in the Cultural Revolution" by Xu Xiangqian in *Renmin De Haozongli* (*The People's Beloved Premier*), p. 1.

[21]*The Xi'an Incident and Comrade Zhou Enlai* by Luo Ruiqing, Lu Zhengcao and Wang Bingnan, People's Publishing House, Beijing, 1978.

[22]*Liaowang* (*Outlook*) weekly, March 5, 1984, Beijing.

[23]Ren Bishi (1904-50) joined the CPC in 1922 and was a top Party leader at the time of his death.

[24]Song Renqiong, born in 1909, voluntarily retired from the Politburo in September 1985 in order to allow younger people to assume more responsibilities in the top Party leadership. He is today a Deputy Director of the CPC Central Advisory Commission.

[25]"The Inside Story of 'the Armed Attack Against the Cultural Revolution Directorate'" in *People's Daily*, March 15, 1979, p. 3. Also "General Fu Chongbi Interviewed" in *Beijing Evening News*, April 12, 1985, p. 1. Fu Chongbi is today Political Commissar of the PLA's Beijing Military Command.

[26]*Beijing Review*, September 3, 1984.

[27]*Resolution on CPC History (1949-81)*, Section 21, paragraph 3.

[28]Two resolutions adopted by the CPC Central Committee were announced on April 7, 1976 — one appointing Hua Guofeng as First Vice-Chairman of the Party and Premier of the State Council and the other dismissing Deng Xiaoping from all positions in the Party and government.

Chapter Ten

[1]Yang Zhengmin is a Deputy Secretary General of the Chinese People's Political Consultative Conference; Deng Yingchao is Chairperson of its National Committee.

[2]"Beloved Premier Zhou Enlai Will Always Live in Our Hearts" in *Remembering Premier Zhou Enlai*, Vol. III, p. 474.

[3]"Premier Zhou Enlai Has Always Concerned Himself with the Country's Publication Work" in *Remembering Premier Zhou Enlai*, Vol. II, p. 372.

[4]"Commemorating Beloved Premier Zhou's First Death Anniversary" in *Remembering Premier Zhou Enlai*, Vol. I, p. 5.

[5]"Unforgettable Memories" by Wang Yeqiu in a collected volume bearing the same title published by People's Daily Press, Beijing, 1979.

[6]Wang Yeqiu's article "Unforgettable Memories" was a catalyst, inspiring several other writers to record their impressions of Yang Du the man. A piece by Xia Yan entitled "A Couple of Things About Comrade Yang Du" also appeared in the collected volume, p. 297.

[7]"Premier Zhou Always Lives in the Hearts of the Tibetan People" in *Remembering Premier Zhou Enlai*, Vol. I, p. 212.

[8]"The Capital's Medical Circles Pay Homage to Beloved Premier Zhou" in *Remembering Premier Zhou Enlai*, Vol. III, p. 439.

[9]"The People of Beijing Will Think of You" in *Remembering Premier Zhou Enlai*, Vol. II, p. 138. Also "Premier Zhou Shows the Way for the Medical Profession to Scale the Heights of Medical Science" in *Remin De Haozongli* (*The People's Beloved Premier*), p. 392.

Note on Spelling

Chinese names are spelt in accordance with *Pinyin*, the Chinese phonetic alphabet. For the benefit of readers not familiar with *Pinyin* spelling, a glossary of personal names and a glossary of place names are given below in both *Pinyin* and their former spelling.

Chinese	Pinyin Spelling	Former Spelling
	Personal Names	
博 古	Bo Gu	Po Ku
薄一波	Bo Yibo	Po I-po
陈伯达	Chen Boda	Chen Po-ta
陈公培	Chen Gongpei	Chen Kung-pei
陈独秀	Chen Duxiu	Chen Tu-hsiu
陈锡联	Chen Xilian	Chen Hsi-lien
陈再道	Chen Zaidao	Chen Tsai-tao
邓 拓	Deng Tuo	Teng To
邓小平	Deng Xiaoping	Teng Hsiao-ping
邓颖超	Deng Yingchao	Teng Ying-chao
董必武	Dong Biwu	Tung Pi-wu
杜月笙	Du Yuesheng	Tu Yueh-sheng
杜聿明	Du Yuming	Tu Yu-ming
段祺瑞	Duan Qirui	Tuan Chi-jui
傅崇碧	Fu Chongbi	Fu Chung-pi

郭沫若	Guo Moruo	Kuo Mo-jo
海 瑞	Hai Rui	Hai Jui
贺 龙	He Long	Ho Lung
何香凝	He Xiangning	Ho Hsiang-ning
华国锋	Hua Guofeng	Hua Kuo-feng
纪登奎	Ji Dengkui	Chi Teng-kuei
江 青	Jiang Qing	Chiang Ching
李大钊	Li Dazhao	Li Ta-chao
李 锐	Li Rui	Li Jui
李少石	Li Shaoshi	Li Shao-shih
李硕勋	Li Shuoxun	Li Shuo-hsun
李宗仁	Li Zongren	Li Tsung-jen
廖承志	Liao Chengzhi	Liao Cheng-chih
廖梦醒	Liao Mengxing	Liao Meng-hsing
廖仲恺	Liao Zhongkai	Liao Chung-kai
林 彪	Lin Biao	Lin Piao
林巧稚	Lin Qiaozhi	Lin Chiao-chih
刘清扬	Liu Qingyang	Liu Ching-yang
刘少奇	Liu Shaoqi	Liu Shao-chi
刘 晓	Liu Xiao	Liu Hsiao
陆定一	Lu Dingyi	Lu Ting-yi
鲁 迅	Lu Xun	Lu Hsun
罗瑞卿	Luo Riuqing	Lo Jui-ching
马思聪	Ma Sicong	Sitson Ma
毛泽东	Mao Zedong	Mao Tse-tung
聂荣臻	Nie Rongzhen	Nieh Jung-chen

彭德怀	Peng Dehuai	Peng Teh-huai
彭 真	Peng Zhen	Peng Chen
任白戈	Ren Baige	Jen Pai-keh
孙维世	Sun Weishi	Sun Wei-shih
田家英	Tian Jiaying	Tien Chia-ying
田纪云	Tian Jiyun	Tien Chi-yun
汪东兴	Wang Dongxing	Wang Tung-hsing
王光美	Wang Guangmei	Wang Kuang-mei
王洪文	Wang Hongwen	Wang Hung-wen
王冶秋	Wang Yeqiu	Wang Yeh-chiu
吴 德	Wu De	Wu Teh
习仲勋	Xi Zhongxun	Hsi Chung-hsun
夏 衍	Xia Yan	Hsia Yen
谢富治	Xie Fuzhi	Hsieh Fu-chih
谢觉哉	Xie Juezai	Hsieh Chueh-tsai
徐向前	Xu Xiangqian	Hsu Hsiang-chien
薛 明	Xue Ming	Hsueh Ming
杨 度	Yang Du	Yang Tu
杨虎城	Yang Hucheng	Yang Hu-cheng
杨拯民	Yang Zhengmin	Yang Cheng-min
叶剑英	Ye Jianying	Yeh Chien-ying
叶 挺	Ye Ting	Yeh Ting
袁世凯	Yuan Shikai	Yuan Shih-kai
张伯苓	Zhang Boling	Chang Po-ling
张春桥	Zhang Chunqiao	Chang Chun-chiao
张国焘	Zhang Guotao	Chang Kuo-tao

张鸿诰	Zhang Honggao	Chang Hung-kao
张申府	Zhang Shenfu	Chang Shen-fu
章士钊	Zhang Shizhao	Chang Shih-chao
张学良	Zhang Xueliang	Chang Hsueh-liang
张治中	Zhang Zhizhong	Chang Chih-chung
赵世炎	Zhao Shiyan	Chao Shih-yen
赵紫阳	Zhao Ziyang	Chao Tzu-yang
钟汉华	Zhong Hanhua	Chung Han-hua
周秉建	Zhou Bingjian	Chou Ping-chien
周恩来	Zhou Enlai	Chou En-lai
周攀龙	Zhou Panlong	Chou Pan-lung
周劭纲	Zhou Shaogang	Chou Shao-kang
周贻淦	Zhou Yigan	Chou Yi-kan
朱 德	Zhu De	Chu Teh

Place Names

北 京	Beijing	Peking
重 庆	Chongqing	Chungking
广 州	Guangzhou	Canton
杭 州	Hangzhou	Hangchow
南 京	Nanjing	Nanking
绍 兴	Shaoxing	Shaohsing
天 津	Tianjin	Tientsin
西 安	Xi'an	Sian
延 安	Yan'an	Yenan
遵 义	Zunyi	Tsunyi

安 徽	Anhui	Anhwei
福 建	Fujian	Fukien
甘 肃	Gansu	Kansu
广 东	Guangdong	Kwangtung
广 西	Guangxi	Kwangsi
贵 州	Guizhou	Kweichow
河 北	Hebei	Hopei
河 南	Henan	Honan
湖 北	Hunan	Hunan
湖 南	Hubei	Hupeh
江 苏	Jiangsu	Kiangsu
江 西	Jiangxi	Kiangsi
陕 西	Shaanxi	Shensi
山 西	Shanxi	Shansi
山 东	Shandong	Shantung
四 川	Sichuan	Szechuan
新 疆	Xinjiang	Sinkiang
浙 江	Zhejiang	Chekiang

Abbreviations at a Glance

CPC   Communist Party of China

NPC   National People's Congress

PLA   People's Liberation Army

CPPCC   Chinese People's Political Consultative Conference

FLP   Foreign Languages Press

KMT   Kuomintang

Chronology

1898   Born on March 5 to a once-prosperous Mandarin family, the descendant of many scholar-officials, in Huaian, Jiangsu Province.

1910-1917 Goes with an uncle to northeast China, attends primary school in Shenyang and Nankai Middle School in Tianjin. Works part time to make ends meet.

1917   Travels to Japan to study and search for answers to China's problems. Takes part in protests against Japanese encroachments on China. Develops serious interest in Marxism.

1919   Returns to China, takes charge of a progressive student newspaper in Tianjin. Becomes a leading force in student sector of famous May 4th Movement against feudal oppression and foreign domination. Is briefly imprisoned and threatened with execution. Meets future wife Deng Yingchao, also active in the movement.

1920-1921 Goes to France on work-study programme. Organizes a Marxist group among Chinese studying or working in France, and another in Germany. Both later link up with Chinese Communist Party, founded in Shanghai in 1921.

1924-1925 Returns to China, becomes political director of the Whampoa Military Academy in Guangdong Province during the period of Communist-KMT co-operation against the northern warlords. Marries Deng Yingchao in 1925.

1927   April: Leads the armed uprising of Shanghai workers which takes the city from warlord forces in anticipation of the arrival of the combined Communist-KMT Northern Expedition

Army. Within a week Chiang Kai-shek turns against his Communist and progressive allies in a bloody massacre. Zhou barely escapes with his life.

August: Organizes the Nanchang Uprising in Jiangxi Province, an event marking the birth of the People's Liberation Army.

1927-1931 Does underground revolutionary work in Shanghai and other places, along with Deng Yingchao.

1931 Becomes one of top leaders of Central Revolutionary Base Area in Jiangxi Province in the southeast.

1934-1935 Helps organize and lead the famous Long March to Yan'an in the northwest (Deng Yingchao is one of the few score women to make the march). At an enlarged Party Politburo meeting in Zunyi, Guizhou Province, in January 1935, decisively supports Mao Zedong as the new leader of the Party and army.

1936 During the Xi'an Incident, represents the Communist side in delicate three-way negotiations with Chiang Kai-shek and two of his own generals who have kidnapped him in an attempt to force him to fight the Japanese invaders instead of the Chinese Communists.

1937-1945 Acts as chief Communist Party spokesman and negotiator during the Communist-KMT united front against Japanese aggression, first in Chongqing and later in Nanjing.

1946 After the victory over Japan and the breakdown of peace talks with the KMT, returns to Yan'an to help formulate the strategy and tactics leading to nationwide victory in the revolutionary struggle.

1949-1976 As Premier of the People's Republic, oversees government administration. Internationally, becomes one of the world's great statesmen, known particularly for his contributions to solidarity among the Third World nations and to the formulation of the Five Principles of Peaceful Coexistence.

1966-1976 During the tumult of the Cultural Revolution, does his best to keep the government and economy operating while trying to protect those unjustly persecuted by Lin Biao and the Gang of

Four. Hospitalized for cancer in 1974, continues to direct affairs of state from his sickbed until his death on January 8, 1976.

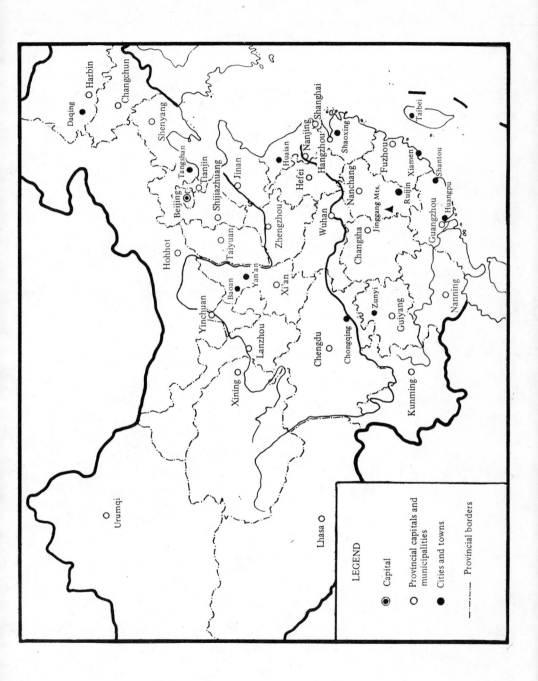

LEGEND

⊙ Capital

○ Provincial capitals and
   municipalities

● Cities and towns

–·–·– Provincial borders

Index

tivities, 24-27; Nanchang Uprising, 30-32; on the Long March. 27, 32-33, 58-59; Zunyi Conference, 58; Xi'an Incident, 33, 46, 96; Chongqing years, 55, 97, 102; beginning of a diplomatic career, 96-99; directing China's foreign affairs, 86-87, 93, 94-95, 99-101, 189-191; in Geneva, 100, 102-107; at Bandung Conference, 100, 107-109; visits to Asian and African countries, 110-113, Sino-Soviet relationship, 113-115; Sino-U.S. relations, 109-110, 115-118; as Premier of the State Council, 34-37, 39-41, 42-50, 80-85, 183-185, 189, 191; on sports, 86, 90, 94-95; the Lushan meeting, 128, 141; the Cultural Revolution, 130, 132-135, 139, 146-148, 151-154, 156, 163, 165-166, 167-168, 170, 172-176; organizing the

government in 1975, 132; friendship with Strong, 90-93; concern for others, 27-28, 33, 40, 43, 70-71, 170, 184, 187, 189; towards his family, 53, 60-65, 67-69; relations with Mao, 122, 133-136; on Mao as China's leader, 137-138; last meeting with foreigners, 190-191; death in 1976, 8; death mourned, 4-5, 11, 197

Zhou Panlong, 12
Zhou Shaogang, 12
Zhou Yigan, 12
Zhu De, 8, 22, 30-32, 58, 63, 72, 96, 119, 154, 160, 172, 181
Zhu Dianhua, 184, 197
Zhu Guang, 58
Zhuo Lin, 179-180
Zhuoxian County, Hebei Province, 12
Zunyi Conference, 58, 120